*A*dventure Guide to

St. Martin & St. Barts

Lynne M. Sullivan

HUNTER

HUNTER PUBLISHING, INC.
130 Campus Drive, Edison NJ 08818
732-225-1900, 800-255-0343, fax 732-417-0482
comments@hunterpublishing.com

4176 Saint-Denis, Montréal, Québec Canada H2W 2M5
514-843-9447; fax 515-843-9448; info@ulysses.com

The Boundary, Wheatley Road, Garsington
Oxford, OX44 9EJ England
01865-361122; fax 01865-361133
windsorbooks@compuserve.com

ISBN 1-58843-348-X

© 2003 Lynne M. Sullivan

Maps by Kim André, Lissa Dailey & Toni Carbone,
© 2003 Hunter Publishing, Inc.

Cartoons by Joe Kohl

Cover photograph:
Great Bay, Sint-Maarten, © Loek Polders/ImageState.
All others by Paul J. Sullivan, unless otherwise indicated. Back
cover photograph: *View from Fort Amsterdam, Saint Martin.*

**For complete information about the hundreds of other
travel guides offered by Hunter Publishing, visit us at
www.hunterpublishing.com**

4 3 2 1

Contents

■ Maps

Introduction

St. Barts and St. Martin are two of the most popular islands in the Caribbean. They are located 20 miles apart, 150 miles east (and slightly south) of Puerto Rico, at the top of an archipelago known as the Lesser Antilles. Think of them as

the pivot joint between the Greater Antilles, which stretch west-to-east from Cuba to the Virgin Islands, and the Lesser Antilles, which extend north-to-south from Anguilla to Grenada.

Saint Barts is a tiny scrap of land covering about eight square miles. It's an overseas *région* of France, and old-timers still call it Saint-Barthélemy (pinch your nose, gargle the "r," and say *sahn bar tay leh MEE*). But most everyone else refers to it as Saint Barts. You may see it spelled Saint-Barth (the French abbreviation), but in this book we abbreviate American/English-style and use simply St. Barts.

Saint Martin is several times larger, with about 36 square miles, divided almost equally between France (20 square miles) and the Netherlands (16 square miles). This is the smallest land area in the world to be governed by two nations. The Dutch call their part **Sint Maarten**. The French call theirs **Saint-Martin**. In this book, we use St. Martin to refer to the island as a whole.

St. Martin is easily reached from the US, and St. Barts is a quick inter-island hop by ferry or plane. You may want to divide your vacation between the two, or choose one island as your home base and take a day-trip to the other. Day-tripping won't allow you a proper visit, but it's easy to do and relatively inexpensive.

■ Which One's Best?

If you ask a dozen visitors who've stayed on both islands which they prefer, you'll get a half-dozen zealous votes for each. Those who favor St. Martin rave about the Dutch-side casinos, French-side restaurants, and sensational duty-free shops. St. Barts fans gush over luxurious little hotels, exquisite meals, chic boutiques, and camera-shy celebrities seen lounging on the beaches.

If you seek a lot of action, go for St. Martin. Need more peace and quiet? St. Barts is for you.

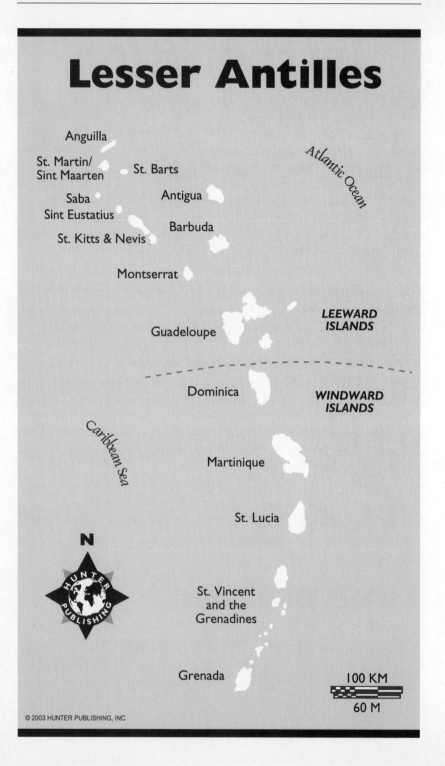

Lesser Antilles

Anguilla

St. Martin/
Sint Maarten   St. Barts

Atlantic Ocean

Saba   Antigua
Sint Eustatius

St. Kitts & Nevis   Barbuda

Montserrat

Guadeloupe   **LEEWARD ISLANDS**

Dominica   **WINDWARD ISLANDS**

Caribbean Sea

Martinique

St. Lucia

N

St. Vincent
and the
Grenadines

Grenada   100 KM

60 M

© 2003 HUNTER PUBLISHING, INC

The Land & Sea

■ Geography, Topography & Ecology

 Honestly, St. Barts and St. Martin are not gorgeous overall. Each has lovely areas, and both have stunning beaches and picturesque vistas, but don't expect breathtaking mountains, cascading waterfalls, lush rainforests, or idyllic rivers and lakes.

Preserving Paradise

Eco-tourists probably will be happier elsewhere in the Caribbean, but St. Martin and St. Barts have made recent strides in the direction of protecting and enhancing what nature provided.

On St. Martin, the **Nature Foundation** (Dutch) and **AGRNSM** (French) have taken on the demanding chore of preserving the island's natural assets for future generations to enjoy. Both the French and the Dutch have set up marine reserves to oversee management of the coral reefs and coastlines, and each government is enforcing new conservation laws. Additional organizations have sprung up to protect wildlife habitats, restore historical sites, encourage sustainable tourism, and clear the island of debris.

On St. Barts, the **Environmental Commission** heads up an ongoing campaign to maintain the island's reputation as a clean, safe vacation destination. Elected officials, the hotel association, and the businesses community are proactive participants in programs designed to handle waste, prevent pollution of the sea, and preserve natural resources. Results of these joint environmental efforts are visible throughout the island. An athletic stadium now sits on ground that was once a trash heap. A revitalized seafront area occupies a former dumping ground for old cars and appliances. The island's incineration plant gives off clean steam that is converted to potable water. Organized volunteer groups periodically spend a morning collecting debris from roadsides, beaches, and public land.

Most of the terrain on St. Martin is low, arid, and covered in desert vegetation or man-made structures. The southwestern part is dominated by **Simpson Bay Lagoon**, one of the largest landlocked bodies of water in the Caribbean; **Philipsburg**, the principal Dutch city, backs up to a huge salt pond. Rolling hills in the center of the island rise to 1,391 feet at **Pic Paradis** (called **Paradise Peak** by English speakers), and lovely bays with sandy beaches cut into the shoreline.

Tiny St. Barts has deep coves with long, golden-sand beaches that are protected from the elements by reefs and bluffs. They ring a dry, rocky interior topped by 938-foot **Morne du Vitet**. **Gustavia,** the capital, is built around a natural harbor prized by sailors seeking shelter for multi-million-dollar yachts. Smaller, well-groomed villages dress up the rolling countryside with charming houses, lovely gardens, and delightful shops. Lavish private vacation villas and year-round homes are tucked discretely among a scattering of palm trees and hibiscus bushes.

■ Weather

Temperatures

 This is the Caribbean. The weather is perfect. You can count on a year-round average temperature of 77°F. Daytime highs occasionally reach 90°, but the average for January is 83° and July's standard is a balmy 86°. Nighttime temperatures have been recorded as low as 55°, but they are usually about 72° in January and 76° in July. The Caribbean Sea maintains a temperature of 80°, plus or minus a degree or two, throughout the year.

Rainfall

You'll notice a greater difference in seasonal rainfall. Summer, which runs from May through November, is rainy season. Winter, from December through April, is dry season. Both St. Martin and St. Barts have an arid terrain, but each still receives up to 40 inches of rain per year (about half of the amount that falls on greener islands). However, even during the wet season, most days have several hours of sunshine, and humidity is offset by steady trade winds.

DID YOU KNOW?

Residents of St. Martin and St. Barts say they enjoy a big season of small rains and a small season of big rains.

Hurricanes

Hurricanes and strong tropical storms get a lot of press, but the truth is that dangerous tempests are rare. Records show that most major hurricanes deteriorate at sea, and only one in three ever reaches land. In fact, you're more likely to encounter a severe storm on the eastern coast of the United States than in the Caribbean.

On the off-chance that nasty weather is brewing, check with reliable sources for the Caribbean forecast just before you leave home. Some of the best reports are posted on the following websites:

The **Caribbean Hurricane Network** – http://stormcarib.com

The **Hurricane Research Division of the Atlantic Oceanographic and Meteorological Laboratory** – www.aoml.noaa.gov/hrd

The **Telecommunication Operations Center of the National Oceanic and Atmospheric Administration** – http:// weather.noaa.gov/weather/current/TNCM.html

The Palm Beach Post (tropical storm information is updated four times a day during peak season) – www.gopbi.com/weather/special/storm/atlantic/outlook.html

National Hurricane Center – www.nhc.noaa.gov

Once a name is given to a tropical depression (an organized system of clouds and thunderstorms with a defined circulation and maximum sustained winds of less than 39 miles per hour), you can follow the storm with the **Hurricane Hunters**, the 53rd Weather Reconnaissance Squadron of the Air Force Reserve (www.hurricanehunters.com). They're based at Keesler Air Force Base in Biloxi, Mississippi, and since 1944 they've been flying directly into storms and hurricanes. You can view their photos at www.hurricanehunters.com

Hurricane Facts

- A hurricane is a storm with winds at a constant speed of 74 miles per hour or more. These winds blow in a large spiral around a relatively calm center of extremely low pressure known as the eye. Around the rim of the eye, winds may gust to more than 200 miles per hour. The storm dominates the ocean surface and lower atmosphere over tens of thousands of square miles.

- Hurricane-force winds flow counterclockwise in the Northern Hemisphere and clockwise in the Southern Hemisphere toward the storm's center. The entire system is pushed by upper-atmosphere winds 10,000 to 40,000 feet above the earth.

- Hurricanes form only over warm tropical oceans, and their force weakens quickly when they move over land or cold water.

- Typhoons and hurricanes are basically the same type of storm. They are called typhoons in the western part of the North Pacific. In the eastern part of the North Pacific, as well as the Atlantic, Caribbean, and Gulf of Mexico, they are called hurricanes. In the rest of the world, they are known as tropical cyclones.

- No hurricane has ever hit California, but they occasionally do hit Mexico's west coast.

- A small hurricane is about 100 miles wide; a large one may be 300 miles across. Some last only a few hours before they weaken, while others maintain hurricane strength for two weeks.

- The period from 1995 to 2000 was the busiest on record, with 79 named storms, of which 49 became hurricanes, and 23 became major hurricanes.

- Forecasters began naming hurricanes in 1950. At first, they used words from the international phonetic alphabet – Able, Baker, Charlie, etc. Women's names common to English-speaking countries started being used in 1953. Beginning in 1979, forecasters began alternating male and female names common to French, English, and Spanish countries.

- The Hurricane Capital of the Caribbean is the island of Bimini in the Bahamas. It has been hit with 16 major hurricanes. Aruba, Bonaire, and Curacao, located off the northern coast of South America, have never been hit by a major hurricane, but 10 named storms have made near-miss passes.

■ Plant Life

 Wind and rain move across St. Martin and St. Barts from east to west, so the western side of both islands is drier than the eastern side. The arid hillsides have shallow, nutrient-poor soil that supports mostly cacti and succulents, but still, the countryside is lovely, especially after a rain shower when wild flowers burst into bloom and grasses turn deep green.

The eastern side of both islands is greener and sustains a variety of plants, trees, and bushes. A study conducted in 1994 classified hundreds of wild indigenous species, as well as naturalized flora that have adapted to local conditions. Although there are no tropical forests, several areas have woodlands with forest-like features. Seagrape trees and palm trees grow in sandy soil along the shores, and a variety of mangroves and shrubs thrive in the salty water and mud found in coastal swamps and inland salt pans.

Some of the plants that are typically regarded as indigenous to the Caribbean were actually brought to the islands by Europeans. For example, the coconut palm was imported to the West Indies from the Pacific islands by British colonists who intended to harvest the fruit as a commercial crop. Today, a wide assortment of palm trees grow on all the Caribbean islands. They are characterized by compound leaves (called fronds) that top a trunk-like stem. New leaves grow from the middle of the stem, as older leaves bow outward and eventually fall off.

As you travel through St. Martin and St. Barts, look for the following plants and trees growing in private gardens and on landscaped resort property, as well as in the countryside:

Flamboyant trees, native to Madagascar, have small feathery leaves and clusters of red-orange flowers. The blooms last from May until September, and black seed pods dangle from bare branches after the tree sheds its leaves and flowers in the fall.

Frangipanis may be bushes or small trees, depending on the variety. They are native to the Antilles and tropical areas of the Americas. During the blooming season in summer, look for pointed waxy leaves and yellow, red, or white flowers with a scent similar to jasmine. The flowers are edible and sometimes used in desserts and jams, but the sap is toxic.

Latanier or **sabal palms** produce fronds used for weaving hats. Although this cottage industry is no longer a significant part of the islands' economy, latanier groves still stand at Lorient on St. Barts.

Gaiac trees or **lignum vitae** are native to the Antilles. These small trees are now a protected species, but the wood was once used in construction. The sap is said to relieve arthritis pain, and the bark was once touted as a treatment for syphilis. You will recognize this tree by its glossy green leaves, purple or blue flowers, and small decorative orange fruit.

Trumpet trees (also called **poui** or **poirier**) are native to tropical parts of the Americas and now grow wild on the islands. They have adjusted well to arid conditions, but cannot survive strong winds. You will see their spectacular mauve, pink, or white flowers only from April to June.

Manchineel trees (also called **mancenillier** and **mancinella**) are tall, native to the West Indies, and often found growing in sandy soil on beaches.

While this is a lovely shade tree, the sap is extremely caustic and can cause burns and blisters if it touches your skin or eyes. Don't stand under the tree during a rain shower, and don't pick up the apple-like fruit, which is extremely poisonous.

The **anaconda** or **geranium tree** is a Caribbean native that grows well in dry soil and salty air. It has gorgeous red flowers that bloom in clustered bouquets year-round, and its fruit looks similar to white plums.

The **royal palm** is, as its name implies, a stately tree and the largest of the many varieties of palms. You will recognize it by its smooth, ringed trunk that bulges in the middle, and its thick fronds, which are made up of long, curved leaves.

Seagrape trees are the shrub-like plants that grow on beaches and along the shoreline. When they grow in more protected inland areas, they often reach heights of 18 to 24 feet. You can eat the small, reddish fruit that grows among the round, waxy leaves, but it's quite acidic.

Aloe or **aloe vera** is a succulent plant that was brought to the islands from Mediterranean countries and is valued for its powerful medicinal qualities. Although its sap is often used as a laxative, you will probably find it more useful for soothing sunburned skin. It grows wild in dry, rocky soil, and gardeners include it in landscapes. It is also grown commercially. Recognize it by its long, fleshy, serrated leaves that grow straight out of the ground. From January to June, it produces yellow flowers.

Night-blooming cereus is the name of the cactus that produces big white flowers late in the afternoon from February to July.

Mamillaria nivosa is a round, fuzzy cactus with yellow thorns that grows among rocks like a ground cover. It is endangered and rarely found on islands other than St. Barts, St. Martin, and Barbuda.

Yellow prickly pear is actually a military hero. In 1773, French residents were asked to plant rows of this barbed cactus along the shores of St. Barts to discourage British invasion by sea. It produces an edible red fruit and bright yellow flowers.

Thornless prickly pear or **barbary fig** is a Mexican cactus with flat, purple, thornless stems that bear orange flowers. It grows well in dry soil and salty air, and you will often see it in landscaped areas.

Stapelia gigantea is often mistaken for a cactus, but it is actually part of the milkweed family. Its small olive-green stems bare large starfish-shaped yellow flowers with reddish stalks. Flies love the stuff and buzz around collecting pollen, which they transport from plant to plant.

Englishman's head is a funny little cactus that grows on rocky cliffs and hillsides. You'll know when you see it because it looks just like its name – a round green *head* wearing a bright red thorny *cap*. You can eat the red fruits, which are tart and similar to cranberries.

Yucca is native to Mexico and the southwestern United States. It has smooth, rigid stems that taper to a point; white flowers cluster in the middle of the plant from April to July.

Golden trumpet or **yellow bell** comes from South America, and its trumpet-shaped yellow flowers are toxic. You often see it climbing rock walls, and gardeners sometimes trim it into a shrub.

Purple allamanda is native to the African tropics and resistent to drought. Its large rose-colored flowers bloom year-round, making it popular with gardeners.

Bougainvillea is synonymous with the Caribbean, although it came to the region from Brazil. The robust thorny vine climbs and creeps everywhere and is easily recognized by its brilliantly colored bracts (leaves) that surround a tiny, inconspicuous white flower.

Cotton was once grown commercially in the Caribbean, and some of the knotty shrubs still grow wild on the islands. You may see birds building nests with the soft, white cotton that surrounds black seeds inside tough green seed pods.

Hibiscus originates from Asia and islands in the Pacific, but grows rampant in the Caribbean. The hardy shrub is often used as a hedge, and diverse varieties produce a profusion of colorful flowers. The spectacular blooms each last only one day.

Mexican creeper is also called **chain of love** because of its tendency to embrace fences, walls, signposts, and other plants. After a rain shower, the twining vine bursts forth with gorgeous pink flowers. You gotta love it.

Oleander flowers are toxic but lovely. The decorative shrub comes from the Mediterranean and produces yellow, white, or pink blooms year-round.

Bengale clockvine, from India, and **bluebird vine**, from tropical areas of the Americas, produce hanging bouquets of flowers. Clockvine blooms are purple. Bluebird blooms are blue. Each has adapted well to the Caribbean, and you will see them in decorative landscapes as well as growing wild along the roadsides.

St. Martin's Legendary Guavaberries

Guavaberry liqueur has been made in St. Martin homes by many generations, but in the mid-1990s it went commercial. The **Guavaberry Emporium** (see page 72), located in an historic cedar house on Frontstreet in Philipsburg, is the primary retailer for the beloved folk drink, which is made from oak-aged rum and wild guavaberries.

The guavaberry is an odd little fruit that grows without stems directly onto the branches of flowering trees found high in the hills at the center of the island. The bittersweet, grape-like berries have a center seed surrounded by juicy transparent flesh and a thin skin that changes from pale green to orange or dark red as they ripen.

While guavaberry trees live on other Caribbean islands, as well as in the Pacific, they aren't widely cultivated because the trees are difficult to grow, the fruit ripens at unpredictable times, and harvesting the berries is a laborious manual chore. After the fruit is gathered, it is washed and put into wooden barrels, where it ages in a mix of rum and sugar. The resulting liqueur has a woody, bittersweet flavor.

■ Wildlife

St. Martin and St. Barts are not inhabited by indigenous land animals, but they do have a few imports. Europeans brought **mongooses** to the islands to eat troublesome snakes and rats, but the skinny, long-tailed carnivores turned out to have a voracious appetite for beneficial reptiles and ground-nesting birds. Since there were no natural predators, the mongooses reproduced beyond expectations and became a real nuisance.

Iguanas were also brought to the islands by European colonists, but these large lizard-like creatures are rare and becoming rarer. You will probably see them only on resort grounds, where they are fed and treated as pets. While iguanas look prehistorically scary, with their spiny backs, they are strict vegetarians and don't care to share space with humans.

At sea, you may spot marine mammals such as **dolphins**, **porpoises**, and **whales**, which migrate through the area from December until May.

Turtles

Sea turtles, while not mammals, do breathe air, and you may see them swimming along the surface of the water. They live in the ocean, except when the females come onto land to lay eggs. All species are endangered and require 15 to 50 years to reach a reproductive age, so their nesting grounds on sandy beaches are protected by wildlife societies.

WORD TO
THE WISE

Despite the ban on hunting sea turtles, you may see products made from their shiny shells in markets. Don't buy them.

Leatherbacks, the largest of the sea turtles, have a leather-like skin over their backs instead of a shell. The largest one on record measured 10 feet from the tip of its nose to the end of its tail, but most are in the five-foot range. A mature leatherback can weigh 1,000 pounds or more. Poachers snatch turtle eggs from nests on beaches, which threatens their dwindling population. In addition, many of them die when they eat discarded plastic bags, which they mistake for jellyfish, their favorite food.

Hawksbill turtles are recognized by their hawk-like beaks. They grow to about three feet in diameter and weigh an average of 130 pounds. You are most likely to see them swimming around reefs, where they dine on crabs and snails and encrusted organisms that they scrape off rocks with their pointed noses.

Green turtles have a rounded head and, like the hawksbill, grow to about three feet in diameter. They are much heavier, however, and prefer to live in tall sea grasses rather than near reefs because they are herbivorous grazers.

■ Birds

 Native and migrating birds are the islands' true wildlife treasure, and you don't need to be a birder to be impressed by the vast number and variety of species that live on or migrate through the Lesser Antilles. They land on your table when you eat outdoors, tease you while you try to nap on the beach, and steal small items off your patio when you're not looking. The following will help you identify a few of the most common winged wildlife:

- The **brown pelican** is grayish-brown with a long neck, long beak, and short legs. It's usually seen feeding along the shore.

- **Magnificent frigate birds** (magnificent is part of its name) have an extraordinary wingspan, which can reach more than six feet. They are jet-black, and you can discern their sex by the color of their throats. The males' are red; the females' are white. These birds are pirates, stealing prey from other birds, and they hunt everywhere on the islands.

- The small **green-backed heron** has a distinctive call and gray-green feathers. The **great heron** has long legs and a long black feather growing from its white head.

- **Snowy egrets** are white with black legs, while **cattle egrets** (usually sitting on cows) have white plumage and a tuft of orange feathers on their head.

- The **kingfisher** is blue with a white breast and a ruffled tuft on its head. It floats in the air looking for food, and dives into the surf to catch fish.

- **Bananaquits** are little birds with dark feathers on its back and a bright yellow throat and breast. They love sugar and will make themselves at home on your out-door table.

- Broad-winged **hawks** are frequently seen soaring in wooded areas.

- Two species of **hummingbird** are often seen feeding among flowers: the **green-throated Carib** and the **Antillean-crested hummingbird**.

- Two types of dove live on the islands: **Zenaida doves**, with brown backs and pink-tinged breasts, neck, and head; and **common turtledoves**, with grayish-brown feathers and black-and-white speckled necks.

■ Marine Life

 The shallow warm waters surrounding St. Martin and St. Barts are teeming with life. **Conch** (say konk) is one of the most versatile and popular sea creatures. Their large, pearly-pink shells are favorite collector's items, and the meat is the key ingredient in many Caribbean recipes. You can often see islanders cleaning the meat from the shells near Bobby's Marina at Great Bay Beach in Philipsburg, St. Martin.

Among the vast number of fish that live in shallow waters close to shore, you're most likely to recognize the following species at popular scuba and snorkeling sites:

- **Sergeant majors**, a four- to six-inch fish that gets its name from the five black stripes that ring its body.

- **Blue chromis,** a brilliant blue three- to four-inch fish with big eyes and a thin deeply-forked tail.

- **Brown chromis**, a brownish-gray three- to six-inch fish with big eyes and a deeply-forked yellow-tipped tail. The border of its dorsal fin is also yellow, and the pectoral fin has a dark spot at its base.

- **Surgeonfish** grow to lengths of six-12 inches. Their overall color changes from blue-gray to dark brown and their tail and fins are edged in blue or white. Some have a pale band of color at the base of their tail.

- **Blue tangs** are blue with a white or yellow spine at the base of their tail and darker blue edging around their fins. They are usually five-10 inches long, but may grow to 15 inches.

- **Trumpetfish** are thin and 1½-2½ feet long. They get their name from their extended trumpet-like snout. Most often, they are brown or reddish-brown, with pale lines and black spots along their body, but they can change their color to various shades of blue and yellow.

On shore, you're likely to spot:

- **Ghost crabs**. They never leave the beach. They tunnel into the sand, then dart out of their holes, zip a few feet across the wet beach, then burrow down again and disappear. At night, they emerge to feed, and during a full moon you can see hordes of them scampering about.

- **Hermit crabs** live on land, but lay their eggs in water. During spawning season, hundreds of them dash down the hillsides to the shore, hoping to become parents. After the baby crabs hatch, they spend a few months in the ocean before trudging onto land, carrying enough water to sustain themselves for awhile. When they grow too big for their backpack homes, they look about for larger dwellings, and sometimes kill other hermits in order to steal their shells. If a suitable shell isn't available, they will move into almost any kind of container. Hermits are known for eating any kind of garbage, including sewage.

The People

Approximately 7,000 people live on eight square miles of land on St. Barts. Since the little island was settled by French citizens and never had economic motivation to open up to outsiders, 95% of its residents are white. The islanders are understandably friendly to tourists, but they have a reputation of being slow to accept newcomers. Illegal immigrants seeking work are quickly deported.

By comparison, St. Martin, with four times more land (36 square miles), has nearly 10 times as many residents (about 69,000). Over the past 20 years, immigrants have poured onto the island looking for work and ideal living conditions, so that now the native Creole population is heavily outnumbered by newcomers. Approximately 70 na-

Introduction

tionalities are represented on the island, but most of the people trace their roots to Africa, France, or the Netherlands. Illegal immigration is an acknowledged problem, and government officials say as many as 30,000 people may be living on the island without proper authorization.

■ Language

The official language on St. Barts is **French**, spoken with a Norman accent, but most residents also speak English, either fluently or functionally. On St. Martin, the official languages are **Dutch** on the Dutch side and **French** on the French side, but most everyone on both sides speaks at least some English. You may hear a small segment of native islanders speaking a French-based patois among themselves. Some residents speak **Papiamento**, the unofficial, but preferred language on Aruba, Bonaire, and Curaçao – islands that are also members of The Kingdom of the Netherlands.

Cuisine

You will eat extremely well on St. Barts and on both sides of St. Martin. Chefs come from Europe, the US, and other Caribbean islands to open restaurants or ply their culinary arts in the kitchens of eateries owned by others. As you might expect, French and West Indian Creole are the most recognized cuisines on the two islands, but Dutch St. Martin has a variety of restaurants featuring Argentinian beef, Indonesian buffets, Mexican combination plates, and Italian pastas.

Everything, except local seafood, is imported. Meat, produce, and some fish are flown in from North America, while wine, cheese, and chocolate come from Europe. Small beach cafés and roadside stands specialize in grilled or fried fresh fish.

West Indian Créole dishes are a mouth-watering melding of French, African, and Indian recipes. You'll want to try the fried fritters, barbecued goat, spicy stuffed shrimp, and grilled langouste (the local lobster).

Common French & Creole Menu Items

Accras or Amarinades	Spicy doughnuts/fritters usually made from cod or other fish, but sometimes from vegetables.
Balaou	Small fried fish.
Bébélé	Dish made of boiled sheep tripe and green bananas.
Beignets	Donut-like sweet fritters.
Bière/bière pression	Beer/draft beer.
Blaff	Spicy lime-and-garlic bouillon used to cook fish. The word is said to come from the sound the fish makes as it hits the boiling liquid.
Blanc-manger	Coconut flan or gelatin dessert.
Boudin Noir	Blood sausage (made from pig's blood mixed with suet, bread crumbs and oatmeal) – not to be confused with Louisiana-style Boudin Blanc, made from pork, rice and onions.
Breadfruit	Large melon-like fruit.
Cabri	Small, bony goat, usually prepared as curry or smoked.
Calalou	Soup made with herbs, vegetables, crab, and pork.
Chadron	Sea urchin.
Chatrou	Small octopus.
Chou coco	Rare dish made from the heart of the coconut tree.
Christophine	Vegetable similar to a potato, particularly delicious when prepared au gratin.
Cirique	Small crab.
Colombo	Curry. In the Caribbean, usually a mild green curry, not as hot as Indian curry. The most common is made from cabri, small goat, but occasionally it's chicken or pork.
Corossol	A white-fleshed fruit.
Court-bouillon	Tomato, pepper, and onion mix.
Crabbe de terre	Land crab cooked with coconut and hot pepper.
Cribiches	Freshwater crayfish.
Déjeuner	Lunch.
Dombre	Small flour croquette.
Entrée	Appetizer, not main course.
Écrevisses	Freshwater crayfish.

Farci	Stuffed land crab.
Féroce	Avocado, hot pepper, and cod salad.
Fruit à pain	Breadfruit.
Giraumon	Pumpkin.
Igname	Any of a wide variety of yams.
Lambi	Conch, a large shellfish.
Langouste	Caribbean lobster, no claws.
Manioc	Cassava/tapioca flour.
Maracudja	Passion fruit.
Matoutou	Crab fricassée.
Migan	Mashed bananas and breadfruit.
Ouassous	Big freshwater crayfish.
Oursin	Sea urchin (chadron).
Pain	Bread.
Pâté en pot	Thick soup usually made with otherwise-unusable parts of a goat, vegetables, capers, white wine, and a splash of rum.
Patate douce	Sweet potato.
Petit déjeuner	Breakfast.
Schrub	A liqueur made by soaking oranges in rum.
Soudons	Sweet clams.
Souskai	Green fruits, grated and macerated in lime juice, salt and hot pepper.
Table d'hôte	Chef's specialty of the day.
Ti-nain	Small banana, cooked like a vegetable because it is not as sweet as the larger variety.
Ti-punch	Drink made of rum, sugar cane syrup, and lime.
Titiris	Tiny fish.
Touffé	Braised.
Z'habitants	Large crayfish.

Music

 People in the Caribbean consider music their *true voice*. Most original rhythms are based on African beats and make extensive use of drums. The region has given birth to calypso, merengue, soca, zouk, and reggae, which have become popular world-wide. The common element in all these musical styles and their variations is an infectious dance rhythm and outrageous lyrics.

Often, favorite musicians and bands come out of competitions held during Carnival, an annual celebration on almost every Caribbean Island. On St. Martin, the annual Carnival competitions culminate in a play-off between 10 finalists and the defending Calypso Monarch from the past year. So far, only men have won the contest, but women may enter, and **Lady Melody** has made it to the finals.

DID YOU KNOW? *On St. Barts and the French side of St. Martin, Carnival is celebrated before Lent; on the Dutch side of St. Martin, Carnival is celebrated after Easter. Residents of St. Barts put as much or more preparation into the celebration of their annual Music Festival each January and their annual Boubou's Festival each August. See page 25 for details on island festivals.*

Currently, local stars on St. Martin include **King Beau Beau** (the Calypso Monarch for many years, who has a BA degree in music from Hofstra University in New York), **Kaiso Brat** (the former multi-year Calypso Monarch), **Neville York** (a steel drummer and the principal member of Jazz Flamboyant, a group that promotes the island's music, dance, literature, and art), **Tanny and the Boys** (an old-timers band that plays calypso, bolero, and merengue with an African accent, using instruments they make themselves), **Colors** (a dance band playing reggae, jazz, funk, and blues), and **Anastascia Larmonie** (a pianist who studied at the Berklee School of Music in Boston and Brabants Conservatorium in The Netherlands).

The 12-night **St. Barts Music Festival** is held every year during mid- to late January. It features live performances by musicians and dancers in an informal setting. The audience is treated to ballet one evening, jazz the next, and perhaps a classical symphony the next. Performers come from internationally acclaimed orchestras, quartets, opera companies, and ballet troupes.

Violinist **Frances De Broff** founded the festival with her friend, the now deceased Charles Magras, in the 1980s. They intended to keep the festival intimate and under-publicized, but word of mouth has increased its popularity and scope. Now, the performances (which are associated with annual concerts held in a 14th-century château in the small village of Ainay, France) draw many visitors, and the festival is large enough to feature large orchestral works.

Boubou's Festival was started in 1999 by the well-known Parisian restaurateur, Christophe Barjetta (nicknamed Boubou), who owns several exotic eateries on St. Barts. The 12-night event in August is growing rapidly and features the music of lesser-known performers. As many as 1,000 spectators show up to enjoy the music each evening.

> *For details on how to make calls on and to the islands, see* Telephones, *page 40.*

For Information & Tickets to Events

Dutch St. Martin is represented by **Sint Maarten Tourism Office**, ☎ 800-786-2278 (in North America), 599-542-2337 (on-island), fax 599-542-2734, www.st-maarten.com.

French St. Martin is represented by **Office du Tourisme de Saint-Martin**, ☎ 0590-87-57-21 (on-island), fax 0590-87-56-43, www.st-martin.org.

St. Barts is represented by **Office Municipal du Tourisme de Saint-Barthèlemy**, ☎ 0590-27-87-27, fax 0590-27-74-47, www.saint-barths.com.

A Shared History

■ Early Times

People lived on the islands of the Lesser Antilles long before Christopher Columbus "discovered" them on his second voyage in 1493. Archeologists have uncovered evidence of ancient civilizations living on St. Martin and St. Barts as early as 3,500 years ago. These original inhabitants were most likely **Ciboney**, Arawak-speaking Indians who migrated through the Caribbean from South America in ocean-going canoes.

Around 800 AD, more advanced sub-groups of Arawak Indians settled on St. Martin. More than 30 archeological sites on the island reveal that these people were peaceful, artistic, and spiritual. Each village had a chief, who lived in a rectangular hut, while tribal members lived in round huts. The dwellings were simple wooden structures with straw roofs, but they were sturdy enough to withstand hurricanes. You can see artifacts from these early villages in the museums in Philipsburg and Marigot. Look for zemis (three-sided stone figures which depict their gods), pottery shards, tools made of stone or shells, and jewelry.

Sometime later, another group of South American Indians arrived on the islands. These people, known as the **Caribs**, were warriors who killed the Arawak men and forced the women into slavery. By the time Columbus passed through the Lesser Antilles in 1493, the Indian population was dominated by Caribs. When he spotted St. Barts, Columbus named it after his brother, Bartolomé.

DID YOU KNOW?

When he discovered a larger island to the north, he named it after Saint Martin of Tours because it was first sighted on the revered saint's feast day, November 11.

■ After Columbus

 After Columbus' discoveries, Pope Alexander VI, who was a Spaniard by birth, decided to divide the New World into two parts and award the larger section to Spain (who, after all, paid for its discovery and, by the way, was a big contributor to the church) and Portugal (Spain's political ally). At first, England, France and the Netherlands didn't object because the New World didn't appear to possess much worth coveting. However, when the Spanish began flaunting gold and the Portuguese bragged of finding spices, furs, and wood, other countries sat up and took notice.

■ European Colonization – the Short Version

In 1623, the French privateer **Pierre Belain d'Esnambuc**, financed by Cardinal Richlieu, sailed for the Caribbean. His ship was attacked by the Spanish and he found refuge on St. Kitts (then called Saint Christopher), which was already under the control of Englishman Thomas Warner.

D'Esnambuc liked what he saw on St. Kitts, returned to France for more money, and founded the **Compagnie Saint-Christophe** to oversee future colonization in the Lesser Antilles. A few years later, Compagnie Saint-Christophe was upgraded to the more encompassing **Compagnie des Îles d'Amérique**, which sought to colonize all the islands between latitude 10° and 30° North (basically from Trinidad to Bermuda).

While the Compagnie des Îles d'Amérique was using peasants from the French provinces of Normandy and Brittany to establish colonies on St. Kitts, St. Barts, St. Martin, Guadeloupe, and Martinique, the **Dutch West Indies Company** had its eye on the Lesser Antilles as a halfway point between their flourishing settlements in Brazil and Nieue Amsterdam (New York). By 1631, the Dutch had set up camps on St. Martin, built Fort Amsterdam to protect themselves, and installed Jan Claeszen van Campen as governor.

The Spanish, who had been content with their lucrative holdings in the Greater Antilles, began to notice the successful French, English, and Dutch settlements springing up in the Lesser Antilles. Remembering their Pope-given rights, thousands of Spanish troops stormed St. Martin in 1638, took control of the island, and built the Old Spanish Fort at Point Blanche.

Six years later, **Peter Stuyvesant** (later the governor of Nieue Amsterdam) directed his Dutch troops in an unsuccessful effort to retake the island.

DID YOU KNOW? *Stuyvesant lost his leg in the attack when he was hit by a cannonball. He replaced it with a wooden prostheses, which earned him the nickname Peg Leg.*

By 1648, the Spanish colonists had tired of defending the minimally valuable island, and abandoned St. Martin. The French and Dutch quickly moved to reoccupy the land and, when both realized the other would not willingly leave, St. Martin was amicably divided between the two countries. The original boundary was moved several times, but eventually the French ended up with 20 square miles on the north side, and the Dutch got 16 square miles on the southern side.

Meanwhile, on St. Barts, the first French settlers weren't doing well, since the island had poor soil, no rivers or lakes, and was inhabited by hostile Carib Indians. The Compagnie des Îles d'Amérique decided the place was too expensive to maintain, and in 1651 sold it, along with St. Kitts and the French section of St. Martin, to the **Knights of Malta**. The sale made no difference to the native Caribs, who were determined to keep their land and continued to make life miserable for the white settlers. Finally, in 1656, the irate Indians raided the European settlement, killed all the colonists, and displayed their victims' heads on poles at Lorient beach.

Amazingly, more French settlers arrived three years later. This time around, the colonies did somewhat better, and St. Barts was included in the "island package" supervised by a new French enterprise called **Companie des Indes Occidentales**. This company, backed by the French monarch, set its sights on developing St. Martin, St. Barts, St. Kitts, Guadeloupe, and Martinique into profitable trade centers to supply the French colonies in the Americas.

While the other Indes Occidentales established profitable sugar plantations, St. Barts didn't have the natural resources to join in. Instead, colonists scratched out a meager living as farmers, and tried to defend themselves against hostile takeovers by foreign troops. One invasion the islanders didn't resist was from pirates and privateers, who brought along ship loads of goodies.

DID YOU KNOW?

Privateer is the politically correct term for a pirate who plunders with government authorization.

Montbars the Exterminator

A French hoodlum who allegedly roamed the seas in search of Spanish galleons during the 1700s, Montbars presumably was one of the infamous corsairs (a French pirate) who found refuge on St. Barts. Island lore says the notorious bad guy buried treasure in the sandy coves of Anse du Gouverneur. When you visit this beach, walk softly and carry a big shovel.

St. Barts limped along stoically as a half-forgotten French colony until 1784 when King Louis XVI allowed one of his ministers to sell the island to Sweden in exchange for trading rights in the port of Gothenburg. This surprise move brought instant prosperity to St. Barts because the Swedes allowed it to operate as a free port during a period when many European countries needed a convenient one-stop trade center.

Sailors could pull up to the sheltered port in Gustavia (named after Swedish King Gustave III), sell anything they had stolen from foreign colonies or ships, resupply their vessels from the overflowing warehouses that surrounded the harbor, enjoy a good French meal, and be on their way. This period of prosperity dwindled as international conflicts declined in the New World and fewer ships sought safe harbor.

The original French settlers, whose numbers had grown over the years, never merged into the Swedish society, so they were pleased when France repurchased their island in 1877. They were even more thrilled by the announcement that the island would remain a duty-free port, a policy that is still honored today.

■ Sugar & Slavery

 Europeans developed a sweet tooth in the 1600s, and St. Martin began cultivating sugar around 1650. Since the settlers couldn't keep up with the demanding work load, they tried to recruit laborers from Europe by offering them land in exchange for 36 months of unpaid work. As tempting as the offer might seem, few Europeans fell for it, and plantation owners were forced to seek another solution. Slaves from West Africa were the only affordable choice.

Hundreds of captured Africans were brought to the island, and the plentiful workforce soon turned the arid countryside green with sugar cane. At first, prospering landowners were too content to notice that they were becoming outnumbered by discontented black workers. When black-slave/white-owner tension became evident, owners adopted strict rules to keep the slaves under control. These policies understandably caused tempers to flair, and the slaves began to rise up against their owners.

To compound the problems on St. Martin, slaves weren't the only group unhappy with their circumstances. Small property owners were organizing to rid themselves of regulations imposed by large property owners. Large property owners wanted to free themselves from restrictions placed on them by France. France was plotting to overthrow its monarchy. The situation was explosive, and in 1789 it did explode with the French Revolution.

While the French were busy with internal matters, the English took advantage of the dissent in the Antilles and overthrew the administration on Guadeloupe, Martinique, and French St. Martin in 1794. Five years later, Frenchman **Victor Hugues**, an outspoken opponent of slavery, was dispatched to the islands to confront the English. He armed the black inhabitants on all three islands and successfully retook the French possessions.

As promised, Hugues freed the slaves. But freedom was bittersweet and short-lived, because the administrators sent to govern the islands took every opportunity to revoke the rights of former slaves. **Napoleon Bonaparte** reinstated slavery during his reign and the blacks were enslaved when England once again retook St. Martin in the early 1800s.

In 1816, France gained lasting sovereignty over Guadeloupe, Martinique, St. Barts, and St. Martin in the **Treaty of Vienna.** Thirty-two years later, Frenchman **Victor Schoelcher** led a successful campaign to permanently abolish slavery in French territory. Slaves on the Dutch side of St. Martin were freed in 1863.

St. Barts never had a plantation society and, thus, very few African slaves. However, immediately after the abolition of slavery, the entire Caribbean region suffered economic problems, and the inhabitants of St. Barts were no exception. The few liberated slaves who lived on the island were forced to leave to look for paid work in more prosperous areas. Consequently, very few current residents are African descendants.

■ The 20th Century

Islanders on St. Barts and French St. Martin gained full benefits granted all French citizens on March 19, 1946 when Guadeloupe and Martinique became overseas *départements* of France, and St. Barts and the northern section of St. Martin were tied administratively to the *préfecture*. Guadeloupe is capital of the *région*, and administrators (called *préfects*) are appointed for each island by the central government in Paris.

Dutch St. Martin is part of **The Netherlands Antilles**, which is divided into two three-island clusters: the "S" islands (St. Maarten, St. Eustatius, and Saba), and the "ABC" islands (Aruba, Bonaire, and Curaçao). Each island has a governor appointed by the sovereign of the Netherlands (Queen Beatrix, currently) on the recommendation of local officials to serve a six-year term. Willemstad, Curaçao serves as the seat of government for the five-island Netherlands Antilles. (Aruba became autonomous in 1986 when it seceded from The Netherlands Antilles, but it remains a part of The Kingdom of the Netherlands.)

Travel Information

When to Go

Winter is the ideal time to visit. The weather is perfect. Lots of events are going on. Everything is open. But planes are packed, hotels are full, traffic is bad, and you must call well in advance to get a dinner reservation. All this, and prices are high too.

Think about visiting during the shoulder seasons, just after Easter until late June and again just after hurricane season but before the winter holidays. Summer is fine, too, but you'll have more rain – you may even encounter a tropical storm – and some businesses may be closed.

Airfares and hotel rates typically fall between April 15 and December 15, and many restaurants and shops drop their prices during that time as well. If you want to watch or participate in some type of celebration or event, check the listings below.

Celebrations, Events & Holidays

The citizens of St. Martin and St. Barts take every opportunity to celebrate their mixed cultures. Dates vary for some holidays and events, so all the tourist offices or check the official island websites to get the exact dates and ticket information for each event. Dutch St. Martin is represented by **Sint Maarten Tourism Office**, ☎ 800-786-2278 (in North America), 599-542-2337 (on-island), fax 599-542-2734, www.st-maarten.com. French St. Martin is represented by **Office du Tourisme de Saint-Martin**, ☎ 0590-87-57-21 (on-island), fax 0590-87-56-43, www.st-martin.org. St. Barts is represented by **Office Municipal du Tourisme de Saint-Barthèlemy**, ☎ 0590-27-87-27, fax 0590-27-74-47, www.saint-barths.com.

 B = St. Barts; D = Dutch St. Martin; F = French St. Martin.

January

January 1 . . . . **New Year's Day** (B/D/F)

Variable . . . . **St. Barts International Music Festival** (B) This 12-night festival is held every year in mid- to late-January. It features live performances by musicians and dancers in an informal setting. The audience is treated to ballet one evening, jazz the next, and perhaps a symphony the next. Performers come from internationally acclaimed orchestras, quartets, opera companies, and ballet troupes. See *Music*, page 18 above, and www.stbartsmusicfestival.org for more information.

February-March

Variable. . . . . **Carnival** (B/F) French Carnival isn't as big as the Dutch extravaganza, but it is celebrated with passion and exuberance. It runs for two weeks before Ash Wednesday and is highlighted by the crowning of a beautiful Carnival Queen, who presides over costume parades, dancing, and music competitions.

Variable . . . . **Ash Wednesday** (B/F) On this, the last day of Carnival, everyone dresses in black (signifying sin) and white (signifying a fresh start) to attend street parties and torch-lit parades.

April

Variable . . . . **Carnival** (D)

April 30. . . . . **Queen's Birthday** (D) Queen Beatrix, the current monarch of the Netherlands, was actually born in January, but that's a lousy time of year in Holland, so citizens (including those living in the Netherlands Antilles) celebrate on the birthday of the former Queen (Juliana), who was born April 30, 1909. It's a national holiday, and Dutch citizens throw parties, while the queen herself makes public appearances in various towns throughout Holland. Most businesses on French St. Martin also close in honor of the Dutch queen.

Variable . . . . **St. Barth Festival of Caribbean Cinema** (B) This is held annually during the week after Easter. It began in 1995 with the objective of presenting films from Caribbean producers so that island residents would have the opportunity to view and discuss works made in and about their area of the world. The event has grown and is now popular with both visitors and islanders. All foreign movies are shown in their original version, with French subtitles.

May

May 1 . . . . **Labor Day** (B/D/F)

May 8. . . . . **Remembrance Day/Armistice Dat WWII** (B/F) More and more, this holiday is a celebration of freedom in general, but it specifically honors military personnel who died during World War II to protect that freedom.

Variable . . . . **Ascencion Day** (B/D/F)

May 27 . . . . **Abolition of Slavery** (B/F)

Variable . . . . **Whitsun** (B/F)

July

July 14 . . . . **Bastille Day** (B/F) This holiday is celebrated by the French much as Independence Day is by Americans. It's a national holiday, with parades, fireworks, and sporting events, which extols the beginning of a new (and better) form of government. French citizens stormed the Bastille (a political prison) on July 14, 1789, marking the start of the French Revolution. Both sides of St. Martin celebrate the day with great zeal.

July 21 . . . . **Victor Schoelcher Day** (B/F) Victor Schoelcher was born in Paris on July 21, 1804 and became a French parliamentarian. He lived and traveled on the islands of Guadeloupe and Martinique, becoming interested in the lives of black slaves. Under his leadership, slavery was abolished in French territory on April 27, 1848. He died in 1893 and is remembered on French Caribbean Islands as a great statesman and humanitarian. His memorial day is celebrated with Anguillan sailboat races at Grand Case, a mini-marathon, and an island-wide bike race ending up in Grand Case.

August

August 15 . . . . **Day of the Assumption** (B/F)

August 24 . . . . **Fête de Saint-Barthélemy** (B)
The feast day of Saint Barthélemy is celebrated with church services, official government ceremonies, boat races, a public dance, and fireworks in Gustavia.

Variable . . . . **Boubou's Music Festival** (B)
See *Music*, page 19, for details on this popular event.

November

November 1. . . . . **All Saints Day** (B/F)
Islanders commemorate this religious holiday by placing lighted candles in all cemeteries.

November 11. . . . . . . **Remembrance Day/Armistice Day WWI** (B/F)

Saint Martin Day/Concordia Day (D/F)
Concordia Day corresponds to the feast day of Saint Martin of Tours, the patron saint of France, for whom the island is named. It is a multi-faceted holiday that simultaneously commemorates the longstanding agreement (Concordia) between Dutch and French citizens, who amicably share the small piece of land, recognizes the day Columbus first sighted the island, honors its namesake, and remembers those who died during World War I. There's a ceremony by government officials at the Border Monument obelisk, followed by parades, a 20-mile "Around the Island" race, dancing, and feasting.

December

December 25 . . . . **Christmas Day** (B/D/F)

December 26 . . . . **Boxing Day** (B/D/F)

Decmber 31. . . . . **New Year's Eve** (B/D/F)

■ Carnival

Every Caribbean island celebrates Carnival, but the traditions and dates vary. On St. Barts and the French side of St. Martin, the festival begins about two weeks before Shrove Tuesday, which is known as Fat Tuesday or *Mardi Gras*. Everything comes to a close on Ash Wednesday or *Mercredi des Cendres*, with the burning of *Vaval*, the King of Carnival.

The Dutch side of St. Martin postpones its Carnival until the last two weeks of April, so the island actually celebrates almost nonstop throughout the winter/spring season. Dutch traditions include electing King Momo (sometimes spelled *Moumou*) and a Carnival Queen to preside over the events, which include music concerts, parades, cooking competitions, and street parties called **jump ups**. The main parade is usually timed to coincide with Queen Juliana's birthday on April 30, a public holiday. As on the French side, an effigy of the King is burned on the final night to end the festivities.

The tradition of electing a king to reign over Carnival began in ancient Rome and Greece, where the week before the holy season of Lent was spent eating, drinking, and making merry. All societal rules were abandoned, and people, whether slaves or masters, disguised themselves with masks and marched through the streets in immodest clothes, sang raunchy songs, and defied laws. The **King of Carnival** mocked authority by suspending all rules and commanding everyone to enjoy themselves.

Today, the king is the winner of a music competition held to select Carnival's official "road song," or theme song. Calypso, and its variations, is the heartbeat of the Caribbean, and each year the islands' musicians try to outshine one another with an original song. Traditionally, the song mocks government officials, laws, or some social situation on the island. The lyrics are always witty and usually rude or risqué.

No one is allowed to be a bystander during Carnival. Residents and visitors all join the dancing, singing, and feasting. On the French side of St. Martin, the streets of Marigot and Grand Case become parade routes, with booming bands, gaily decorated floats, and participants marching along in outrageously elaborate costumes – towering headdresses, colorful feathers, and glitzy jewels. Similar parades and parties take place in Gustavia on St. Barts.

Carnival Village, set up two blocks from Front Street in Philipsburg during the Dutch-side celebration, features more than 100 game and food booths. Best-selling Caribbean favorites include dumplings, johnny cakes, barbecue chicken, conch fritters, and icy drinks. Local and well-known international bands perform almost non-stop on a central stage.

The highlight of both the French and Dutch Carnivals is the **Grand Parade**. Bands, floats, and marchers jam the roads for miles, and everyone on the entire island turns out to sing, dance, and celebrate. In the end, a straw figure representing the King of Carnival is burned. According to legend, this ceremonial blaze also destroys everyone's sins and leaves the islands pure.

Customs

When traveling outside the continental boundaries of your home country, always carry a valid passport, even if you aren't required to present one. Since regulations are subject to change, especially during times when international security is on high alert, it's also a good idea to check with the tourist office of the country you'll be visiting to verify current documentation requirements. Although you may not be asked to present it, immigration officials also require all visitors to St. Martin and St. Barts to possess a round-trip or onward-transit ticket, as well as proof of sufficient funds for their stay on the islands.

Get a Passport

Find out where to apply for a **US** passport by entering your zip code or state in the search box at http://iafdb.travel. state.gov, or ☎ 900-225-5674 and use the automated service for 35¢ per minute. You can also call ☎ 888-362-8668 to talk to an someone who will help you for a $4.95 flat fee. Additional information is available at http://travel.state.gov/ passport_services.html.

Canadians can get passport information by contacting ☎ 800-507-6868, www.dfait-maeci.gc.ca/passport.

UK citizens can call ☎ 0990-210-410, or visit www.ukpa.gov.uk.

Australians can apply for a passport at any post office or make inquiries by calling ☎ 131-232. Additional information is available at www.passports.gov.au.

Currently, citizens of the **United States**, **Canada**, and the **European Union** may enter St. Barts and St. Martin for a period of up to three months by presenting either a passport or a certified birth certificate plus a government-issued photo ID. Citizens of all other countries should check with their local French or Dutch embassy or the islands' tourist offices.

If you lose your passport, contact the local police and the nearest embassy or consulate of your country in the Caribbean. Citizens of the United States can contact **US Consul General T.J. Rose** on Barbados, ☎ 246-431-0225, fax 246-431-0179, or call the **US Embassy** on Barbados, ☎ 246-436-4950. Canadian citizens should contact the **Consulate of Canada** on St. Martin, ☎ 599-544-5211, fax 599-544-3242. Travelers from the United Kingdom can contact the **British High Commission** on Barbados, ☎ 246-430-7836, fax 246-430-7860.

WORD TO THE WISE

Remember that if you visit both islands, you will be required to present your documentation on each, even if you're just making a day-trip. However, there's no real border between the French and Dutch territories on St. Martin, so you don't have to show ID or declare purchases as you travel from one side to the other.

Protect the Kids

France and The Netherlands Antilles, like many other countries, strive to prevent international child abduction by requiring anyone traveling with a minor to provide documentary evidence of relationship and permission for the child to travel from the parent or legal guardian, if they are not present. Travelers may also be asked to present these documents when they return to their own country. Carrying these documents when you vacation with a child may prevent travel delays and inconveniences.

■ Arrival

Foreign-made personal items taken out of the US are subject to duty each time they are brought back into the country. Avoid this expense by registering watches, cameras, and other expensive articles that shout "foreign" with the Customs Office before you leave the US. You can also carry the dated sales receipt, insurance policy, or jeweler's appraisal to prove prior possession. To find the nearest Customs Office, ☎ 202-354-1000, www.customs.gov.

Citizens of the United States and Canada, who are 17 years of age or older, may bring a liter of liquor or two liters of wine and 200 cigarettes onto the islands. Citizens of the European Union may bring in 1.5 liters of liquor, four liters of wine, and 300 cigarettes.

Do not try to enter the Caribbean with illegal drugs, including marijuana. Possessing even a small amount will land you in jail and cost you more than you'll want to pay to get out. If you take prescription medications, carry them in the original labeled container, and if they contain narcotics, get a note from your doctor or carry a copy of the prescription.

■ Returning Home

Make your trip through Customs quick and hassle-free by packing all items that you bought on the islands together in the same bag and having all receipts readily available for Customs officials. Remember that you must declare everything that was given to you as a gift, as well as everything that you bought. If you had merchandise shipped home, you must declare these items when you go through Customs.

Each country has its own regulations for taxing and exempting purchases made by residents traveling to a foreign country. If you think you may buy more than a T-shirt, request a copy of rules from the Customs Service before you leave home.

Citizens of the **UK** can obtain a copy of regulations by contacting the National Advice Service of The UK Customs and Excise Center, ☎ 0845-010-9000, www.hmce.gov.uk.

Canadians living in all provinces can get a summary of regulations by contacting the Canada Customs and Revenue Agency, ☎ 800-461-9999, www.ccra-adrc.gc.ca.

Each resident of the **United States** is allowed to return home with $600 worth of duty-free goods every 30 days, and families traveling together may fill out a joint declaration form. If you arrive with new items worth more than the allowable credit, you will be charged a flat rate of 10% on the excess.

US citizens who are at least 21 years old may reenter the country with one liter of duty-free alcohol, and all residents may bring back 200 cigarettes and 200 cigars, as long as the cigars are not from Cuba.

Up to $200 worth of duty-free merchandise may be sent home from abroad, but only one package may be sent to each address per day, and alcohol, tobacco products, and perfume valued at more than $5 are not allowed. Each parcel must be labeled *Personal Use*, and an itemized list of the contents and the retail value must be attached.

Duty-free gifts to friends and family may be sent from foreign countries, but the limit is only one package per address per day, and the value must not exceed $100. Mark parcels *Unsolicited Gift*.

The government publishes a valuable pamphlet for travelers called ***Know Before You Go***. It's free, and may save you time, money, and stress when you travel outside the country. Request a copy from the US Customs Service, ☎ 202-354-1000, www.customs.gov.

■ Departure Tax

You will be charged a $20 departure tax when you leave St. Martin, even if you're going to St. Barts or one of the other nearby islands. The only exception is for travelers going to another island within the Netherlands Antilles, such as Saba or St. Eustatias, in which case the tax is only $5. Expect to pay your tax at a separate window after you check in, but before you enter the departure lounge.

St. Barts charges a $5 per person departure tax, but it is included in the cost of your airline or ferry ticket, so you don't have to pay it as you leave the island.

Health & Safety

St. Martin and St. Barts are clean, modern, and safe. That said, there are some common precautions that you should take.

- The **water** that comes from indoor taps is desalinated sea water or purified rain water. It tastes fine. Restaurants will pretend that they do not serve tap water, but insist, unless you prefer bottled water, which may cost more than soda or wine. Do not drink water meant for irrigation from outdoor taps.

- Food in almost all eating establishments is free of disease-causing bacteria and contamination. Eat hot foods hot and cold foods cold.

Do not eat from a buffet that has been sitting out more than two hours, unless the food has been kept covered and at the correct temperature with heating or cooling apparatus. Avoid prepared food sold by street vendors, and wash all fresh fruits and vegetables before eating.

■ Most health-reporting agencies include all Caribbean islands in one general category without considering the conditions on individual islands. St. Martin and St. Barts are among the more healthful islands in the region, so keep that in mind when you check the following agencies for information about infection outbreaks, health concerns, and suggested vaccines:

The Bureau of Consular Affairs, http://travel.state.gov/.

The US Centers for Disease Control and Prevention, ☎ 404-332-4559 (in the US), or internationally at 877-394-8747, fax 888-232-3299, www.cdc.gov/travel.

The Medical Advisory Services for Travelers Abroad (MASTA) provides health tips and useful links for minimizing risks while traveling. www.masta.org.

The World Health Organization, www.who.int.

Health Canada, www.hc-sc.gc.ca.

WORD TO THE WISE

If you become seriously ill or injured while on the islands, your country's consular or embassy office in the Caribbean may be able to assist you. Also, your health insurer and most major credit card companies can suggest names of qualified doctors and certified hospitals in the Caribbean. For a list of hospitals and medical clinics, see the Facts & Numbers *section at the end of each island in this book.*

■ Remember that the Caribbean **sun** is stronger than in North America or Europe. Wear a high sun-protection-factor (SPF) cream containing zinc oxide or titanium dioxide, sunglasses, and a hat or visor during daylight hours. If you get burned anyway, drink plenty of water to prevent dehydration and smooth on a coat of aloe vera gel. If you feel dizzy or develop a fever, headache, or nausea, you may have experienced sunstroke. Seek medical attention.

- **Mosquitoes** are usually kept away by the steady winds, but at night and on calm days, you may want to use an insect repellent containing DEET. Some people claim that Avon's *Skin-So-Soft* is the best insect repellent, but scientists can't duplicate results in the lab. A product called *Bite Blocker,* made from soybean oil, protected wearers for about an hour and a half during lab testing. Eucalyptus oil products (*Fite Bite* and *Repel Lemon Eucalyptus Insect Repellent* are two) tested a bit better and protected wearers for about two hours. Try the nontoxic stuff and decide for yourself. If precautions don't work and you're still bitten, use a product such as *Sting-Eze* to relieve the itch.

■ Crime

 Thieves are among us, even in paradise. St. Martin and St. Barts are not known for aggressive pick pockets or *sand bandits* who steal your stuff off the beach while you're in the water. However, the islands are becoming more populated and unemployment is a current problem, especially on St. Martin, so watch your valuables and always, always lock your car.

On a recent trip, we heard the following stories from fellow visitors:

A doctor and his wife were driving back to their hotel after dinner one evening when they saw a woman lying beside the road. Thinking she was injured, they stopped to help her. Yeah, you guessed it – a group of boys jumped out of nearby bushes, took everything and fled.

Another man and his wife stopped at a lookout point, stepped a few feet away from their car to take a picture, and heard the car doors slamming closed as a thief started the engine and sped away with their wallets, airline tickets, passports, and a beach bag full of clothes.

One local blames the growing petty crime problem on youths who have nothing better to do. Whatever the reason, take common precautions to guarantee your safety, and watch for clever schemes.

Time Shares

Speaking of clever schemes, this falls into the annoying, but not dangerous category.

Timeshare salespeople have a rather novel approach on St. Martin. Young, clean-cut, cheerful couples travel together, either on foot or by motor scooter or jeep, and stop unsuspecting tourists with various believable stories that always end with the tourist sitting through a sales pitch in order to receive a "prize."

During a recent visit, we were approached several times before we caught on. On our first and best encounter, a chipper college-aged man pulled his little jeep in front of our car parked at the border marker on a hill between the French and Dutch territories. His pert girlfriend jumped from the car and ran back waving her hands to announce breathlessly that we perhaps had won a $500 radio promotion. All we had to do was scratch off the protective cover on a small card to reveal a series of numbers. If any three numbers matched, we had won.

Of course, we uncovered three sevens. In order to collect the $500 prize, we simply presented the winning card at the sales office of a new luxury resort. And, by the way, we would be treated to a fabulous hour-and-a-half tour of the resort and information about how we could own a part of it. Even if we weren't interested, please, please stop by for at least 45 minutes so Miss Pert could collect her $50 bonus, the money she used to put herself through college.

Similar incidents occurred while we took pictures in Marigot, at a stoplight in Philipsburg, coming out of a restaurant in Simpson Bay, and during a sunset happy hour on the beach. If you're interested in this sort of thing, no problem. Otherwise, wave away all cute young couples who seem overeager to meet you with a polite "No thank you."

Money Matters

■ Currency

As strange as it may seem on an island that doesn't even have a proper border between its two nations, French St. Martin doesn't accept Dutch St. Martin's florins, and Dutch St. Martin won't take French St. Martin's euros.

However, businesses on both sides of St. Martin and throughout St. Barts accept US dollars, though they usually give change in local currency. Visitors from the United States don't need to convert dollars into euros or florins. Visitors from Canada will want to convert Canadian dollars into either US dollars or euros and florins, depending on the exchange rate. European visitors who plan to spend time on Dutch St. Martin should convert enough euros to florins for daily expenses.

The best advice for everyone is to charge as much as possible to your credit card, and let the banks do the math. This will eliminate inaccurate exchange rates, you'll have a detailed record of where you spent your vacation money, and your pockets won't be loaded down with a variety of mixed currency.

If the merchant charges your purchase in euros or florins, check to be sure the use of local currency is clearly marked on the charge slip. While it doesn't make much difference when you're dealing in euros, you will be paying double if your account is charged in dollars for what you bought in florins. It is to your advantage to be charged in local currency, because merchants use a less favorable conversion rate than banks when they write up the bill in US dollars.

If you do pay for goods or services with cash in US dollars, expect change in local currency, and assume the exchange rate will not be in your favor. Also, before you make a purchase, be sure you know which currency prices are quoted in.

At publication, one euro was equal to almost exactly one US dollar, and a Netherlands Antilles florin was worth about 56¢. The prices given in this book are in US dollars.

■ ATMs & Banks

ATMs are located outside the arrival terminal at Princess Juliana Airport on St. Martin, at the cruise-ship dock and Bobby's Marina in Philipsburg, and at most banks in Philipsburg, Marigot, and Grand Case. The Food Center grocery stores have machines and are located on Union Road in Cole Bay, on Bush Road and Airport Road in Simpson Bay. Shopping centers and resorts have begun to install ATMs, as well, so ask around. Find a more complete list of ATMs and banks in *Island Facts and Numbers* at the end of the St. Martin and St. Barts chapters, pages 150 and 218.

On St. Barts, ATMs are located at Banque Française Commerciale in Gustavia and St. Jean, and at Banque National de Paris in Gustavia.

Dutch-side ATMs dispense US dollars. French ATMs dispense euros. Some machines give you a choice of currency.

Banks on both sides of St. Martin and on St. Barts commonly close weekends and holidays. On St. Barts and French St. Martin, most banks are open Monday-Friday, 8 am-noon and 2-4 pm, but hours vary somewhat, especially in the afternoon. On Dutch St. Martin, banks operate Monday-Friday, 8:30 am-3:30 pm, and most stay open an hour later on Friday afternoon. The bank at Princess Juliana Airport is open daily, 8:30 am-5:30 pm.

WORD TO THE WISE *If possible, avoid exchanging money at hotels or currency exchange offices. They don't charge a commission, but the exchange rate is worse than at banks or ATMs.*

Going Metric

US citizens continue to have trouble with temperature, distance, and quantity measured in anything other than "American." Use this chart and avoid the shame.

Pounds vs. Kilos	
At the market, if you want a pound of fruit, ask for half a kilo. Need more or less? You do the math.	
I kilogram	2.2046 pounds
I pound	0.4536 kilograms
On the Road	
When you buy gas, you'll need almost four liters to make a gallon. The distance from one town to the next may be 10 kilometers, but that's only a little over six miles.	
I liter	1.06 quarts or 0.264 gallons
3.8 liters	4 quarts or one gallon
1.6 kilometers	I mile

Is It Hot in Here?	
Temperature is converted from °C to °F by multiplying the Celsius temperature by nine, dividing the result by five and adding 32.	
15°C	59°F
20°C	68°F
25°C	77°F
30°C	86°F
35°C	95°F

 It's easy to remember that 28°C = 82°F.

Electricity

 On St. Barts and French St. Martin, electricity operates at 220 volts/60 cycles, as in Europe and South America. On Dutch St. Martin, electricity runs at 110 volts/60 cycles, as in the US and Canada. Many resorts provide a hair dryer and an electric shaver outlet in their bathrooms, but check before you leave home. Ask also about the plug, since you may need an adapter if the hotel has French or Dutch outlets.

Use a surge protector for sensitive equipment, such as computers, on both islands, and watch for overheating if you're using a convertor. Charge your dive and photographic equipment, such as strobes, at the regulated outlets at dive shops.

Time

 St. Martin and St. Barts are both on Atlantic Standard Time, which is four hours earlier than Greenwich Mean Time. They do not observe Daylight Savings Time. When the US is in standard time, the islands are one hour later than Eastern Standard Time. When the US is observing Daylight Savings Time, it is the same time on the islands as in New York and other East Coast cities.

Travel Information

Telephones

Telephones, like currency, are an area where the French and Dutch don't jibe, thus making a simple thing quite difficult. The area code for **St. Barts** is **590**. The area code for **French St. Martin** is also **590**, but when you call the French side from the Dutch side you must dial 00, then 590, then 590 again, plus the six-digit number. (Example: 00-590-590-xx-xx-xx.)

When you call within the **French** overseas territory, you must dial a **0** before the area code. For example, if you are on the French side of St. Martin and wish to call St. Barts (or even next door), you must dial 0590 + six-digit number.

The area code for **Dutch** St. Martin is **599**, and when you call from the French side, you must dial 00 + 599 + the seven-digit number.

Got that?

Making an **international call** is simpler. From either Dutch or French St. Martin or St. Barts, access the international service by dialing 00, then enter the country code plus the number you wish to reach. To call the **US** or **Canada**, dial 00 + 1 + area code + the number. To call anywhere in **Great Britain**, dial 00 + 44 + the area code + the number. You can find all other country codes listed along with long-distance rates in the TELEDOM phone directory that's available at hotels.

WORD TO THE WISE
You may have to wait for a second tone after dialing 00 before dialing the country code and local number, especially on St. Barts.

■ On-Island Phone Cards

Public phone booths don't accept coins. Use a **Télécarte**, which looks like a credit card, to make local and international calls when you're in **French** territory. Use a similar-looking **TELCard,** when you're on **Dutch** soil. This is less expensive than phoning from your hotel. You can buy a card on St. Barts at the post offices in Gustavia, St. Jean, and Lorient, and at the gas station near the airport. On St. Martin, TELCards are readily available at convenience stores, gas stations, and hotel desks on the Dutch side. A Télécarte may be harder to find on the French side, but most resorts and many shops in the larger towns have them.

> *Major credit cards can be used for long distance calls from some phone booths on both islands, but the rates are higher than with a prepaid calling card.*

■ To Call the Islands

To call from the US or Canada, dial 011 to get international service, then the area code (590 for St. Barts and French St. Martin; 599 for Dutch St. Martin) plus the on-island nine-digit number, which means dialing 590 twice. When calling the islands from Great Britain, dial 00 to get international service, then the area code plus the on-island nine-digit number, which means you will dial 590 twice. (Example 00-590-590-xx-xx-xx.)

WORD TO THE WISE

> *The number for directory assistance on Dutch St. Martin is 542-2211; on French St. Martin and St. Barts it is 1012.*

Planning Your Trip

You can gather quite a stack of information online, by phone, and through the mail from the tourist information offices for each island. If you have a specific question or just want general information, talk to an English-speaking staff member before you leave home, then check with the on-island office for current events, new attractions, and special offers.

■ French Tourism Offices

Information on the Web: www.saint-barths.com.

In the US

Maison de la France
444 Madison Ave., 16th Floor
New York, NY 10022
☎ 212-838-7800, fax 212-838-7855

In Canada

Maison de la France
1981 Avenue McGill College
Montréal, Québec, H3A 2W9
☎ 514-288-4264, fax 514-845-4868

In England

Maison de la France
178 Piccadilly
London W1J 9AL
☎ 09068-244-123, fax 207-493-6594

On St. Martin

Office du Tourisme de Saint-Martin
Route de Sandy Ground
Marigot
☎ 0590-87-57-21, fax 0590-87-56-43

On St. Barts

Office du Tourisme de Saint-Barthelemy
Quai du Général De Gaulle
Gustavia, 97095
☎ 0590-27-87-27, fax 0590-27-74-47

■ Dutch Tourism Offices

Information on the Web: www.st-martin.org

In the US

Sint Maarten Tourist Office
675 Third Avenue, Suite 1806
New York, NY 10017
☎ 800-786-2278 or 212-953-2084, fax 212-953-2145

In Canada

Sint Maarten Tourist Office
703 Evans Avenue, Suite 106
Toronto, Ontario
M9C 5E9
☎ 416-622-4300

On St. Martin

Sint Maarten Tourist Bureau
Imperial Building
23 Walter Nisbeth Road
Philipsburg
☎ 599-542-2337, fax 599-542-2734

■ Making Reservations

Transportation and hotel rates change often and vary between vendors. Never accept the first price you receive. If your time and patience are limited, contact at least two certified travel agents who specialize in the Caribbean, then double-check their quotes with a bit of Internet research before you agree to anything. With infinite time and diligence, you can uncover numerous bargains and packaged arrangements for yourself, especially off-season.

Once you make a decision, pay by credit card. While trip insurance is the only way to fully protect yourself from unforeseeable events, a credit card purchase will give you some measure of protection and a means of protesting the charge if an airline, hotel, or travel agency goes out of business. Never pay an agency for travel arrangements with cash or a check.

■ Finding & Evaluating a Travel Agent

Find an agent near you by clicking on the interactive map at www. doitcaribbean.com/travelagents.

The **Institute of Certified Travel Agents** (ICTA, www.icta.com) is an organization that accredits travel-agent schools in the US and issues credentials to qualified graduates. ICTA awards Certified Travel Agent (CTA) status to professionals who have worked in the industry for at least 1½ years. The Certified Travel Counselor (CTC) status is granted to those with at least five years of experience in the industry. **Cruise Lines International Associated** (CLIA, www.cruising.org) is a worldwide association for certified agents who specialize in cruises. See page 50 for a list of cruise specialists.

In addition to verifying certification, ask if your potential travel agent is a member of any professional associations. Two of the best-known in the US are the **American Society of Travel Agents** (ASTA, www.astanet.com) and the **Association of Retail Travel Agents** (ARTA, www.artaonline.com). Members of the **Caribbean Travel Organization** (CTO), www.onecaribbean.org, have a particular interest in the region, and those who have completed a destination-specialist course will have considerable knowledge of the islands' history, culture, main tourist attractions, lodging, restaurants, and activities.

■ Insure Your Trip

Before you pay for any type of travel insurance, check your existing health and homeowner's policies to see if you're covered while on vacation. If you need additional coverage, consider one of the following health, trip, or lost-luggage insurers. Some travel agencies, tour organizers, and cruise lines offer their own insurance, which may allow you to cancel your trip for any reason without charge. However, remember that these types of policies will not help if the company itself goes bankrupt.

Traveler's Medical Assistance Insurance

These health-care policies take care of things such as emergency evacuation, hospital care, and doctor's charges. Some provide 24-hour telephone contacts and immediate aid if you become ill. Others reimburse you for medical expenses after you file the necessary papers on your return home. Both services may be covered under your existing health insurance program, but few will pay for emergency travel back home. You must purchase additional med-evac insurance for this benefit, which is rarely needed but can cost $10,000 or more.

Most government-supported programs, including Social Security Medicare for US citizens, do not provide coverage for medical costs outside the home country. Supplemental plans must be purchased.

Never leave home without your ID card that shows proof of your health insurance coverage.

For a list of companies that sell travelers' health insurance, ask your travel agent or check the website maintained by the **US Department of State Bureau of Consular Affairs**: http://travel.state.gov/medical.html.

*Students, teachers, and anyone between the ages of 12 and 25 may purchase a **Council Travel** ID for $22. The ID includes insurance that covers hospital stays, accident medical expenses, emergency evacuation, accidental death and dismemberment, repatriation of remains, passport protection and baggage delay insurance. Numerous worldwide discounts are also available with the ID. ☎ 800-2COUNCIL, www.counciltravel.com / idcards.*

Lost-Luggage Insurance

Many homeowner or apartment-renter policies cover personal items that are lost or stolen while you're on vacation. In addition, airlines pay international travelers about $9.07 per pound or $20 per kilo, up to a maximum of $640 per bag, if checked luggage is lost. Unchecked luggage is covered for a total of $400 per passenger. Additional coverage may be purchased in advance from the airline for more valuable articles. Most travelers do not need more protection than this, but if you do, contact your current insurer about buying a rider for your existing policy.

Trip-Cancellation Insurance

This is the one type of insurance that can be valuable for many travelers. If you pay for all or portions of your trip in advance, then must cancel because of illness or a death in the family, the policy will reimburse most or all of the costs. Some policies also cover cancellation in the event of illness, injury, or the death of your travel companion. Most policies exclude trip cancellation in the event of war or other hostilities, including terrorism and natural disasters. Some policies also exclude travel to specific destinations that are prone to political unrest.

Many comprehensive travel insurance policies now include coverage if your tour operator defaults but, if you buy a policy directly from your tour provider, you will not be covered for default of that provider. Some policies only cover tour operator default if the operator files for bankruptcy.

Non-Refundable Ticket Insurance

If you buy a non-refundable airline ticket through a travel agent that uses Worldspan Network, you can purchase insurance that will reimburse the cost if you are not able to use the ticket. You are covered whether you simply do not want to reschedule the trip and pay the $100 change fee, or don't want to take the trip at all.

Travel Insurance Agencies

In the US

The following agencies are a few of the well-known and reputable suppliers of travel insurance listed by, but not endorsed by, the US Department of State:

Travelex Insurance Services, ☎ 800-228-9792, www. traveles-insurance.com.

International Health & Travel Insurance Quotes, ☎ 800-909-7476, www.nwinc.com.

Access America, ☎ 800-284-8300, www.accessamerica. com.

Travel Guard America, ☎ 800-826-4919, www. travelguard.com.

In the UK

UK Long and Short Stay Travel Insurance, ☎ 01702 587003, www.coeconnections.co.uk.

Worldwide

Mercury International, ☎ 01273 205703 (in the UK), fax 01273 733719, www.mercuryint.co.uk.

■ Travelers With Special Needs

Several organizations offer information and assistance to older travelers and persons with health problems. If you have special needs, contact one of these groups:

AARP offers 50-and-older members discounts on airfares, hotels, and rental cars, ☎ 800-424-3410, www.aarp.com.

Access-Able Travel Source is an online publication that helps make travel easier for mature and disabled people by providing information about accessibility at hotels and attractions around the world. You won't find much specifically about the Caribbean, but look for details on cruise ships, travel agents, equipment rental, and packing. www.access-able.com.

Society for Accessible Travel & Hospitality is a clearinghouse for disability-access information. They also publish the magazine *Open World*. ☎ 212-447-7284, fax 212-725-8253, www.sath.org.

Emerging Horizons, an accessible travel magazine and newsletter, has feature articles and a section with advice on accessible tours, lodging, transportation, and recreation. http://emerginghorizons. com.

In the US alone, more than 15 million people have diabetes, and almost 20% of senior citizens suffer from the disease. While travel is more difficult for diabetics, it's not impossible. Get information on how to prepare for a trip and manage while on vacation from **The American Diabetes Association**, ☎ 800-DIABETES, www.diabetes.org; or **The Canadian Diabetes Association**, ☎ 800-BANTING www.diabetes.ca.

Getting There

■ By Air

 St. Martin constantly vies for increased air service from Europe and the Americas. For the best fares and most direct routing, search the Internet in addition to checking with a certified travel agent who has extensive knowledge of the Caribbean.

Air service is frequent from several North American and European cities, and regional or commuter flights are available from San Juan and other islands within the Caribbean. St. Martin has two airports, **L'Espérance** (☎ 590-87-53-03) on the French side, and **Princess Juliana** (☎ 599-545-4211) on the Dutch side. Since L'Espérance (airport code SFG) only accepts small aircraft, most international visitors land at Princess Juliana (airport code SXM).

You must first land on St. Martin, St. Thomas, or Guadeloupe, before you can continue on to the tiny **St. Bart's Airport** (☎ 0590-27-65-41, airport code SBH). It's also possible to take a ferry from St. Martin to St. Barts, but through-passengers won't find this practical since it entails transferring luggage from the airport to a ferry dock by taxi.

Airline Contact Information	
International Carriers	
Air Canada	☎ 800-776-3000 (US), 888-247-2262 (Canada), 599-542-3316 (St. Martin), www.aircanada.ca
Air France	☎ 800-237-2747 (US/Canada), 599-545-4212 (St. Martin), www.airfrance.com
American Airlines/ American Eagle	☎ 800-433-7300 (US/Canada), 599-545-2040 (SMX St. Martin), www.aa.com
Continental Airlines	☎ 800-523-3273 (US), www.flycontinental.com
Delta Air Lines	☎ 800-325-1999 (US/Canada), www.delta-air.com
KLM	☎ 0870-5074-074 (UK), 800-447-4747 (US/ Canada), 31-20-4-747-747 (The Netherlands), www.klmuk.com
Northwest Airlines	☎ 800-447-4747 (US), www.nwa.com
United Airlines	☎ 800-241-6522 (US), www.ual.com
US Airways	☎ 800-428-4322 (US), www.usair.com

WORD TO THE WISE

Some international carriers have code-share arrangements with regional airlines, allowing them to book you through to your destination on connecting flights. As an example, US Airways has an agreement with Winair for flights from St. Maarten to Anguilla, Antigua, Saba, St. Barts, St. Eustatius, St. Kitts and Nevis. They also have an agreement with Nevis Express linking San Juan with St. Kitts and Nevis. Other airlines have similar agreements, so ask your carrier about connections in the Caribbean.

Regional & Commuter Airlines & Air Taxis

Air Caraibes	☎ 0590-87-10-36 (SFG St. Martin), www.aircaraibes.com
Air Culebra	☎ 787-268-6951 (San Juan), www.airculebra.com
Air Mango	☎ 0590-27-88-81 (St. Barts), www.st-barths.com/air-mango
Air St. Thomas	☎ 800-522-3084 (North America), 340-776-2722 (St. Thomas) 0590-27-71-76 (St. Barts), www.airstthomas.com
Caribbean Star Airlines	☎ 800-744-7827 (in the Caribbean), www.flycaribbeanstar.com
LIAT	☎ 800-468-0482 (US) 599-545-5428 (SMX St. Martin), www.liat.com
St. Barth Commuter	☎ 0590-27-54-54 (St. Barts), www.st-barths.com/stbarth-commuter/index.html
Winair	☎ 0590-27-61-01 (St. Barts), 599-545-2568 (SMX St. Martin), www.fly-winair.com

■ By Cruise Ship

 Several international cruise lines make stops at both St. Martin and St. Barts. You won't have time to really explore the islands on a short layover, but cruising is a good way to sample several destinations on one trip. Later, you can return for a longer stay on the islands you like best.

Smaller ships, such as those on the **American Canadian Caribbean Line**, spend several days cruising one area with multiple stops or multiple-day stays on each island. This allows you to island-hop and spend more time at each destination, without the hassle of unpacking more than once.

The **National Association of Cruise Oriented Agencies** (NACOA) is an organization of certified travel agents who have made a serious commitment to helping travelers find the cruise vacation that best suits their expectations. To find a cruise-travel specialist in your area, go online to www.nacoaonline.com/frame_supplier.htm and type your zip code, area code, or city into the *Find* window.

The website for the **Cruise Lines International Association** (CLIA) gives cruisers information, current news, and ship profiles. Find them at www.cruising.org.

Travel Information

The following websites provide additional information for cruise-ship passengers:

- Find descriptions of cruise ships, destinations, and schedules online at **www2.i-cruise.com/shipinfo. htm**.

- Read *The SeaLetter,* an Internet publication that covers cruising: **www.sealetter.com**.

- Check out *Cruise News Daily* for information, rates, and tips on shore excursions at: **www.cruisenewsdaily. com**.

Destinations change as new ships come on-line and cruise companies adjust their itineraries, but the following lines are most likely to offer stops on islands covered in this guide.

Cruise Lines	
American Canadian Caribbean Line	☎ 800-556-7450 or 401-247-0955, www.accl-smallships.com
Carnival Cruise Lines	☎ 888-CARNIVAL, www.carnival.com
Celebrity Cruises	☎ 800-CELEBRITY, www.celebritycruises.com.
Cunard Line	☎ 800-728-6273, www.cunardline.com
Holland America	☎ 877-932-4259, www.hollandamerica.com
MSC Italian Cruises	☎ 888-278-4737, www.msccruisesusa.com
Norwegian Cruise Line	☎ 800-327-7030, www.ncl.com
Princess Cruises	☎ 800-PRINCESS, www.princess.com
Radisson Seven Seas	☎ 800-477-7500, www.rssc.com
Royal Caribbean Cruise Line	☎ 800-398-9819, www.royalcaribbean.com
Seabourn Cruise Line	☎ 800-929-9595, www.seabourn.com
Windjammer Barefoot Cruises	☎ 800-327-2601, www.winjammer.com

■ Package Vacations

Many visitors book a package deal that includes transportation and accommodations. Often, these bundled arrangements cost less than separately booked hotel or airfare.

Start with the airlines. They frequently throw in multi-night hotel arrangements at a great price when you book your flight. Or go the other way and check with the hotel of your choice for a package deal that includes airfare.

Tour-scan computerizes all the published package trips to the Caribbean according to season, then selects the best values for each island. You can search for your trip by destination, cost, hotel rating, and preferred activity. This can save you a lot of time, but if you want to search for yourself, using a search engine such as www.google.com, you may find unpublished packages at even better rates. Search the website or order a 52-page $4 catalog at ☎ 800-962-2080, www.tourscan.com.

Vacationpackager.com is, of course, an online company. It leads you to dozens of other companies that offer package vacations to many Caribbean destinations, including St. Martin and St. Barts. Their website also lists toll-free phone numbers and Internet addresses for a variety of travel-related organizations and businesses. www.vacationpackager.com.

Getting Around

Hotels do not operate shuttle service to and from the airports, but if you're on a charter flight or package vacation, transfers to and from your hotel are often included. Taxis wait for arriving passengers just outside the arrival terminal, and most car rental companies will either deliver your car to you at the airport or pick you up and take you to their off-site location.

■ By Car

International Car Rental Companies	
Avis	☎ 800-331-1212, www.avis.com
Budget	☎ 800-472-3325, www.drivebudget.com
Dollar	☎ 800-800-4000, www.dollar.com
Hertz	☎ 800-654-3001, www.hertz.com
National	☎ 800-CAR-RENT, www.nationalcar.com
Thrifty	☎ 800-THRIFTY, www.thrifty.com

See Getting Around *in each island's section for local numbers of international companies and listings for local rental agencies.*

■ By Taxi

Taxis are plentiful at the airport and ferry docks on both islands. Drivers are licensed by either the Dutch or French government and carry a published rate sheet, which lists authorized fares between many common destinations, such as from the airport to major hotels. Ask to see it. Daytime rates apply from 7 am to 9 pm. An additional 25% is added to the base fare until midnight; 50% is added to the base fare from midnight to 7 am. If your destination isn't listed, negotiate a price before you get into the cab, confirm the currency and whether the rate is quoted per trip or per passenger.

Unless the driver overcharges, is rude, or takes you out of your way, add at least a 10% tip to the fare. Tip a little extra if the driver gives information about the island as you travel or helps you with your luggage (50¢ to $1 per bag is standard, depending on the size and weight of each piece). US dollars and local currency are accepted, but don't expect the driver to have change for large-denomination bills.

WORD TO
THE WISE

Most drivers will not allow you to get into their taxi wearing a wet swimsuit, so make sure you're dry and wearing some type of coverup.

The **Taxi Dispatch Hotline** number is 147 on St. Martin. You can also call individual taxi stands:

- in **Philipsburg**, Dutch St. Martin, ☎ 599-542-2359.

- at the **airport** on Dutch St. Martin, ☎ 599-5435-4317.

- in **Marigot**, French St. Martin, ☎ 0590-87-56-54.

- at the airport in **Grand Case**, French St. Martin, ☎ 0590-87-75-79; in **Gustavia**, St. Barts, ☎ 0590-27-66-31.

- in **St. Jean**, St. Barts, ☎ 0590-27-75-81.

■ By Mini-Van

Public transportation on St. Martin is by private mini-buses and vans, which travel the main roads between Philipsburg, Marigot, Grand Case, and the large residential areas. Fares are inexpensive – around $1 or $2, depending on the distance – but you may have to change vehicles several times to reach your destination. Since the service is used heavily by local workers, expect the buses/vans to be crowded during morning and afternoon transit times. Few or no vehicles provide service at night. There's no public transportation on St. Barts.

■ Inter-Island Ferries

Most people take a 10-minute, 15-mile airplane ride between St. Martin and St. Barts, but you also can take a ferry or high-speed catamaran for about $50-$60 round-trip, plus $7 port tax. If you love the sea, the trip is spectacular.

WORD TO THE WISE

If you are prone to motion sickness don't go to St. Barts by sea. It is always rough, especially heading toward St. Barts when the winds are strong. Consider taking a half-dose of a medication, such as Dramamine, an hour before you depart. Or swallow two or more capsules of ginger root an hour before your trip. You can buy this at most pharmacies, including the one across from the ferry dock in Gustavia. Some passengers on a recent trip had good luck with acupressure wrist bands purchased at a health food shop.

Voyager I and *Voyager II* are 125-passenger ferries that run a regular schedule between both Marigot and Philipsburg on St. Martin and Gustavia on St. Barts. They also offer scheduled trips to Saba. Make your reservation well in advance, especially during high season. Contact them at Bobby's Marina in Philipsburg, ☎ 599-542-4096, fax 599-542-2858, at the waterfront in Marigot, ☎ 059-87-10-68, fax 0590-29-34-79, or at the Port of Gustavia. ☎ 0590-27-54-10, fax 0590-29-34-79, www.voyager-st-barths.com.

The Oyster Line operates round-trip ferry service every day except Monday between Captain Oliver's Resort at Oyster Pond on Dutch St. Martin and Gustavia, St. Barts. Contact them for times and reservations, ☎ 0590-87-46-13. The crossing takes 45 minutes and costs $48 or 53 euros round-trip.

The Edge is a 62-foot high-speed catamaran that leaves Pelican Marina on the Dutch side of St. Martin in the morning and returns from Gustavia in the afternoon. It makes the trip in 45-50 minutes, which is about half the time of the other ferries. A sister boat makes daytrips to Saba. Contact them for reservations through **Aqua Mania Adventures**, ☎ 599-544-2640, fax 599-544-2476, www.stmaarten-activities.com/trips/edge.htm.

Marine Service offers charter boat service between St. Martin and St. Barts. Contact them at Gustavia Harbor, ☎ 0590-27-70-34, fax 0590-27-70-36, www.st-barths.com/marine.service/snorkleframe.html.

St. Martin

Planes from North America and Europe deliver hundreds of vacationers to St. Martin several times a day. Many more come by cruise ship. So, what's the tremendous attraction?

Great beaches and year-round sunshine come to mind. But many places in the Caribbean have that.

Fabulous bargains at duty-free shops are a factor. But Charlotte Amalie on St. Thomas is almost as good.

Certainly, nature lovers can find better choices, and anyone looking for Dutch culture should continue traveling south to Curaçao.

Many North Americans come to St. Martin for a fast French fix without the long plane ride or the hassle of communicating in a foreign language. Others set up headquarters on the easily reached island and make quick day-trips to the neighboring islands. And then, there are those adventurous types who simply love the fast-paced, highly developed, two-nation isle.

Variety, then, is the great attraction. No other island in the Caribbean can offer you more choices.

It is impossible to overlook the fact that little St. Martin is divided in half and governed by two nations. There's no border crossing as such between French Saint Martin to the north and Dutch Sint Maarten to the south, but you'll know when you cross from one side to the other.

The roads are different. France does asphalt better. They line it, sign it, and maintain it better, too. And, the atmosphere is different. The Dutch specialize in high-rise glitz, big-time gambling, and rambunctious partying. The French have perfected the gentle art of bistro dining, boutique shopping, and bare-all sunbathing.

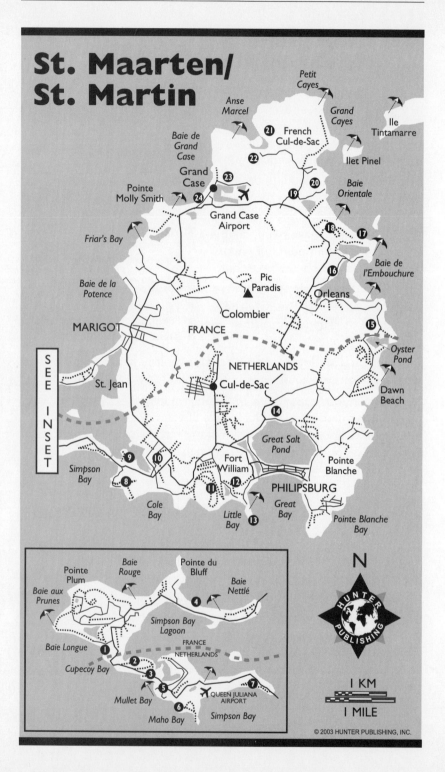

St. Maarten/
St. Martin

Petit
Cayes

Anse
Marcel

Grand
Cayes

Ile
Tintamarre

㉑ French
Cul-de-Sac

Baie de
Grand
Case

㉒

Ilet Pinel

Grand
Case ㉓

㉚ ㉘ Baie
Orientale

Pointe
Molly Smith ㉔

Grand Case
Airport

㉙

㉘

㉗

Friar's Bay

Baie de
l'Embouchure

Baie de la
Potence

Pic
Paradis ㉖

▲

Colombier

Orleans

MARIGOT

FRANCE

㉕

Oyster
Pond

S E E   I N S E T

St. Jean

NETHERLANDS

Cul-de-Sac

Dawn
Beach

㉔

Great Salt
Pond

Pointe
Blanche

㉙

㉚

Simpson
Bay

㉘

Fort
William

㉒

PHILIPSBURG

Cole
Bay

㉑

Little
Bay ㉓

Great
Bay

Pointe Blanche
Bay

Pointe
Plum

Baie
Rouge

Pointe du
Bluff

Baie
Nettlé

Baie aux
Prunes

④

Simpson Bay
Lagoon

FRANCE
NETHERLANDS

Baie Longue ①

②

Cupecoy Bay

③

Mullet Bay ⑤

⑦

⑥

QUEEN JULIANA
AIRPORT

Maho Bay

Simpson Bay

N

HUNTER PUBLISHING

I KM

I MILE

© 2003 HUNTER PUBLISHING, INC.

St. Maarten/St. Martin Map Key

1. La Samanna, Cupecoy Beach Club, Ocean Club, Sapphire Beach Club
2. Summit Resort Hotel
3. Towers at Mullet Bay
4. Royal Beach, Mercure Simson Beach, Nettlé Bay Beach Club, Anchorage Margot Hotel, Le Flamboyant Resort
5. Royal Islander, Maho Beach Hotel & Casino
6. Caravanserai Hotel
7. Horny Toad Guesthouse, La Chatelaine, Mary's Boon Beach Plantation
8. Flamingo Beach Resort, La Vista, Pelican Resort & Casino
9. Atrium Resort, Royal Palm Beach Club, Turquoise Shell
10. Carl's Unique Inn
11. Sea Breeze Hotel
12. Belair Beach Hotel, Divi Little Bay Beach Resort
13. Fort Amsterdam
14. Zoo Sint Maarten
15. Blue Beach, Captain Oliver's
16. Butterfly Farm
17. Club Orient
18. Cap Caraïbes, Esmeralda Resort, Green Cay Village, La Plantation
19. Alizéa
20. Anchorage Little Key, Hotel Mont Vernon
21. Le Méridien L'Habitation, Hotel Privilège, La Résidence de Lonvilliers
22. Privilège Resort & Spa
23. Grand Case Beach Club, L'Esplanade Caraïbes
24. Pavillon Beach

———— Paved Road   ▪ ▪ ▪ ▪ Border

············ Unpaved Road   ⏃ Beaches

St. Martin

Top Temptations

- **Duty-free shopping** in Philipsburg and Marigot.

- **Dining** on gourmet French food in Grand Case.

- **Sunbathing** at clothing-optional Orient Bay Beach.

- Trying your luck at one of the **big casinos**.

- Escaping to a **luxurious villa**.

- **Diving and snorkeling** the marine reserves.

- **Hiking** Pic Paradis (Paradise Peak).

- **Picnicking** on Dutch cheese and French wine in an isolated cove.

- Studying ancient **Indian artifacts** in Marigot's Museum.

- **Day-tripping** to St. Barts, Saba, Anguilla, and St. Eustatius.

The French-Dutch Split

 How did this small piece of land become the home of two nations? Quite amicably, it seems, but not in the beginning.

First, the Indians ruled. Then Columbus arrived, claimed everything for Spain, and the Pope said that was fine. A few hundred years later, Dutch sailors came along, found the saline ponds, and began exporting salt back to The Netherlands. When the French found out how nice things were in the Caribbean, they sent settlers to colonize the entire region. With their European foes moving in, the Spanish quickly lost interest and returned to their enterprises in the Greater Antilles. French and Dutch settlers returned to St. Martin, and agreed to share nicely. Of course, the Indians did not fare well during all this back-and-forth Old World bickering.

By the time Europeans found out they could grow cash crops on the islands, all the Indians had been killed or banished, and the land owners were hurting for workers. The solution? African slaves. Boatloads were delivered to the plantations, and soon black slaves outnumbered white owners.

Again, St. Martin became a battleground as French and Dutch settlers snatched each other's land and the English joined in, just for the
sport of it. Between 1648 (when the first fair-share agreement was
signed on Mount Concordia) and 1815 (when the post-Napoleonic
Treaty of Vienna put an end to all French hostilities with the British),
St. Martin changed hands 16 times.

Finally, after the English left, the French and Dutch settled into a
complacent relationship (but they didn't like each other enough to
build a decent road between the two halves of the island until the
1900s). The French freed their slaves in 1848. The Dutch hung onto
theirs until 1863. In the end, the fall of free labor destroyed the economy on both sides.

St. Martin deteriorated badly during the late 1800s and early 1900s,
but began to profit from tourism when Princess Juliana International
Airport opened on the Dutch side in 1943 with the region's longest
airstrip. Understandably, the French side also benefitted from the
airport, as did neighboring islands. Over the past 60 years, the dual-
nation island has experienced a building boom, developed a healthy
economy, and become home to a large, diverse population.

The Dutch side developed faster, and is still ahead of the French side,
but not by much. While St. Martin as a whole is one of the most
densely populated islands in the Caribbean, the Dutch side packs
about 10,000 more residents into four fewer square miles.

On our most recent visit, we found the island looking good and working on its tourist appeal. Philipsburg has been spruced up a bit:
there's a new cruise terminal; many store fronts have a fresh coat of
paint; and sand has been trucked in to restore the hurricane-battered
city beach. Marigot has a new shopping mall. You'll have unavoidable
traffic jams going into and out of both capital cities, but traffic circles
and signal lights have cars moving fairly smoothly through most areas. Rural roads are rarely congested, and you can bypass the towns,
unless you want to shop.

Official Business

Dutch St. Martin is divided into two three-island clusters. The "S"
islands (St. Maarten, St. Eustatius, and Saba) lie just east of the
Virgin Islands between Anguilla and St. Kitts. The "ABC" islands
(Aruba, Bonaire, and Curaçao) lie along the northwestern coast of

Venezuela. Both groups are part of the Kingdom of the Netherlands, which includes Holland.

Curaçao is the capitol of The Netherlands Antilles, which were granted political autonomy within the Kingdom of the Netherlands in 1954. Each island has its own Parliament and elects its own officials to manage domestic affairs, but depends on Holland for defense and foreign policies. A representative governor is appointed for a six-year term by the sovereign of the Netherlands on the recommendation of local officials.

In 1986, Aruba withdrew from the Netherlands Antilles and became an autonomous member of the Kingdom of the Netherlands. Since then, residents on St. Martin and the other four Dutch islands have discussed the benefits of also seeking *status aparte*. However, the majority consistently votes for *status quo* and continued ties with Holland and its current reigning monarch, Queen Beatrix.

Citizens of Dutch St. Martin are Dutch nationals and carry passports issued by the European Union. Citizens of French St. Martin are French nationals and carry passports issued by the European Union.

French St. Martin is part of the *sous-préfecture* which includes Tintamarre (just over a mile off St. Martin's northeast coast) and St. Barts (about 18 miles south of St. Martin) and is overseen by Guadeloupe, a *département français d'outremer.* Four elected representatives speak for this overseas department in the French Assemblée Nationale, and two elected senators hold seats in the Sénat. Residents enjoy all the social programs available to French citizens living on the continent, but are heavily dependent on France economically as well as politically. Residents of Guadeloupe regularly lobby for autonomy, but St. Martin, Tintamarre, and St. Barts appear content with their status as French possessions.

Getting There

■ By Air

See page 48 for airline contact information.

Unless you depart from another Caribbean island, you will arrive at **Princess Juliana International Airport** (SMX, ☎ 599-545-4211), located on the skinny strip of Dutch land that separates Simpson Bay from the Caribbean Sea. This is the second busiest airport in the Caribbean (San Juan, Puerto Rico records more takeoffs and landings), and it has one of the few landing strips in the region long enough to accommodate jumbo jets.

DID YOU KNOW?

The international airport is sometimes called Queen Juliana Airport, because Juliana became queen of the Netherlands in 1948, five years after the airport was built. She reigned until 1980, when she abdicated in favor of her eldest daughter, Beatrix, who is the current queen.

L'Espérance Airport (SFG, ☎ 590-87-53-03), on the French side, accepts smaller aircraft arriving from other islands within the Caribbean.

WORD TO
THE WISE

Do not misplace the Immigration Card you receive on arrival. You will need it when you depart.

St. Martin

Getting Around

■ By Inter-Island Ferry

Voyager I and **Voyager II**, ☎ 599-542-4096 (Philipsburg), 059-87-10-68 (Marigot), 0590-27-54-10 (Gustavia).

The Oyster Line, ☎ 0590-87-46-13.

The Edge, ☎ 599-544-2640.

Marine Service, ☎ 0590-27-70-34.

You can find additional information about inter-island ferry service on page 53.

■ By Bus

Bus service on St. Martin is essentially nonexistent. Privately owned vans and mini-buses do run between the main towns and large residential areas, but they are meant for locals traveling to work, doctor's appointments, and grocery stores. You may certainly catch a ride on them for a dollar or two, but it's not the best way to get around.

If you want to give it a try, wait beside the bus-stop sign for the non-scheduled vehicles to arrive on Back Street in **Philipsburg**, at the corner of Rue Président Kennedy and Rue de Hollande in **Marigot**, and anywhere along the main road in **Grand Case**. You can also flag down a bus or mini-van anywhere along the road. (You can identify them by the destination sign in the front window.) They'll stop, if they have room to squeeze you in. Service is infrequent after dark and stops completely between midnight and 6 am.

∎ By Taxi

The **Taxi Dispatch Hotline** number is 147. You can also call the individual taxi stands: in **Philipsburg**, Dutch St. Martin, ☎ 599-542-2359; at the **airport** on Dutch St. Martin, ☎ 599-5435-4317; in **Marigot**, French St. Martin, ☎ 0590-87-56-54; at the airport in **Grand Case**, French St. Martin, ☎ 0590-87-75-79.

∎ Driving on St. Martin

Roads are in good condition on most parts of the island, and international road signs are posted, so getting around by car is easy. All the rental agencies will accept US, Canadian, or European licenses. You must have held the license for a minimum of two years.

Car Rental & Driving Tips

- Driving is on the **right** side of the road, as in the US and Canada.

- International **road signs** are posted along with local signs written in French, English, or Dutch.

- **Speed limits** are set in kilometers at 40 (25 mph) in urban areas, and 60 (37 mph) in rural areas.

- Most rental-car speedometers register in **kilometers**.

- **Right turns** are not allowed on red lights anywhere on the island.

- Plan to pay with a major credit card and ask before you leave home about included **insurance** on rentals charged to the card.

- If you pay cash, you will be required to leave a $500 **deposit**.

- **Age restrictions** for renters vary somewhat among companies, but in general, the minimum age is either 21 or 25 and the maximum is 65 to 70. If you fall within these two age groups, verify the company policy before you book a car.

- Always **lock your car doors** and use any theft-prevention device the rental company supplies. Don't leave valuables visible inside the car.

Rental Car Companies

Below are local contact numbers. See page 52 for international and toll-free telephone numbers and website addresses of major car rental companies.

Rental rates vary season-to-season, but they average about $35 per day for a small car with manual transmission, air conditioning and unlimited mileage. You pay about $65 per day for a larger car or one with automatic transmission or four-wheel-drive. Weekly rates are available and usually work out to be less per day. Insurance add-ons begin at $10 per day, but you may be responsible for $500 worth of damage anyway. Check before you sign up.

WORD TO THE WISE

If you decline insurance coverage offered by the agency, verify in advance that the credit card you will be using covers you if you have an accident or damage the car. American Express and Visa Gold Card customers are not covered when they rent a sports car or four-wheel-drive vehicle.

International Car Rental Companies	
Alamo	☎ 599-545-5546
Avis	☎ 599-2847 or 0590-87-50-60
Budget	☎ 599-545-4030, 0590-87-38-22
Dollar	☎ 599-545-3281
Europcar	☎ 599-544-2168, 0590-77-10-46
Hertz	☎ 599-545-4541, 0590-87-83-71
National	☎ 599-544-2168 (associated with Europcar)
Thrifty	☎ 599-545-2393
Local Car Rental Companies	
Adventure Car Rental	☎ 599-544-3688
Best Deal Car Rental	☎ 599-545-3061
Cannegie Car Rental	☎ 599-544-4329
Executive Car Rental	☎ 599-545-4028

AAA Car Rental	☎ 0590-87-37-17
Moke Alizées	☎ 0590-87-78-54
Route 66 Jeeps and SUVs	☎ 0590-29-65-88
Saint Louis Car Rental	☎ 0590-87-45-71
Sens Unique Smart Cars	☎ 0590-87-22-88

DID YOU KNOW?

Numbers beginning with area code 599 connect to an office on the Dutch side; numbers beginning with area code 0590 connect to an office on the French side.

■ By Scooter & Motorcycle

The best way to get around the island is by car, but St. Martin's roads are in good condition, so scooters and motorcycles are often used. Traffic in Philipsburg and Marigot is heavy, especially when a cruise ship is in port, and the main highways are busy during hours when locals are going to or from work. Unless you're a skilled, experienced biker, stick to side-roads.

You'll pay about $35 per day for a scooter, and $45 to $100 per day for a motorcycle. If you want to roar around the island on a Harley, plan to spend around $150 per day during high season.

WORD TO THE WISE

A reader writes that she and her husband were riding a motorcycle on a main road during daylight hours on the French side of St. Martin, when boys on another motorcycle pulled up beside them. The boy on the back of the second cycle repeatedly kicked the reader until she and her husband fell. While they lay injured on the road, more cycle-riding youths appeared and attempted to steal the motorcycle. They were able to fend off their attackers, but sustained additional injuries. They spent time in the hospital emergency room, but got no help from the police, who said these motorcycle attacks were becoming more common on the island.

St. Martin

Motorcycle Rentals	
Eugène Moto	☎ 0590-29-65-89 or 0590-87-13-97
Location 2 Roues	☎ 0590-87-20-59
Harley Davidson	☎ 599-544-2704 or 599-542-6565
Rodael Rental	☎ 599-542-5155
Yamaha Power Center	☎ 599-544-3249

■ By Bicycle

 While off-road riding is a popular sport on St. Martin, most streets have no shoulder and too much traffic to allow safe biking. If you want to bike to secluded beaches or tour the countryside, sign up for a guided tour with someone who knows the terrain. The following offer a variety of guided tours, kayak/bike combo trips, and bike rentals. You will pay about $18 per day to rent a mountain bike; $39-$49 for a two- or three-hour tour, including bike, helmet, and water bottle; and around $100 for a full-day combo trip that includes all equipment and lunch.

Bike Tours & Rentals	
Authentic French Tours	Marigot, ☎ 590-87-05-11, fax 590-87-99-47
Caribbean Mountain Bike Adventures	Marigot, ☎ 590-87-05-11, fax 590-87-25-54
Tri Sport	Airport Road, Simpson Bay, ☎ 599-545-4384, fax 599-545-4385, www.stmartinstmaarten.com/trisport

Getting Married

Honeymooning on St. Martin is terrific. Getting legally married there is another story. Don't consider a wedding on the French side, unless you're a French citizen. The requirements and paperwork are just too difficult. You can, however, have the official ceremony on the Dutch side and celebrate on the French side.

For 127 years, Dutch St. Martin had a law that prohibited non-residents from getting married on the island. But in 1997, this injunction was repealed, so you're free to tie the knot. Allow a couple of months to make plans and process the documents. A wedding consultant can save you time and headaches, and there are several on the island.

Tropical Weddings and Honeymoons, ask for Lucie Davis, ☎ 599-544-4143, fax 599-544-4863, www.sintmaarten-wedding.com.

Caribbean Wedding Consultants, ask for Joan Bethune or Marie Williams, ☎ 599-547-2067.

Enchanté Weddings, ask for Henneke Lee, ☎ 599-543-6900, fax 599-543-6007, www.enchanteweddings.com.

Weddings In St. Maarten, ask for Jean Rich, ☎ 599-544-3021, fax 599-544-3201, www.weddings-in-stmaarten.com.

Documents You Need to Get Hitched

You will be required to submit the following documents to the Chief Registrar at the Census Office on Soualiga Road in Philipsburg (☎ 599-542-2457, fax 599-542-4267):

- A **birth certificate** for both the bride and groom bearing a raised official stamp.

- A **declaration** of marital status for both the bride and groom that is no older than three months and stating that both are single. Forms are available from most attorneys, some notaries, and from wedding consultants.

- People under 18 years of age, must have written **parental approval** for marriage.

- The **legal address** of both the bride and groom.

- Proof of **length of stay** on St. Martin (the bride and groom must be on the island for at least a week).

- If either the bride or groom is widowed or divorced, he or she must provide **death** or **divorce certificates**.

- Valid **passports** for both the bride and groom.

The official marriage will be performed by the Officer of the Civil Registry, but you can have a clergyman perform a religious service afterwards in the Marriage Hall of the Philipsburg Census Office.

St. Martin

Marriages held outside of the Marriage Hall in Philipsburg must be observed by six witnesses. Weddings inside the Marriage Hall require two witnesses.

Exploring the Island

■ Taxi Tours

 If you want a private orientation tour of both sides of St. Martin, consider hiring a member of either the Dutch or French taxi association as a guide. You can find drivers at Wathey Square in Philipsburg or at the taxi kiosk near the waterfront market in Marigot. Staff members at your hotel reception desk and the owners or managers of good restaurants are another good source of guide recommendations. Be sure to request an English-speaking driver who knows both sides of the island well, and agree on a fee before you start out. Expect to pay about $35 for a two- to three-hour tour for two people. On a recent visit, drivers on the Dutch side were charging a bit less, so make a couple of calls and compare the itineraries before you decide on a guide. You may also want to speak directly with the driver, either in person or by phone, to make sure you understand his accent.

> **Dutch St. Maarten Taxi Association**, ☎ 147 (hotline) or 599- 545-4317.

> **French St. Martin's Taxi Service & Information Center** (Marigot), ☎ 590-87-56-54.

■ Group Sightseeing Tours

Several reputable companies run scheduled sightseeing tours from both sides of the island. Be sure the tour you sign up for has an English-speaking or bilingual guide. During high season, many resorts organize tours for guests at special prices, so check with the activities director before you book something on your own.

If you want to save precious vacation time, do a little research before you leave home, and book one or more tours that you know you'll enjoy. Request current information by fax or e-mail to save the expense of making long-distance calls.

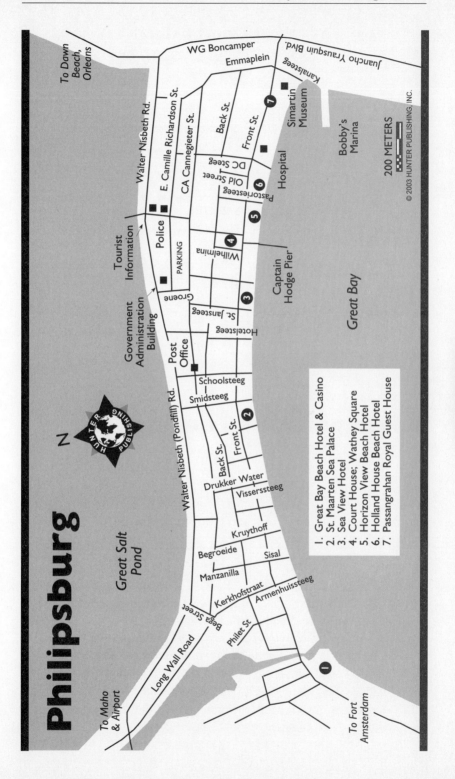

Philipsburg

Great Salt Pond

To Maho
& Airport

To Dawn
Beach,
Orleans

WG Boncamper

Emmaplein

Juancho Yrausquin Blvd.

Kanalsteeg

Simartin
Museum

Bobby's
Marina

Great Bay

Captain
Hodge Pier

Hospital

Walter Nisbeth Rd.

E. Camille Richardson St.

CA Cannegieter St.

Back St.

Front St.

Old Street

DC Steeg

Pastoriesteeg

Wilhelmina

St. Jansteeg

Groene

Hotelsteeg

Tourist
Information

Government
Administration
Building

Police

PARKING

Post
Office

Schoolsteeg

Smidsteeg

Front St.

Back St.

Drukker Water

Visserssteeg

Kruythoff

Begroeide

Manzanilla

Sisal

Kerkhofstraat

Armenhuissteeg

Bega Street

Long Wall Road

Walter Nisbeth (Pondfill) Rd.

Philet St.

To Fort
Amsterdam

200 METERS

© 2003 HUNTER PUBLISHING, INC.

1. Great Bay Beach Hotel & Casino
2. St. Maarten Sea Palace
3. Sea View Hotel
4. Court House; Wathey Square
5. Horizon View Beach Hotel
6. Holland House Beach Hotel
7. Passangrahan Royal Guest House

N

St. Martin

Tour Companies	
R & J Tours	Colombier, ☎ 590-87-56-20, fax 590-87-52-98
Elle Si Belle	Simpson Bay, ☎ 599-545-2271, fax 599-545-2273
Transco	Quartier d'Orléans, ☎ 590-87-30-16, fax 590-87-39-30
Winston Sightseeing Tours	Quartier d'Orléans, ☎ 590-87-25-61, fax 590-87-25-6
Artsen Travel and Tours	Simpson Bay, ☎ 599-545-4193, fax 599-545-4194
Calypso Tours	Cole Bay, ☎ 599-544-2858, fax 599-544-2858
Mack Sightseeing	Lower Princess Quarter, ☎ 599-542-3070, fax 542-2702
Sint Maarten Sightseeing Tours	Simpson Bay, ☎ 599-545-2646, fax 545-2645
TriSport Eco-adventures	Simpson Bay, ☎ 599-545-4384, fax 599-545-4385, trisport@stmartinstmaarten.com, www.saintmartinsintmaarten.com/trisport

■ Independent Touring

If you have a car or motorcycle, you can easily tour the entire island in a day. This is good for cruise-ship passengers with limited time, but if you're staying for several days, consider dividing your tour into smaller excursions. Ideally, you'll want to schedule time to explore Philipsburg and Marigot at leisure, linger awhile in Grand Case, and take frequent beach breaks.

A Walking Tour of Philipsburg

 The principal city of Dutch Sint Maarten is second only to Charlotte Amalie on St. Thomas (US Virgin Islands) for popularity among duty-free shoppers. If you don't stop to shop, you can walk the town and see its few sights in less than an hour. But no one ever walks through without stopping, so plan on spending most of a morning or afternoon browsing.

Philipsburg is built on a narrow stretch of land that separates the natural harbor of Great Bay from the marshy Great Salt Pond. John Philips, a Scotsman who served as a commander in the Dutch military, founded the town in 1763, and over the next 200 years residents survived by fishing and selling salt extracted from the pond. Back then, Philipsburg was wide enough for only two parallel streets, **Voorstraat**, which bordered the sea, and **Achterstraat**, one block north bordering the Great Salt Pond. The principal public buildings were built around **De Ruyterplein**, the town square.

Today, landfill has almost doubled Philipsburg's width, and four roads now run parallel from one end of town to the other, but Voorstraat (now called **Front Street**) and Achterstraat (now called **Back Street**) still hold the most interest for visitors. Traffic travels one way, west to east, along Front and one way toward the west along Back. **Walter Nisbet Road** (also called **Pondfill Road**) brings traffic in and out of town along the southern edge of Great Salt Pond. **Cannegeiter Street**, also two-way, runs the length of town between Nisbet and Back. Narrow north-south lanes (*steegjes*) with names ending in *steeg* connect the four main thoroughfares.

You can park free near the police station on Walter Nesbeth Road. (Watch for signs pointing the way as you enter town.) Paid parking is available a block closer to Front Street at the corner of Peterson Street and Cannegieter Street, just south of the Government Building. Rates are $1 per hour, up to $14 for a full day. Limited parking is available along the streets, but you'll have to arrive very early in the morning – or be very lucky – to snag a spot.

A good place to begin your tour is **Cyrus Wathey** (say watty) **Square**, the former De Ruyterplein, site of **Captain Hodge Pier**, where shuttle boats drop off passengers from cruise ships docked in the harbor. The pier was given a $1.7 million makeover after Hurricane Luis ripped through the island in 1995, and tourist-friendly conveniences now include a tourist information office, an ATM, restrooms, and telephones. If a cruise ship is in port, the area will be especially crowded with taxi drivers, tour operators, hair-braiding artisans, and people hawking timeshares and fruit drinks.

The covered pier sits opposite the historic and picturesque **Courthouse**, designed by John Handleigh and built first in 1792 by Willem Hendrik Rink, Dutch commander of the island, then rebuilt in 1825 after the original structure was damaged by a hurricane in 1819. The green-trimmed, white, two-story building faces the square. It is topped by a bell tower, surrounded by a quaint picket fence, and shaded by a palm tree. Over the years, it has been used as a fire station, prison, and a post office.

On the square, a signpost points the way to casinos, shops, and restaurants. Turn toward the east and follow the one-way automobile traffic along Front Street toward what is locally known as the "Head of Town." All the buildings face inward, toward the street, so you won't have the pleasure of walking along the lovely beach unless you turn down one of the narrow access passages or cut through a hotel lobby.

WORD TO THE WISE

Old Street is a personal favorite. This pedestrian-only shopping arcade is off the north side of Front Street, east of Wathey Square, between Colombian Emeralds and Oro de Sol jewelry stores. Plants and potted palms line the block-long lane that houses specialty boutiques and a French café.

Among the mostly characterless architecture of the duty-free shops, take notice of the few traditional buildings and gingerbread-design houses. The **Pasanggrahan Hotel** at 15 Front Street is the oldest inn on the island and the original structure was the home of St. Martin's first governor. Pasanggrahan is an Indonesian word meaning "guest house," and the West Indies-style inn hosted Queen Wilhelmina of the Netherlands for a short time during World War II when she was en route to Canada after being exiled from her country by the Nazis. Walk through the antiques-furnished lobby to the veranda facing Great Bay Beach, where you can enjoy a quiet drink, stop by Wilhelmina's old room (which has been converted into the Sydney Greenstreet Bar) or have lunch in the jungle-like setting of the hotel's restaurant (☎ 542-3588).

The **Guavaberry Emporium**, which occupies a late 18th-century cedar townhouse at 8-10 Front Street, was built on the site of a former synagogue. It's a busy place, with shoppers zipping in and out of the colorful old former governor's home to buy flavored liqueurs made with the local guavaberry fruit and rum. Old timers remember when the legendary folk liqueur was made in private homes and quaffed on holidays and during cultural celebrations. Stop in for a free sample of the bittersweet drink. If you like it, order a guavaberry colada to sip while you browse through the shop's other island-made products (☎ 542-2965).

The Sint Maarten Museum at Museum Arcade, 7 Front Street, occupies a restored two-story house built in the 1800s. Spend a few minutes looking over old photographs, antique maps, shards of Arawak pottery, plantation-era artifacts, items retrieved from the *HMS Proselyte* (a ship that sank off Fort Amsterdam in 1801), and an exhibit on damage caused by Hurricane Luis in 1995. You can browse the street-level gift shop without charge and visit the second-floor displays by paying a $1 fee (free for children). They are open Monday-Friday, 10 am-4 pm, and Saturday, 10 am-2 pm, ☎ 542-4917.

Just east of the museum, turn right toward the water into the **Sea Street Arcade**, a pedestrian-only brick-paved lane lined with specialty shops and cafés. Pick up a snack and carry it down to the sand, where you can watch men shelling conch. (**Monk Kok Seafood Bar** sells burgers and sandwiches; **Caliente Beach Bar** makes fresh-fruit drinks.) If your timing's right, you may spot one of the sailboats that competed in past America's Cup competitions leaving the docks at **Bobby's Marina** (☎ 542-2366) for a short-course race. You can sign up to join one of the crews for a three-hour sail by stopping at the **12 Metre Challenge** office (☎ 542-0045) at the marina. (See *Adventures on Water*, page 94, for more information.)

To get back to Cyrus Wathey Square, walk along **Great Bay Beach**, one of the nicest city beaches in the Caribbean. The beach is about 65 feet wide, and the mix of crushed shells and golden sand makes for easy strolling. On a clear day, you may be able to spot Saba in the distance.

A Walking Tour of Marigot

The capital of French Saint Martin is far more charming than its Dutch counterpart, Philipsburg. But of course. *C'est Français, n'est-ce pas?*

Marigot (say *mar-ee-go*) means "backwater" in French and refers to the swampy conditions the first colonists found when they arrived on the island's western shore in the 1600s. If it weren't for the natural harbor provided by wind-protected Marigot Bay, the French probably would have left the marshy mangrove to the birds and settled elsewhere. But sailors then, as now, were willing to suffer most anything for love of their boats and the sea, so today we have a lovely town built along the sandy curve of a yacht-filled bay.

Commercialism is less apparent here than in Philipsburg, and for the most part, the town has retained much of its innate French charm and West Indian style. Contemporary boutiques have moved into colonial buildings and Creole homes, and new development blends esthetically with the old. A modern shopping complex, anchored by a

St. Martin

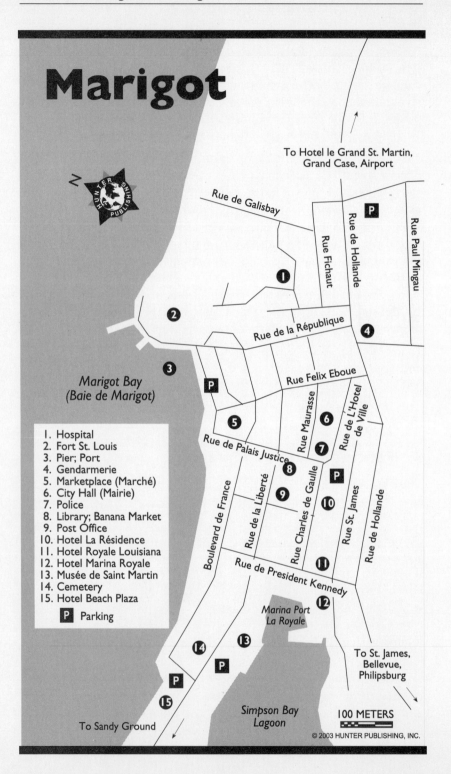

Marigot

To Hotel le Grand St. Martin,
Grand Case, Airport

*Marigot Bay
(Baie de Marigot)*

1. Hospital
2. Fort St. Louis
3. Pier; Port
4. Gendarmerie
5. Marketplace (Marché)
6. City Hall (Mairie)
7. Police
8. Library; Banana Market
9. Post Office
10. Hotel La Résidence
11. Hotel Royale Louisiana
12. Hotel Marina Royale
13. Musée de Saint Martin
14. Cemetery
15. Hotel Beach Plaza

P Parking

Rue de Galisbay
Rue Fichaut
Rue de Hollande
Rue Paul Mingau
Rue de la République
Rue Felix Eboue
Rue Maurasse
Rue de L'Hotel de Ville
Rue de Palais Justice
Boulevard de France
Rue de la Liberté
Rue Charles de Gaulle
Rue St. James
Rue de Hollande
Rue de President Kennedy

*Marina Port
La Royale*

To St. James,
Bellevue,
Philipsburg

*Simpson Bay
Lagoon*

To Sandy Ground

100 METERS

© 2003 HUNTER PUBLISHING, INC.

Match supermarket, is at the northeast edge of town, and an air-conditioned shopping mall and office complex rises above the waterfront below Fort Saint-Louis.

WORD TO THE WISE

*If you drive into town, **park free** in front of the Office du Tourisme on Rue du Morne, the road leading into town from Sandy Ground to the south, or in the waterfront lot near the market on Blvd. de France.*

You can walk nonstop through the small town in about an hour, but Marigot is meant to be savored slowly in small sips. Allot an entire morning or afternoon for strolling through the shops and lingering over lunch. Return in the evening to dine by candlelight at one of the waterfront restaurants and enjoy nighttime entertainment.

Begin your walking tour at the **Office du Tourisme** at the south end of town on the main road leading into town from Sandy Ground. Here you can pick up maps and brochures and ask one of the friendly English-speaking representatives for information. The office is open Monday-Friday, 8:30 am-1 pm and 2:30-5:30 pm; Saturday, 8 am-noon. ☎ 87-57-23.

Before you leave the area, stop by the history and archeology **museum** called **Sur les Traces des Arawaks** (On the Trail of the Arawaks), which shares a parking lot with the tourist office. Inside, the exhibits (labeled in English and French) include tools made from shells, pieces of pottery, and jewelry crafted by indigenous inhabitants as far back as 1800 BC. The pieces were dug up during archeological excavations made by the Hope Estate Archaeological Society and, by comparing their design, experts are able to link tribes that once lived on the island with natives of South America and follow their trail of migration from the Orinoco River basin in present-day Venezuela.

Other pre-Colombian exhibits include a reproduction of a 1,500-year-old burial site that was discovered at the excavation site in 1994. More recent history is depicted through numerous artifacts from the island's colonial period, and through photographs and antique maps from the last century. Contemporary local art and handmade crafts are displayed in the gift shop on the second floor. Ask about a group or private tour with one of the English-speaking guides, or visit on your own, 9 am-1 pm and 3-7 pm, Monday-Saturday, ☎ 29-22-84. Entrance fees are $5 for adults and $2 for children.

St. Martin

WORD TO THE WISE

If you're interested in obtaining more information about the ongoing excavations at Hope Estate in the hills near Grand Case, contact the Archeological Society, ☎ 29-22-84.

Port Royale is an easy walk from the Office du Tourisme and the museum. Just head north in the direction of town and watch for a passageway on your right that leads to the waterfront on Simpson Bay Lagoon. This is the best people-watching spot on the island. Lovely boats fill the marina, and boutiques and restaurants face the water along a U-shaped portion of the lagoon. You will feel as if you're in a small village on the French Riviera as you browse the chic shops, linger over café au lait at an outdoor café, or enjoy a gourmet meal at one of the petit restaurants. On Thursday evenings during high season, bands, jugglers, mimes, magicians, and dancers entertain along the boardwalk.

Leaving Port Royale, walk west toward the sea and turn north onto Boulevard de France, which parallels Marigot Bay. This will take you to a large square where the **public market** is held on Wednesday and Saturday mornings. A taxi stand and public restrooms are nearby, and the busy harbor is across the street. Stop to admire the oversized statue of an island woman sitting at the head of the marketplace. This lovely piece was sculpted by Martin Lynn, who lives with his wife, Caribbean painter Gloria Lynn, on the main street in Grand Case.

Boulevard de France ends at Rue de la République, one of Marigot's best shopping streets. The new enclosed and air-conditioned **West Indies Mall** sits opposite the harbor, and the road stretches east past a serious assortment of sassy shops. Even if you don't want to buy anything, stroll up and down the narrow roads that run more or less parallel to each other south of République. (Rue de la Liberté, Rue Maurasse, and Rue du Général de Gaulle are the main streets.) The quality and quantity of French goods will impress you. If you get tired or bored, pop into a little bar for a glass of French wine.

Allow your energy level to dictate your route after you finish exploring downtown. If you're still going strong, follow Rue Fichaut north off Rue de la République to Rue de l'Eglise, which leads up the hill to **Fort Saint-Louis**, overlooking the harbor above the West Indies Mall. If you don't want to make the 10-minute uphill hike, return to your car and drive up. The view is terrific.

The French built the stone fort between 1767 and 1789, during the turbulent time that led up to the French Revolution. British troops took advantage of the unstable political situation and slavery problems on St. Martin to attack and conquer the fort in 1794. The English held the fort, and controlled the island, for two years until Victor Hugues, backed by slaves who hoped to be freed, liberated the island and reclaimed Fort Saint-Louis. The fortress was abandoned after 1815 when the Treaty of Vienna put an end to English-French competition for Caribbean territory.

A Walking Tour of Grand Case

This will be short and sweet. Grand Case (say *grawn caz*) is tiny and has one main road that runs for about a mile down the center of town. It's a picturesque Creole village with a fine beach and a number of excellent eateries. Most of the European-trained gourmet chefs are set up in authentic West Indies houses, while local cooks serve island specialties from open-air *lo-los* (snack shacks). The contrast creates a festive atmosphere.

 See Where to Eat, *page 134, for information on individual restaurants.*

On many weekends and holidays, boat races and jump-ups (outdoor dance parties) add to the convivial spirit. On alternating Saturdays throughout the year, St. Martin fishermen compete against Anguilla fishermen for bragging rights – and, perhaps, a beer. Spectators gather on the sand to cheer for the sailors, and often local bands play near the pier. Aéroport de L'Espérance is located at the salt pond on the east side of town, and small planes on final approach come in low over the beach, adding to the noise and excitement. Tourists fit right in, so don't hesitate to join the fun.

*As you wander down Boulevard de Grand Case (the main street), watch on the east side for number 83, the home studio of **Gloria and Martin Lynn**. Their artist sons, Robert and Peter, no longer live full time on the island, but some of their work is on display at the house along with Gloria's and Martin's. Martin is best known for his large sculpture of a West Indies woman that sits beside the public market in Marigot. All paint scenes of island life, and their colorful work is sold in galleries. The gregarious Lynns welcome visitors "by appointment or by chance." If you see paintings outside on the covered front porch, and the door is open, drop in. Otherwise, call ahead, ☎ 590-87-77-24.*

After dark, Grand Case grows quiet and glitters with lights from **restaurant row**. During high season, reservations are essential, but during the summer, you can stroll along at dusk checking out the menus posted outside each restaurant, until you find one that suits your tastes and budget. Prices are a bit high, but not excessive. Remember, you'll be enjoying exquisite cuisine prepared by a European-trained chef from products flown in from the US, Holland, or France.

Island Highlights – A Driving Tour

One highway more or less circles St. Martin and connects the Dutch capital (Philipsburg), on the south coast, with the French capital (Marigot), on the west coast. Along the way, it swings off to Simpson Bay and Princess Juliana Airport. As it loops across the northern part of the island, it scrapes by Grand Case, then heads back south past Orient Bay and Oyster Pond.

You can do the circuit in one long day, but this is one of the busiest highways in the Caribbean, so plan your route to avoid rush-hour traffic. Also, allow plenty of time for photo stops. The shore is lined with gorgeous bays, and the rolling countryside is sprinkled with flowers in flaming colors. Look for picturesque scenes at the following sites:

- **Guana Bay**, off the secondary road that leads to the east coast from Great Salt Pond in Philipsburg. This is a high-end residential area with lovely homes set in the hills above the Atlantic.

- **Falaise aux Oiseaux** (Cliff of the Birds), a steep ridge overlooking the Caribbean on the northern edge of Terres Basses (Low Lands), a small bit of ground that would be an island if it were not connected to St. Martin by thin ribbons of land that form the north and south shores of Simpson Bay Lagoon. You can get out to Terres Basses by taking Airport Road from Philipsburg or the Sandy Ground Road from Marigot. Beautiful homes are scattered along Falaise aux Oiseaux between **Baie Rouge** (Red Bay) and **Baie des Prunes** (Plum Bay).

- **Colombier**, northeast of Marigot, inland from Friars Bay, is named for the woodpigeons or doves that once inhabited this hilly area. The valley at the foot of Pic Paradis produces the fruit and vegetables sold at the public market in Marigot. At one time, landowners produced large crops in this area, and you may spot 100-year-old mango trees, a few stalks of sugar cane, and perhaps a row of cotton or a coffee bush. Goats and cows graze along the dead-end road that runs past a scattering of Creole houses surrounded by flowers and herb gardens.

- **Pic Paradis** (Paradise Peak), the island's highest point at 1,391 feet, offers awesome views. You can drive there on a steep, rutted road (off the main highway north of Marigot) that leads east through the village of Rambaud. Many cars can't make it, so be prepared to turn back if the going gets too rough. The paved road becomes a single lane as you climb, so if you meet another car coming head-on, one of you will have to back up until you find a spot that is suitable for pulling over. Eventually, the single lane becomes a rocky track. It helps to have a four-wheel-drive vehicle with plenty of horsepower.

You can also hike to the top on the **Sentier des Crêtes,** a strenuous trail that begins on the west end of Colombier. Once you're at the summit, you can see Marigot, Philipsburg, the entire coastline, and across the ocean to St. Barts, Tintamarre, and Anguilla.

- **St. Louis**, off the main road south of Grand Case, is a small village above Friar's Bay that has majestic views of the western coastline.

St. Martin

- **Anse Marcel**, reached by a secondary road off the main highway just past L'Espérance airport, northeast of Grand Case, is a secluded village in the hills along a lovely bay. You'll pass a guard gate, but probably won't be stopped, unless you look like trouble. Residents in the area simply like to keep track of who's roaming about.

Worth a Visit

La Ferme des Papillons (The Butterfly Farm). Don't miss this on the French side just north of the town of Orleans. It's a 3,000-square-foot mesh-enclosed garden with waterfalls and stocked fish ponds. Hundreds of majestic butterflies from all over the world flutter freely to new-age music and land weightlessly on visitors' bodies. Try to visit when the doors first open in order to witness new babies being born and get in on the most active part of a butterfly's day. The $10 admission fee includes complimentary return visits, so make this stop early in your vacation. Take the guided tour to learn amazing facts and hear amusing stories about these gorgeous little creatures.

Before you leave, scoop up a couple of unique souvenirs from the gift shop and linger in the outside courtyard to enjoy refreshments in the company of liberated butterflies. The farm is open daily 9 am-4:30 pm, with the last tour at 3:30. Look for the sign on the main highway as you approach Orient Beach. Turn toward La Plage du Galion (Galion Beach), which is on Baie de l'Embouchure, north of Orleans, ☎ 590-87-31-21, www.thebutterflyfarm.com.

The St. Maarten Zoological & Botanical Park. If you're traveling with kids, or you happen to be an animal lover, make a visit to the zoo. It has a surprising number of unusual tropical animals, as well as lots of turtles and iguanas, and more than 180 parrots (recently relocated from the now-closed Parrot Jungle) that fly freely throughout the three-acre park. One of the most interesting animals is the golden lion tamarin, a long-tailed monkey with a lion-like mane, which is one of the rarest endangered species in the world. Most of the animals are in open concrete enclosures with no fence. Monkeys, of course, are behind a fence, and birds are completely enclosed, but you can walk into the aviary cages.

General Manager Franck Caulet has big plans for the zoological park, which includes developing a pleasing environment for the preservation of Caribbean animals. Recently, additional trees and plants have gone in along new paths that lead to the animal enclosures, Monkey Island, and the Bat Cage. Also, a new gift shop and restaurant have opened.

Watch for yellow signs pointing the way to the zoo, which is on Arch Road on the north side of Great Salt Pond, directly across from Philipsburg, in the residential area of Madame Estate. It's open daily, 10 am-6 pm. The entrance fee is $10 for adults, $5 for children two-12 years of age, and your ticket includes complimentary return visits. Stop by early in your vacation, then come back as often as you like to revisit your favorite animals. ☎ 599-543-2030.

Loterie Farm. You don't have to be a hiker to love this 150-acre compound built in a dense secondary tropical forest. It's a true step back in time, and you shouldn't miss the opportunity. The original farmhouse was discovered in 1995 after Hurricane Luis blew away vegetation that had been hiding it for several generations. Many people come here to eat at the **Hidden Forest Café,** part of the restored 18th-century sugar plantation. Much of the fantastic food served in the open-air dining room is grown in the farm's garden and creatively prepared by Chef Julie. (Don't pass up the cheesecake.) If you do want to hike, a 1½-hour guided interpretive tour leaves on several mornings from the café. You can also explore on your own, and experienced hikers will want to go all the way to the top of Pic Paradis. The set charge for guided tours is $25 per person, and you will be asked for a $5 "preserve-the-farm" donation if you explore on your own. The café is open Tuesday-Saturday, 11 am-3 pm and 6-11 pm, and on Sundays, 11 am-11 pm (last orders are taken around 9 pm). You can hike the trails from sunup to sundown. Look for signs to the farm off the main highway between Marigot and Grand Case, which leads east through the village of Rambaud. Call for information about the guided hikes, which usually depart around 10 am on three or four mornings per week. ☎ 590-87-86-16.

Old House. This museum is set up in a large green and white Creole house at the top of a hill. It was once the great house of an 18th-century sugar plantation and is worth a visit when you're in the Orient Bay area. The garden and house display tools and machines used in cultivating sugar cane and making rum, as well as interesting household objects from the plantation period, rare lithographs, and ancient maps. Look for the giant *Old House* sign suspended high between two poles on the road between Orleans and Orient Bay. Admission is $5 for adults and $2.50 for children under the age of 12. Schedule about 45 minutes to an hour to tour the house and garden, which is open Tuesday-Sunday, 9 am-4 pm. ☎ 590-87-32-67.

St. Martin

Adventures on Water

■ Best Beaches

St. Martin has 36 beaches, about one for every square mile of land. Those on the windward Atlantic side usually have more waves, unless they are in a protected cove. The Caribbean beaches tend to be calmer. All are open to the public, even those behind the guarded gates of posh resorts. Of course, only hotel guests are welcome to use the lounge chairs and umbrellas set up along these private stretches, but you can usually rent chairs if you don't want to simply spread a towel on the sand. A few beaches can only be reached via public-access trails that bypass the resorts.

WORD TO THE WISE

You've probably heard about the nude beaches on St. Martin. Actually, only one is known for total nudity, Baie Orientale (Orient Beach). At other French-side beaches and pools, many women go topless, and you may see an occasional naturalist sunning au naturel. On the Dutch side, discreet topless sunbathing is tolerated, and one section of Cupecoy Beach is popular with nudists.

Orient Bay Beach (Baie Orientale)

If you only visit one beach on St. Martin, make it Orient. Of course, you'll have plenty of company, but this highly developed mile-long stretch of powdery white sand is just too much fun to miss. The calm waters are always filled with colorful Jet Skis, windsurfers and Hobie Cats, and laughing kids run in and out of the waves. Parasails glide overhead and gorgeously bronzed bodies stroll the shore, browse at the open-air boutiques, and loll on the beach. Tiki-hut snack bars and full-service restaurants provide plenty to eat and drink. On many days, local bands set up on the beach to play original tunes and long-time island favorites with a calypso beat.

Club Orient (☎ 590-87-33-85), at the south end of the crescent-shaped beach, is the famous nudist resort. You can strip and join the guests (the resort has changing rooms), or just stand around in your swimsuit and gawk like a North American tourist. When you're bored with naked bodies, take your snorkel and mask out for a spin around the bay. The water is tranquil and clear most days, and the protective coral reef just off the beach is teeming with critters.

All the activity will make you hungry, and numerous bars and restaurants are open throughout the day and evening to provide a variety of food. Some are more like day resorts, with watersports, chair and umbrella rentals, massage huts, a boutique, and open-air showers or enclosed restrooms where you can dress before dinner.

Try **Bikini Beach** (☎ 590-87-43-25) for a pricey but dependably good casual meal; **Boo Boo Jam** (☎ 590-66-17-99) for pizza and burgers, especially on Sundays, when the band plays; **Kontiki** (☎ 590-87-43-27) for grilled fish and sushi in a Polynesian setting; **Waikiki Beach** (☎ 590-87-43-19) for grilled freshly caught lobster; **Kakao Beach** (☎ 590-87-43-26) for pizza, steaks, and seafood; **Coco Beach** (☎ 590-87-34-62) for breakfast, fajitas, pasta, and frozen drinks.

For a quick meal or specialty drink, choose from a variety of feet-in-the-sand café/bars. These don't have any facilities, but the food and drinks are every bit as tasty. Try **Paradisio** (☎ 590-27-49-87) for fantastic drinks, kosher dishes, and under-$10 sandwiches and salads; **Pedro's** (no phone) for colder-than-cold beer, drinks with names that'll make you chuckle, and live music anytime a cruise ship is in port; **Pirate** (no phone) for outstanding blender drinks made by Glen and served right to your lounge chair by Frank, some of the friendliest guys on the beach.

All the restaurants and bars are within walking distance along the beach, so just stroll along reading menus until you find something that sounds good. Hours vary from place to place, but you'll find something open from around 8 am until about 9 pm. Off-season, call ahead to check on closing hours if you want to have dinner, and be aware that some businesses close for several weeks during late summer. During peak season, phone for dinner reservations at the larger restaurants to guarantee a table.

From shore, you'll see the tiny isles of Green Cay, Tintamarre, and Pinel. You can take a water taxi from **Kontiki Watersports** (☎ 590-87-46-89) to Green Cay or Pinel for a day of snorkeling and sunning on the secluded beaches. Pinel has a restaurant, but Green Cay is deserted, except for day tourists. The round-trip cost is $10 to Green Cay and $15 to Pinel. Call ahead for information or to schedule a trip.

Tiko Tiko, a luxury catamaran, sails to Tintamarre for an all-day beach party. Make arrangements through **Dolphin Watersports** (☎ 590-87-28-75) at Club Orient, and be aware that this is a clothing-optional event, which gives a whole new meaning to the term bare boating. High-season rates are in the $85 per person range, and they offer special deals during the summer.

It's easy to find Orient Beach because the restaurants and watersports outfitters post signs along the highway. Take the main road east from Grand Case or north from Philipsburg, and watch for signs to Baie Orientale.

Cupecoy Bay Beach

This is totally different from Orient, and absolutely gorgeous. It's almost on the French-Dutch border that runs through Terres Basses (the Low Lands) just west of the airport and is noted for its cliffs and caves. The water is too rough for children, so adults (including gays and nudists seeking privacy) enjoy plenty of laid-back peace and quiet. There are no watersports operations or bars, but you can rent an umbrella or pick up a snack from the guys who run a mobile operation on the north end of the beach. You can also stop at the **Cliffside Beach Bar**, up the stairs leading to the villas of the Cupecoy Beach Club (☎ 599-545-2243) for snacks, drinks, and umbrellas.

It's easy to stake out your own little piece of sand, especially early on a weekday. Just park in the lot next to the Cupecoy Beach sign and walk through the opening in the low wall to a path leading to the sand. The beach changes all the time as sand washes in and out with the tide. Look for the picturesque **Cupecoy Boulder**, a big double-humped rock that juts from the sea. This marks the midway point, and you can walk either direction from there to find a good place to spread a towel. There's a steep drop-off and lots of rocks, which makes getting into the water a little tricky.

Maho & Mullet Bay Beaches

Located between the airport and Cupecoy Bay, these Dutch-side beaches are popular and often quite crowded, due to the nearby resorts, restaurants, casinos, and bars. You can walk from one beach to the other – they are similar, but different enough that each has its own fans. The star of Maho's shady rock-strewn beach is **The Sunset Beach Bar** (☎ 599-545-3998), a favorite happy-hour gathering place that roars with the sound of island music and 747 jet engines. The water can be rough at times, but it's fun to float on your back and watch the jumbo jets glide directly over you. Mullet has a mile-long beach with calmer water, but enough waves to be fun. When conditions are right, surfers turn out to ride the challenging swells. Palms provide shade, making this a favorite spot for local families on weekends. The island's only golf course is nearby, but all the buildings are still closed due to hurricane damage several years ago, so the place has a run-down, almost spooky appearance.

Simpson Bay Beach

This crescent-shaped beach extends from the airport east to Pelican Key, but is one of the least visited on the island. Its location near the busy Airport Road probably accounts for this, but you may enjoy the privacy. It's a great place to jog or stroll. There are no watersports operators or resorts, but the nearby village provides lots of places to eat. **Pelican Keys/Pelican Beach**, at the far eastern end of the bay, has a timeshare resort and a large watersports outfitter (**Aqua Mania**, ☎ 599-544-2640) offering equipment rentals, scuba diving, and sailing excursions. The sand is protected by rock jetties on both sides, and you can use the lounge chairs near the two beach bars without charge.

On the west end of Simpson Bay, refreshments are available from the pool-side bar at **Mary's Boon Beach Plantation** (☎ 599-545-4235).

Great Bay Beach

Philipsburg's city beach is surprisingly nice. It's completely developed, with the shops, restaurants, and hotels facing inward toward Front Street. Fresh sand has replaced that which Hurricane Lenny blew away in 1999, allowing you to stroll the beach from one end of town to the other. Beach bars are set up right on the sand, and several restaurants offer patio seating overlooking the sea. You can shop for awhile, then take a swim or nap on the sand.

Dawn Beach

Some of the island's best snorkeling and diving is on the easily accessible coral reefs just off lovely Dawn Beach. The water is too rough sometimes, but if you hit a calm day, snorkel out from the center of the beach, cross over some dead coral, and begin looking for schools of fish and squid.

The beach is long, with white sand that meets the inlet to Oyster Pond at Babit Point on the north end. You can see St. Barts in the distance. This is a wonderful place to spend the day, and early birds will want to arrive in time to watch the fabulous sunrise. If you don't make it out this early, consider a moonlit stroll after dinner.

St. Martin

Look for the lumpy, bumpy road leading to Dawn Beach off the signed secondary road to Oyster Pond. Park at **Scavenger's Beach Bar**, a good place for burgers.

DID YOU KNOW?

*Oyster Pond isn't a pond at all, but rather a half-French, half-Dutch, shell-shaped bay that is almost completely surrounded by land. The French side is a well-developed yachting center and home to the popular **Captain Oliver's Marina** (☎ 590-87-40-84). Guests at Captain Oliver's are water-taxied over to Dawn Beach for swimming, sunning, and snorkeling.*

Le Galion Beach

This beach on **Baie de l'Embouchure**, just south of Orient Bay, is locally known as **Coconut Grove**, because of the stand of coconut palms that shaded the beach when Le Galion Hotel was still open (it closed in 1990). Both the hotel and the trees are long gone, and efforts by residents to reestablish the grove have failed because thieves (landscapers for the new resorts are prime suspects) steal new trees as soon as they are planted.

Regardless of what you call it, this is the island's best windsurfing beach. Kids like it too because of the shallow, calm waters near shore.

Residents voted the beach "Best for Kids" in a recent survey conducted by the local newspaper, The Daily Herald.

Windsurfing and kitesurfing rentals and lessons are available, and you'll enjoy watching others, even if you don't try surfing yourself. Drop by **Chez Pat** (☎ 590-87-37-25) and talk with Pat Turner about your watersport options. He's a US citizen, born in Rio de Janeiro, who's lived on the island more than 20 years and owned a watersports operation most of that time. If he can't teach you to windsurf, you just can't learn.

Anse Marcel

A splendid 1,600-foot white sand beach lines this narrow cove cut deep into the northern shore. Some of the island's poshest resorts are tucked into the 150-acre nature preserve, along with **Port de Lonvilliers**, one of the classiest marinas on the island. There are luxurious shops and exquisite restaurants, as well as a cluster of French resorts: **L'Habitation, Le Meridien,** and **Le Domaine**. The only way to get onto the beach is through the hotels and, while everyone knows all beaches are public, the guard at the front gate may pretend to be clueless. Just tell him you're going to one of the restaurants for lunch, then walk right through the lobby and out to the vast gardens that border the sand. Of course, you'll find every amenity, and if you wish to use them, speak to someone at the activities desk or at the pool bar about paying a day-use fee. If you actually do have lunch, you'll probably be allowed to use the pool, beach chairs and other goodies.

The jig-jag mountain roads between Anse Marcel and Cul de Sac, on the east coast north of Orient Bay, and Grand Case, on the west coast, are a thrill and offer panoramic views.

Grand Case

Almost as much fun as Orient Bay, but not nearly as nice, this town beach is lined with some of the island's best gourmet restaurants. On weekends and holidays, the residents have boat races, local bands play near the pier, and snack shacks (*lo-los*) serve up tasty West Indies dishes and grilled meats. The sand is narrow and slopes toward the water, so setting up a level lounge chair is a challenge. The water is calm and snorkeling is good, especially around Creole Rock, which is off the north end of the cove and accessible by boat. Several scuba outfitters take novice divers and snorkelers there, and you may be able to catch a ride with a local fisherman if you ask around.

The activities desk at **Grand Case Beach Club** (☎ 590-87-51-87) organizes boat trips to Creole Rock several times a week, and they will allow non-guests to sign up if there's space. **Petite Plage,** next to the main beach at Grand Case Beach Club, is small and rocky, but quiet, with some shade. Park on the road across from the Beach Club and follow the path down to the beach.

Friar's Bay Beach

If you happen to visit St. Martin during a full moon, don't miss the party at **Kali's Beach Bar** (☎ 590-49-06-81) on Friar's Beach. At other times, the small protected stretch of sand is fairly quiet and uncrowded. Families and young locals show up on weekends to play volleyball and listen to boom-box music, and **Friar's Bay Beach Club** (☎ 590-87-83-81), at the other end of the short beach, usually features a local band on Sunday afternoons. On weekdays, you may have the whole place to yourself. Kali's and the Beach Club serve burgers, sandwiches, salads, and ice cold drinks at inexpensive prices. It's down a rough and winding road, off the main highway between Marigot and Grand Case.

An easy 10-minute walk to the north from Friar's Beach will bring you to **Happy Beach**, a secluded stretch of white sand strewn with black rocks and shaded by palms. There's no road to the beach, so only those in the know can find it.

Long Bay, Plum Bay, Red Bay

This trio of lovely beaches lines the north and west coasts of Terres Basses, south of Marigot. **Long Bay (Baie Longue)** is the longest stretch of beach on the island. It starts below the cliffs supporting luxurious **La Samanna Resort** (☎ 590-87-64-00), just across the French-Dutch border from Cupecoy Beach, and runs continuously to **Pointe du Canonnier** at the far western tip of the low lands. There are no watersports or other facilities, and you'll probably have a vast span of sand all to yourself.

Plum Bay (Baie aux Prunes) has lovely dunes and soft sand that sprawls across the western edge of Terres Basses, giving it full afternoon sun. Since the beach is wild and undeveloped, with only a few houses beyond the dunes, this is an excellent spot for acquiring an all-over tan. You can walk there from Long Bay by rounding the point that juts out into the sea separating the two beaches. When conditions are right, surfers congregate at the north end to ride the waves near Falaises des Oiseaux (Bird Cliffs). If you don't want to walk from Long Bay, follow the main road to the sign and guardhouse between Baie Rouge and Baie Longue. The guard will look you over and wave you through. When the road forks, go left for about a mile to a high wall, where you turn right onto an intersecting road. Your first left will lead down a winding road to the beach.

Red Bay (Baie Rouge) has lost some sand, but the beach is still spectacular. Huge rocks that appear to be placed as decoration and abundant greenery add to the beauty. Unfortunately, tour buses stop here, so there's often a crowd, especially when cruise ships are docked in town. You can rent chairs and umbrellas ($5 each) and purchase snacks and drinks from the mobile vendors or *lo-los* that set up each day, but there are no real restaurants or beach bars. The water is calm and clear in most areas – ideal for snorkeling and swimming. Try to visit early in the day, before anyone else arrives. Get there on a signed road about a mile from Baie aux Prunes. On a recent visit, we noticed a security guard patrolling the parking lot. Still, be sure to lock up and leave nothing visible inside your car.

Simpson Bay Beach

Crescent-shaped Simpson Bay extends east from the airport to Pelican Key. The western end, called Simpson Bay Beach, has few visitors, probably due to its location near busy Airport Road. You may enjoy the privacy and find it a great place to jog or stroll. There are no watersports or resorts, but you can get refreshments from the poolside bar at **Mary's Boon Beach Plantation** (☎ 599-545-4235), and the nearby town has lots of restaurants.

Pelican Keys/Pelican Beach

Located at the far eastern end of Simpson Bay, Pelican Beach has a timeshare resort (**Pelican Resort**, ☎ 599-544-2503) and a large watersports outfitter (**Aqua Mania**, ☎ 599-544-2640), offering equipment rentals, scuba diving, and sailing excursions. The sand is protected by rock jetties at both ends, and you can use the free lounge chairs and umbrellas. Two beach bars serve burgers, snacks, and drinks throughout the day, while **Pelican Reef Steak and Seafood House** (☎ 599-544-2616) offers full-service waterfront dining.

Seaside Solitude

If you want to find a rarely visited patch of sand for a solitary stroll or uninterrupted romance, try **Cay Bay**, at the foot of Cay Hill between Little Bay and Cole Bay. It's a favorite with horseback riders and hikers, but on most days no one's around. A small road off the main highway leads to Cay Bay, and you can follow the dirt horse path down to the beach. The water is calm and perfect for snorkeling.

Offshore islands are another option. From **Cul de Sac**, on the northeast coast, and nearby **Orient Bay**, you can get a water taxi to **Ilet Pinel**, where you will find excellent snorkeling. Since it's fairly easy to get there, you'll probably have company, but you can get away by walking over the hill to the north shore. Unlike the south shore, which faces St. Martin and has gentle rolling waves, the north shore is battered by crashing surf. Don't plan to go into the water, but do stroll along the pebbly coast and explore the fascinating rock formations. Back on the south shore, you'll find a couple of Robinson Crusoe-type snack shacks and a watersports hut along the white sand beach.

St. Martin

DID YOU KNOW? ***Kontiki Watersports,*** ☎ *590-87-46-89, at Orient Bay, will take you to Ilet Pinel for $15 per person round-trip.*

Tintamarre is a bit farther away and accessible by larger boats. If you want to go over for the day, check with the dive shops about scheduled trips. They may allow you to go along to snorkel, even if you don't scuba. Day charters to the island run about $80-$90 per person, including lunch, drinks, and snorkel equipment. You can also take a water taxi from Cul de Sac.

Tintamarre is 200 acres of deserted desert ringed by white sand beaches. As part of the marine reserve, the underwater world is teeming with fish and other sea animals.

Tintamarre, also called Flat Island by St. Martin residents, was inhabited off and on over the years. In the early 1900s, a few people lived there to protest taxation. Between 1946 and 1950, an airline known as Compagnie Aerienne Antillaise (CCA) flew light planes from Tinatamarre's 1,500-foot airstrip. Hurricanes have destroyed the buildings, but you can still find evidence of their existence in tumble-down rock walls and a clearing where the airstrip used to be along **White Bay Beach**.

Natural Reserves

The entire coastline and everything under the water around Tintamarre is protected by the Réserve Naturelle de Saint-Martin and the Marine Park of Sint Maarten, which have been overseeing nature protection on the island since the early 1990s. This protection extends to the smaller islands of Tintamarre, Green Cay, and Pinel, as well as the reefs surrounding Creole rock. The environmental agencies, and other organizations such as the Sea Turtle Watch Group are interested in preserving the coastal and inland ecosystems (marshes, mangroves, and cliffs) that shelter marine animals and birds, as well as maintaining the fragile coral reefs that act as ocean buffers for St. Martin's beaches. Boating and watersport activities are restricted in some areas, so check posted regulations at marinas and beach entrances.

Old Street, Philipsburg, St. Martin

Courthouse, Philipsburg, St. Martin

Princess Casino, Cole Bay, St. Martin

Above: Guavaberry Emporium, Philipsburg, St. Martin
Below: Racing the America's Cup Yachts, seen from Fort Amsterdam

Above: Oyster Bay Beach Resort, Dawn Beach, St. Martin
Below: View of Marigot from Fort St. Louis, St. Martin

Above: Restaurants on Marigot Harbor, St. Martin
Below: Orient Beach, St. Martin

Friar's Bay Beach, St. Martin

Flamboyant tree, St. Martin

Above: Calmos Café, Grand Case, St. Martin

Below: Grand Case Beach and restaurants, St. Martin

Above: Le Tastevin Restaurant, Grand Case, St. Martin

Below: Shops at St. Jean, St. Martin

Anse des Flamands, St. Barts

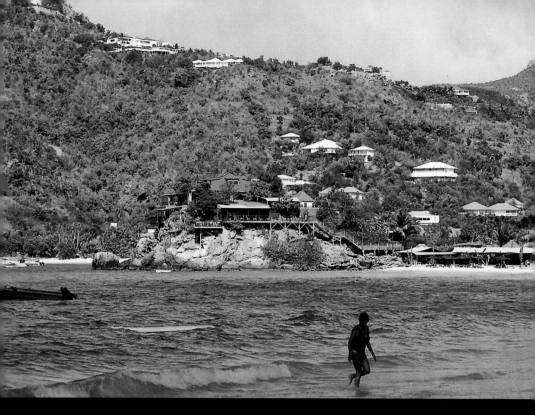

Above: Eden Rock Hotel, St. Barts

Below: Shell Beach, Gustavia, St. Barts

Above: Baie de St. Jean, St. Barts

Below: Anse de Grand Colombier, St. Barts

Above: St. Barts Beach Hotel & Restaurant, St. Barts

Below: Gustavia Harbor, St. Barts

Hotel St. Barth, Isle de France, St. Barts

Shops of Gustavia, St. Barts

■ Boardsurfing, Windsurfing & Kiteboarding

 You'll see people surfing off many of the island's beaches, but the best spot for both beginners and experienced wave riders is Orient Bay Beach. This two-mile stretch of white sand offers various conditions both inside and outside the protected bay. Dependable east and southeast trade winds create a good-to-excellent sailing environment year-round, with the strongest winds blowing from late November through March.

Orient's southern end is protected by a shallow reef and two nearby islands, Pinel and Green Cay, which guarantees smooth water on most days. A bit to the north, the conditions turn somewhat choppy and, outside the bay, Atlantic swells provide big thrills.

The annual **SXM Challenge** is held at Orient Bay in March, with international windsurfers competing in five divisions. Kiteboarders hold a less formal event, with the winner crowned Red Stripe King of the Bay.

For information on the Challenge, wind- or kite-surfing instruction, or equipment rental, contact one of the outfitters below. Expect to pay about $50 for a one-hour private windsurfing lesson, including equipment, and about $60 per day to rent a windsurf board. Kiteboarding lessons cost about $70 for a two-hour private lesson, including equipment. Surf boards and boards with kites rent for about $25 per hour. You'll need to prove that you know how to handle the equipment before you take it out. Package prices on lessons and rentals are substantially less per hour.

Club Nathalie Simon/Wind Adventure
Orient Bay Resort
☎ 590-29-41-57, fax 590-29-58-08, www.wind-adventures.com

Surf'ace
14 Rue du Général de Gaulle, Marigot
☎ 590-87-93-24, fax 590-87-93-24

Tropical Wave/Chez Pat
Le Galion Beach, Baie de l'Embouchure
☎ 590-87-37-25, fax 590-87-37-29

Windy Reef/SXM Water Boys Surf Club
Le Galion Beach, Baie de l'Embouchure
☎ 590-52-58-18, fax 590-87-08-37

St. Martin

*The calm water of Simpson Bay Lagoon is ideal for **kayaking**. You can rent equipment or join a guided tour by contacting **Tri-Sports** (☎ 599-545-4384) at 14 Airport Road in Simpson Bay. Paddle out to Great Key, a tiny island in the lagoon, for a picnic, or travel all the way across the water to Marigot or the resort beaches on Baie Nettlé.*

■ Sailing

St. Martin takes sailing seriously. Each March, the island hosts the **Heineken Regatta** (www.heinekenregatta. com), one of the largest and most exciting sailboat races in the Caribbean. The three-day extravaganza draws more than 200 boats from over two dozen countries to races in 20 categories, from small catamarans to 50-foot vessels. Spectators follow the event as it progresses from Philipsburg to Marigot on the first day, Marigot to Philipsburg on the second day, and a spectacular around-the-island race on the final day. Parties follow each day's competition.

The Heineken Regatta, which began in 1980 with 12 entries, now attracts America's Cup competitors, as well as neophyte sailors. For more information, contact the Regatta Office at **Sint Maarten Yacht Club** in Philipsburg, ☎ 599-0544-2079, fax 599-544-2091, office@heinekenregatta.com, or visit the website at www. heinekenregatta.com.

Throughout the year, smaller racing events draw boat owners and renters. The most popular are the **St. Martin's Day Regatta** on November 11, and the **Guavaberry Full Moon Regatta** to from St. Martin to St. Kitts and Nevis in May. Get more information about all of the island's regattas by contacting the **Sint Maarten Yacht Club** on the Dutch side (see information above) or **Dockside Management** at Bobby's Marina in Philipsburg, ☎ 599-542-4096, fax 599-542-2858.

If you want to participate or spectate from the water, and aren't bringing your own vessel, be sure to reserve a boat early. Multi-day charters are in high demand throughout the year because of St. Martin's excellent marinas, good winds, moderate seas, sheltered bays, and short-sail neighboring isles.

Charters

The following companies arrange both crewed and bareboat multi-day charters. Prices vary widely depending on the type of boat and length of charter.

Nautors Swan Charters
Grand Case
☎ 800-356-7926 (US), 590-87-35-48 (St. Martin), fax 590-87-35-50

The Moorings
Captain Oliver's, Oyster Pond
☎ 800-521-1126 (US), 590-87-32-55 (St. Martin), fax 590-87-32-54

Sunsail
Captain Oliver's, Oyster Pond
☎ 800-327-2276 (US), 250-758-5965 (Canada), 590-87-83-41 (St. Martin), fax 590-87-11-61

Day-Sails

The highlight of your trip may well be a day-sail around St. Martin or to another nearby island. Most half-day cruise prices include snorkeling equipment and drinks, while longer sails include lunch or dinner, and, perhaps, time on a private beach.

You may be able to buy reduced-price tickets through the **Discount Activity Center** on Airport Road, Simpson Bay (☎ 599-544-5536 or 599-557-6232) and on Orient Beach (☎ 590-27-15-63). If they don't offer what you want, contact the activity desk at your resort or **Aqua Mania Adventures** at Pelican Marina, Simpson Bay (☎ 599-544-2640 or 599-544-2631).

Three-hour snorkeling trips run about $35 per person, full-day cruises are in the $70 per person range, and a sunset dinner sail will cost about $50 per person. However, rates vary depending on the season, type of boat, destination, planned activities, and food service. Popular boats include:

> *Golden Eagle*, Bobby's Marina, Philipsburg, ☎ 599-543-0068. This 76-foot custom-designed catamaran is a real beauty, with fabulous creature comforts. It sails to Tintamarre, where you may relax, snorkel, and swim. Open bar and snacks are included in the price.

> *Lagoon Princess*, Turtle Pier, Simpson Bay Lagoon, ☎ 599-545-2562. The 28-foot motorized *Princess* takes you around

St. Martin

Simpson Bay Lagoon. While you enjoy beverages from the open bar, the crew entertains you with island gossip and points out the yachts and homes of the rich and famous. For an extra charge, you can have dinner at Turtle Pier Restaurant after the cruise.

Celine, Turtle Pier, Simpson Bay Lagoon, ☎ 599-545-3961 or 599-556-8806. Neil Roebert built this 40-foot catamaran in South Africa and sailed it to St. Martin in 1996. Sign up for a sunset or day cruises on this spacious handcrafted beauty.

Random Wind, Little Bay, ☎ 599-557-5742 or 599-544-5148. This three masted 54-foot clipper offers a variety of excursions, from half-day snorkeling cruises, to sunset sails, to private charters for groups of up to 18 people.

Tahuna I and *Tahuna II*, Marigot, ☎ 590-62-99-39, 599-544-4354 or 590-27-33-43 (cell). Take your pick of full-day trips to Anguilla, Prickly Pear, Sandy Island, Tintamarre, or St. Barts on these spacious catamarans. Lunch, open bar, and snorkeling equipment is included.

Lambada and *Tango*, Pelican Marina, Simpson Bay, ☎ 599-544-2640 or 599-544-2631. Spend the day on Prickly Pear, an uninhabited island with perfect beaches. Or sail into the sunset while relaxing with a drink and enjoying a buffet dinner. Both are possible aboard these comfortable catamarans. Open decks provide plenty of room for sunning, but shade is available when you've had enough.

Scoobidoo, Anse Marcel and Grand Case, ☎ 590-52-02-53 or 590-29-15-76. You may have seen this spiffy catamaran on the Travel Channel. It cruises the waters between French St. Martin and Anguilla, sometimes stopping at Prickly Pear or Tintamarre. Take the sunset cruise, which features excellent appetizers and an open bar.

Take the 12-Metre Challenge...

... if you think you're up to it. Whether you're a novice or an experienced sailor, you'll have a blast as a working member of the crew on one of the five 12-meter yachts that have competed in the America's Cup, the mother of all yacht races. Dennis Conner's USA winner, *Stars & Strips*, is among the retired "greyhounds of the sea" that challenge each other daily in a mini-race off St. Martin's shores. The sleek, aluminum, single-mast boats are custom-designed to cut through the water like a wind-powered racehorse. If you sign on as a member of the crew, hang on for the ride of your life. You'll be required to do your share of jibbing and tacking, too, which makes the thrills all the more exhilarating.

Allow half a day for this adventure. It begins with a pre-race briefing and ends with both winners and losers enjoying America's Cup – filled with Caribbean rum punch. The cost is $70 per person. Sign on for duty at **Bobby's Marina** in Philipsburg. ☎ 599-542-0045.

■ Motorboat Trips & Rentals

 Sailboats are great, but sometimes you just want a little motor power. You can join a scheduled trip or rent your own boat, with or without a skipper. Organized group trips are priced about the same as sailboat cruises, and boats rent for around $80 per hour without a skipper, $90 with. If you rent for several hours or a full day, you'll get a break on the hourly rates.

Sand Dollar
Aqua Mania Adventures, Pelican Marina, Simpson Bay
☎ 599-544-2640 or 599-544-2631
This motorboat with a shade canopy and diving platform travels to Creole Rock, where you can snorkel and relax during the three-hour excursion.

Aqua World
Royal Village, Simpson Bay
☎ 599-544-3233
Rent an 18-foot Glaston with ski-tow options and a shade canopy for trips to neighboring islands or just cruising the coast.

Any Way Marine
Marina Port la Royale, Marigot
☎ 590-87-91-41, fax 590-29-34-76
Rent all kinds of boats at this outfitter, from a small motorboat to a huge catamaran.

Scorpion Offshore Adventures
Marigot
☎ 590-65-16-16 or 590-87-78-54

St. Martin

Take a cigarette boat for a spin along the coast or to one of the nearby isles. Great fun!

Seaworld Explorer XI

This 49-foot semi-submarine allows you to stay comfortable and dry while you observe underwater reefs and marine life through a large window. The trip leaves from Grand Case and travels along the coast to Creole Rock, where a scuba diver explains everything you see five feet below sea level through your own viewing window. Only the observation level is submerged; the top of the ship remains above water at all times. Tickets are $30 for adults and $20 for children age two-12. For information and reservations, call **Atlantis Adventures**, ☎ 599 542-4078.

■ Water Toys

 Watersports operators are as abundant as beach bars on Orient Bay. You can stroll along the sand and view a colorful display of Jet Skis, Hobie Cats, and banana boats. Outfitters are less concentrated on other beaches around the island. Expect to pay about $45 per half-hour for a Jet Ski, $45 per 15-minute parasail ride, and about $50 per hour to rent a small Hobie Cat. Instruction and guided excursions are available and adapted to your skill level.

Orient Bay Beach

Kontiki Watersports, ☎ 599-557-0776 or 590-87-46-89, www.sxm-game.com/wspen.html

Bikini Watersport, ☎ 590-27-07-48

Boo Boo Jam Parasail, ☎ 590-56-99-01

Kakao Watersports, ☎ 590-27-49-94, www.sxm-game.com/wspen.html

Club Orient Watersports, ☎ 590-87-33-85, www.cluborient.com/cluborient-ang/watersports/dolphinwatersports.htm

Wind Adventures, ☎ 590-29-41-57, www.wind-adventures.com

Elsewhere on the Island

Aqua Mania Adventures, Pelican Beach, Simpson Bay, ☎ 599-544-2640, www.stmaarten-activities.com/trips/edge.htm

Westport Watersports, Simpson Bay, ☎ 599-544-2557

Fat Wake Zone, Mercure Hotel, Baie Nettlé, ☎ 590-64-18-28

Flamboyant Watersports, Hotel Le Flamboyant, Baie Nettlé, ☎ 590-87-60-43, www.sxmtravelguide.com/flamboya.htm

Méridien Watersports, Hotel Méridien, Anse Marcel, ☎ 590-87-67-90, www.lemeridien-lhabitation.com/Facilities.asp

Nico's Watersports, Baie Nettlé, ☎ 590-87-92-11

Tropical Wave, Le Galion Beach, Baie de l'Embouchure, ☎ 590-87-37-25

Rhino Rider Safari

This is the most fun you can have on the water. You drive your own two-passenger inflatable motorized watercraft and zip along behind a wild-and-crazy but absolutely dependable guide, who leads you across the rolling surf from Simpson Bay to Creole Rock. There, you snorkel and swim, then head for a rest break at a nearby beach before returning along the coast to base camp. Single riders pay $80 per person, and buddies who ride double pay $45 each. The whole adventure takes about 2½ hours, and you can choose either a morning or afternoon safari. Book early for this popular outing by calling the **Rhino Office** on Airport Road in Simpson Bay, ☎ 599-557-4466 or 590-27-44-66.

■ Deep-Sea Fishing

 Someting's always bitin' in St. Martin. Set out to sea and you're sure to return with a big sailfish, marlin, wahoo, or tuna. Boat captains design the trip to fit your skills and experience, so you'll have fun on the high seas, even if you don't catch a thing.

Private charters cost from $350-$600 for a half-day and $650-$1,000 for a full day, depending on the boat and number of people in your party. Prices include all your gear and drinks, and usually some type

of lunch on an all-day trip. The catch belongs to the captain, but most will clean, filet, and give you enough to cook for dinner.

Find a deep-sea fishing outfitter by strolling along the docks at any of the marinas. You can check out the boat, and possibly meet the captain before you sign on for a trip. You can also make advance reservations through your travel agent or hotel. The following fishing operators can be contacted by phone or through their e-mail.

Rudy's Deep-Sea Fishing, Captain Rudy Sierens, Simpson Bay, ☎ 599-545-2177 (phone/fax) or 599-522-7120 (cell), www. rudysdeepseafishing.com

Blue Water Sport Fishing, Simpson Bay, ☎ 599-545-3230

Virginia Gentleman, Captain George Shetter, Simpson Bay, ☎ 599-545-3230 or 599-547-1468

Lee's Deep-Sea Fishing, Airport Road, ☎ 599-544-4233. Lee owns Lee's Roadside Grill and he will cook your catch for you at the restaurant after the fishing trip.

Freedom Deep-Sea Fishing, Captain Jan, Simpson Bay, ☎ 599-557-4778

Taylor Made Charters, Captain Dougie, Simpson Bay, ☎ 599-552-7539

Kratuna, Pelican Beach, ☎ 599-544-2640

Samaco, Baie Orientale, ☎ 590-87-33-27

Big Sailfish Too, Anse Marcel, ☎ 590-27-40-90

La Compagnie des Vagues, Grand Case, ☎ 590-87-77-46

Luxe Caraïbes, Marina Port la Royale, Marigot, ☎ 590-29-51-93

Major Fishing, Captain Bernard, Anse Marcel, ☎ 590-87-96-76

Adventures Underwater

 Both the French and Dutch sides of St. Martin have a wide variety of dive and scuba sites, mostly off the west and south coasts. Count on lovely reefs with drop-offs, swim-throughs, and caves. Sunken wrecks, both accidental and deliberate, are plentiful and most are at depths of 40 to 60

feet. Some of the favorite sites are rock formations or dead coral reefs covered with new-growth sponges and corals.

The most famous of more than 40 official dive sites is the wreck of the English ship *HMS Proselyte*, which struck the reef and went down in Philipsburg's Great Bay in 1801. Divers can explore the remains of the 133-foot frigate and its coral-encrusted cannons and anchors. **Proselyte Reef**, on which the ship's remains rest, has elkhorn corals that are visited by groups of sergeant majors and yellowtail snappers.

The freighter *Teigland* was sunk deliberately on nearby **Cable Reef** in 1993, and vegetation growing on its hull has begun to attract a variety of fish, including schools of angelfish and an occasional eagle ray. Small caves within the reef formation harbor lobsters and eels. Nurse sharks and turtles also visit the area.

DID YOU KNOW?

Eight species of coral have been identified under the waters surrounding St. Martin: mustard hill, lettuce, brain, fire, great mound, box fire, elkhorn, and elliptical star.

Most dive operators schedule trips to a basic list of 10 to 12 sites, and many go to locations off Saba, St. Eustatius, St. Barts, and Anguilla. If you aren't certified, check into a *Discover Scuba* introductory course that includes a shallow dive to about 30 feet. Also, most dive boats will allow snorkelers to go along if there's room. (If you want to snorkel on your own, the best spots are off Little Bay Beach, Dawn Beach, and Maho Bay Beach.)

■ Popular Dive Sites

Pelican Reef and **Molly Beday Island** are located in close proximity off the southeast coast around Oyster Pond. Molly juts about 100 feet above the surface of the water, and both have good coral formations. Lobsters live in crevices of the rocks, and shrimp and crabs dart among the coral.

Hens and Chickens (also called **Hens and Chicks**), southeast of Pointe Blanche Bay, is divided into a north and south area. The reef is alive with coral, sponges, and various sea plants. Visibility is usually good, but the site can be reached only when the ocean is calm. Rocks protrude above the waterline, and the reef has beautiful elkhorn forests at depths of 20 feet. The reef descends to 70 feet, creating a wall that ends at the sandy bottom.

Creole Rock, in Grand Case Bay, is ideal for novice divers and all snorkelers. There's a sandy bottom and plenty to see at shallow depths. The reef isn't in great shape, thanks to Hurricane Luis, heavy boat traffic, and uncontrolled beginner kicking, but there are lots of fish and an occasional turtle. Several dive shop operators bring groups to the rock, and you can catch a boat ride from Grand Case Beach Club (☎ 590-87-51-87) for about $25, including snorkeling gear.

French Reef, off the far south coast near Little Bay, is close to shore and has large numbers of fish at shallow depths; perfect for beginners. Snorkelers can enter the water off Little Bay Beach and view colorful tropical fish on the reef in 12 to 25 feet of water.

Tug Boat *Anny* stands upright on the sandy bottom of Simpson Bay. Fish have become accustomed to people and surround divers who descend to the 40-foot boat that's submerged in about 25 feet of water. This is a great place for underwater snapshots and night dives.

Fuh Sheng is a wrecked 120-foot fishing vessel from Taiwan. It's lying on its side on the sandy bottom of Cupecoy Bay at a depth of 110 feet. This is a favorite with experienced divers.

Shark Park

For something a bit different, consider going along with the folks at Dive Safaris to their shark park, a specially developed playground populated by about 20 reef and milk sharks. This isn't all about thrills. You'll also learn about the creatures and their lifestyle, with the hopes that you will appreciate their good qualities and spread the word that they're not really such scary bad guys. By the time you descend among them, you should feel comfortable as well as awed.

The people who've developed this site are aware of all the potential problems, and they won't do anything to harm either sharks or humans. They limit feeding to around 20 pounds of food per week, or one pound per shark – not even a good-sized snack for an animal that devours the equivalent of 10% of its body weight per week. There's no danger that this small amount of food, offered piece-by-piece from the end of a long stick, will stop the sharks from hunting for meals.

Speak with Whitney Keogh at **Dive Safaris** for all the details, ☎ 599-545-3213.

Dive Operators

The following dive shops offer first-class instruction, multi-level certification, guided dive trips, and equipment rental. Most operators schedule two boat trips daily and arrange instruction courses to suit student needs.

You'll pay $45-$65 for a one-tank dive, $70-$90 for a two-tank dive, and about $80 for an introductory resort-course dive. Prices may vary with the season, and multiple-dive packages average less per dive.

Ocean Explorers is the oldest dive shop on the island. It's run by Dominique and LeRoy French, who take small groups of 10 or fewer out on their 26-foot Robalo dive boat, powered by twin 150 hp engines to guarantee a smooth and speedy ride to the sites. Contact them on Simpson Bay Beach, ☎ 599-544-5252, www.stmaartendiving.com.

Dive Safaris and **The Scuba Shop** have three locations with two well-stocked retail stores. In addition to shark dives, they specialize in equipment rentals, provide information on shore dives, and they are certified to guide handicapped divers. Contact the shop nearest your hotel or mooring: Dive Safaris, La Palapa Marina, Simpson Bay, ☎ 599-545 3213, fax 599-545 3209; Dive Safaris, Bobby's Marina, Philipsburg, ☎ 599-542 9001, fax 599-542 8983; The Scuba Shop, Captain Olivers Marina, Oyster Pond, ☎ 590-87-48-01, fax 590-87-48-01, www.diveguide.com/divesafaris or www.thescubashop.net.

Scuba Fun Caraïbes is located at the Port Lonvilliers Marina in Anse Marcel. If diving will be a big part of your vacation, check out their package deals with Le Privilège and Le Méridien hotels. In addition to the retail store and dive facility at Anse Marcel, the multilingual staff offers dive departures from Simpson Bay and will pick up divers at Divi Little Bay and Great Bay Marina in Philipsburg. Two specially outfitted boats take divers to a variety of sites – a 36-foot mono hull with a 300 hp inboard diesel motor that accommodates 20, and a 28-foot inflatable with a 250 hp outboard engine that is also suitable for up to 20 divers. ☎ 590-87-36-13, fax 590-87-36-52, www.scubafun.com.

WORD TO THE WISE

Aqua Mania Adventures is the main watersports company on Dutch St. Martin. You can book almost every water-related activity through them, including scuba. The multilingual instructors and guides take small groups to all the best sites in customized 28- and 35-foot boats. They are at Pelican Marina on Simpson Bay, ☎ 599-544-2640, fax 599-544-2476, www.stmaarten-activities.com.

St. Martin

Blue Ocean Watersports and Dive Center plans dives around the skills of each small group that it takes on its customized 30-foot boat, powered by a 250 hp motor. Divers enjoy an open bar on the ride back home, and can rent an underwater camera to record the fun. Snorkelers are welcome, as long as there's room on the boat, and divers who haven't been down in more than a year are encouraged to take the adaptation dive, which goes a bit slower and offers additional assistance. Ask about night dives and multiple-dive packages when you call the shop on the main road in Baie Nettlé, ☎ 590-87-89-73, fax 590-87-26-36, www.blueocean.catamarans.ws.

O2 Limits, at Grand Case Beach Club and Orient Bay, offers introductory classes, trips for certified divers, and training at all levels, including Nitrox and Rebreather. They also have propulsion vehicles (underwater scooters). The French staff is multilingual, so give them a call, ☎ 590-50-04-00 or 590-50-16-32, www.o2limits.com.

Neptune Dive Center, at La Playa Restaurant on Orient Bay Beach, makes three 1½-hour dives per day. Their high-powered 22-foot boat allows them to get to great sites in 10 to 20 minutes, allowing a full 50 minutes underwater. Groups are small, up to six people, so everyone gets plenty of individual attention with no waiting-around time. Look for them on the beach between Bikini Beach Restaurant and Waikiki Restaurant or ☎ 590-50-98-51, fax 590-27-69-75, www.neptune-dive.com.

Octoplus Dive Center, on Grand Case Beach, has outstanding instructors who have plenty of around-the-world diving experiences recorded in their log books, including adventures in the Red Sea, Indian Ocean, and Thailand. The center is a member of the St. Martin Ecotourism Association and the friendly, bilingual dive team (Philippe, Cecile, and Jean-Michel) holds a variety of certifications. Contact them about their small-group classes and dive trips, ☎ 590-87-20-62, fax 590-87-20-63.

DID YOU KNOW?

Most resorts have on-site dive facilities or affiliations with a nearby dive shop. Ask at the activities center or front desk for information, or call one of the dive operators listed above. Many will pick you up at your hotel.

Adventures on Land

■ Horseback Riding

Bayside Riding Club
Le Galion, Baie de l'Embouchure
☎ 590-887-36-64 or 599-557-6822
Choose from a one-hour ride along the beach ($40) or a two-hour ride and horseback swim ($60). Other choices include a romantic ride for two, including champagne ($70), and a sunset beach ride ($50). Call the club, next to the Butterfly Farm across from the salt pond at Orient Bay, for reservations and information about riding lessons and departure times.

Caid et Isa
Anse Marcel
☎ 590-87-45-70, fax 590-87-45-71
www.caid-isa.com
Ride along the beach or through the nature park with experienced guides. See the island from a whole different viewpoint.

■ Hiking

Exploring St. Martin's countryside on foot is a terrific way to escape the traffic jams, beach crowds, and city shoppers. Hiking trails crisscross the island and lead to mountain-top vistas and coastal seclusion.

One of the most popular hikes is through **Loterie Farm** to the summit of **Pic Paradis** (Paradise Peak), the island's highest point. You can stroll the lush lower levels of the 150-acre farm's forest, or take the 1½-hour uphill trek to the peak. The view from the top is worth every sweaty minute. A guide leads a narrative hike several mornings each week, and you can also go on your own, if you prefer. Look for signs to the farm off the main highway between Marigot and Grand Case, which leads east through the village of Rambaud, ☎ 590-87-86-16.

You may also hike up Pic Paradis along the rutted trail that pretends to be a dirt access road, but is really suitable only for four-wheel-drive vehicles. Find it off the main road out of Marigot, going toward Colombier, just past a road sign pointing the way to St. Louis. Drive as far up the road as you wish (or as far as your car can manage), then continue on foot. As you climb, the vegetation becomes more lush, since more rain falls at the higher elevation. When you get to the radio tower at the top, you'll have unbeatable views of the west coast. A little trail to the left of the fence enclosing the tower (as you face it from the road) will take you to a viewing point of the east coast and Philipsburg, to the south. On a clear day, you may be able to see St. Barts.

A group called **Action Nature** (Marigot, ☎ 590-29-22-84) maintains a network of trails through the island's countryside and leads organized hikes on weekends. Call for a current schedule. Local hikers turn out for the weekly excursions, and you're welcome to go along, but you may prefer a private hike with a professional member of **AGRP (Association des Guides Randonneurs)** ☎ 590-29-2020. The trained teen guides charge $25 per person for a half-day hike that leaves from the Tourism Office in Marigot at 8 am daily.

Tri-Sports (☎ 599-545-4384), on Simpson Bay, also leads eco-adventure hikes. They can put you on the right track for an independent hike or sign you up for a guided excursion geared toward your experience and endurance level. They also carry any type of sporting equipment you may need, and know about road races and other events scheduled on the island. You may want to just drop by their store at 14 Airport Road to check out what's going in, whether you're a sports spectator or participant.

■ Mountain & Off-Road Biking

Don't bike along St. Martin's roadways. The streets are narrow and there's too much traffic. However, off-road biking is terrific. You can rent a bike, pick up maps, and get route information from **Tri-Sport** in Simpson Bay or **Frog Legs Bike Shop** in Marigot. The staff can take you on guided tours along the popular single-track mountain trails that run from the Dutch to the French side of the island, or arrange to have your bike delivered to your hotel or trail site.

Rates are about $18 per day or $90 per week to rent a 21-speed front-suspension mountain bike with a helmet, lock, and water bottle.

Bike Rental

Tri-Sport, 14 Airport Road, Simpson Bay
Monday-Friday 9 am-6 pm, Saturday 10 am
☎ 599-545-4384, fax 599-545-4385

Frog Legs Bike Shop, 183 Rue de Hollande, Marigot
☎ 590-87-05-11, fax 590-87-25-54

■ Tennis

 Many resorts, villas, and hotels on both sides of the island have tennis courts, and playing conditions are good except when the wind kicks up. Check with your travel agent or your resort for information about the availability of courts, condition of the facilities, equipment rental, and the possibilities for organized tournaments, lessons, or games with the staff pro.

If your resort doesn't have courts or the courts aren't lighted for night play, you can usually arrange to play for a fee at another resort nearby. **Privilège**, with six courts, and **Le Meridien**, with four courts, are two of the hotels that welcome paying non-guests. In addition, you can contact the local tennis clubs about the possibility of renting a court or setting up a game with club members.

Tennis Clubs

Tennis Club Caraïbes, Anse Marcel, ☎ 590-27-40-03

Tennis Club Esmeralda, Baie Orientale, ☎ 590-87-36-36

Tennis Club Municipal, Sandy Ground, ☎ 590-87-98-47

Resorts with Tennis Courts

Hôtel Privilège Resort and Spa, Anse Marcel, ☎ 590-87-37-37

Le Flamboyant Resort, Baie Nettlé, ☎ 590-87-60-00

Grand Case Beach Club, Grand Case, ☎ 590-87-51-87

Divi Little Bay Beach Resort, Little Bay, ☎ 599-542-2333

Pelican Resort, Simpson Bay, ☎ 599-544-2503

Caravanserai Beach Resort, Beacon Hill, ☎ 599-545-4000

Great Bay Beach Hotel, Great Bay, ☎ 599-542-2446

Maho Beach Resort, Maho Bay, ☎ 599-545-2115

Princess Port de Plaisance Resort, Cole Bay, ☎ 599-544-5222

Summit Resort, Lowlands, ☎ 599-545-2150

St. Martin

■ Golf

 Unfortunately, St. Martin is not a golfing destination. Its only golf course, which was a good one, was attached to the Mullet Bay Resort, and that was destroyed by Hurricane Luis in 1995. The resort has still not reopened, and the government has been disputing with various developers for years about the future of the land.

However, the heavily damaged golf course is still playable, and much of its vegetation has recovered. The location is naturally beautiful, but the course probably will not be well cared for until the resort issue is settled and new owners come on board. Golfers will still appreciate the challenge, especially of the back nine and the lagoon water holes.

The course opens daily at 7 am, and the last tee-time is 1:30 pm. Fees are $108 per person for 18 holes and $62 per person for nine holes, including cart rental. Club rentals run $26. Phone in advance for a tee time, ☎ 599-545-2801.

Shopping

Along with Charlotte Amalie on St. Thomas, Philipsburg is well known as a duty-free bargain paradise for shoppers. While some of the claims are overblown, you can find terrific buys on imported merchandise and local products. Since goods are free of import duty and local sales tax, and each citizen of the US can bring back up to $600 worth of duty-free goods (see *Returning Home*, page 32, for additional information), the final cost of many items is much less than if you'd bought them at home.

Loose gemstones, local arts and crafts, and porcelain figurines such as Lladro pieces recently have been granted additional exemptions, so you may now bring these items home without paying duty or counting them toward your total duty-free allowance.

Liquor, European china and crystal, and jewelry are some of the best buys. If you're serious about getting a good bargain on specific merchandise, check prices and quality in shops and discount outlets at home, so you'll come to St. Martin as an informed shopper. You're likely to save 30% on perfumes, luxury watches, European ready-to-wear clothing, and advanced-technology cameras. Local art and products that aren't available in your hometown make wonderful gifts and cherished souvenirs, so they are a bargain at any price.

WORD TO THE WISE

Most stores on the Dutch side are open Monday-Saturday, 9 am-6 pm. On the French side, stores open Monday-Saturday, 8:30 am-12:30 pm and 2-7 pm, with a mid-day break for déjeuner. Many shops extend their hours and also open on Sunday if a load of cruise-ship passengers is expected. During low season, hours of operation may be reduced, especially on days when no ship is in port. Some proprietors close for several weeks during late summer, board up their windows against hurricanes, and go off on a vacation of their own.

■ Top Shops in Philipsburg

AUTHOR'S PICK

Park free near the police station on Walter Nesbeth Road. (Watch for signs pointing the way as you enter town.) Paid parking is available a block closer to Front Street at the corner of Peterson Street and Cannegieter Street, just south of the Government Building. Rates are $1 per hour up to $14 for a full day.

Open-air vendors set up near the paid parking lot and on Great Bay Beach. You can get some good deals on souvenirs and T-shirts from these local businessmen, but browse a bit before you start buying.

The majority of shops are lined up along Front Street, with storefronts facing inward on both sides of the road. Recent refurbishing has improved the curb appeal somewhat, but, for the most part, the stores look fairly weathered and shabby on the outside.

A conspicuous exception is Old Street Mall (☎ 599-542-8895) a narrow brick-paved alley lined with two-story faux-Dutch buildings and potted palms. The stores here are some of the most exquisite, including **Oro de Sol** (jewelry, ☎ 599-542-8895), **Colombian Emeralds** (jewelry, ☎ 599-542-39-33), **Tommy Hilfiger** (the designer's clothing and accessories, ☎ 599-542-6315), **Dutch Delfts Blue Gallery** (Holland's famous porcelain and tile, ☎ 599-542-2737), and the wickedly delicious **Belgian Chocolate Shop**, ☎ 599-542-8863.

While it's impossible to describe or even list all the best buys and worthy stores along Philipsburg's Front Street, the following are our favorites for either good prices, great atmosphere, or unusual merchandise.

St. Martin

Jewelry

Joe's Jewelry International, 92 A Front Street, ☎ 599-543-7020.
You can't walk more than a few feet along Front Street without spotting a Joe's. In addition to **Jewelry International** at #92A, there's **Joe's Blue Diamond** at #68, **Joe's Diamonds** at #60, and **Joe's Jewelry** at #40B, #46, #65A and #66. Each store is a bit different from the others, but the theme at all locations is customer education and satisfaction. One of the knowledgeable sales staff will bring you up to speed on the various colors of gold (white, yellow, and combo) and explain how 18 karat is the best for jewelry (even though it's only 75% pure), whereas pure gold (24K) is too soft for wearable art, and platinum is stronger than all gold – thus ideal as the head setting for rings.

If you don't have time to visit each shop, be sure to drop by Blue Diamond to see the awesome collection of blue-and-white diamond rings and earrings.

Artistic Jewelers, 61 Front Street, ☎ 599-542-3456.
If you're the type that likes to change the look of your jewelry every time you change clothes, check out this store's assortment of mix-and-match rings and bracelets that can be worn alone or stacked in various arrangements. They come in white or yellow gold (18K) and platinum, and some are set with diamonds. Individual pieces make great special-occasion gifts to collect for yourself or give to others. Also, browse their selection of pricey Mikimoto pearls.

WORD TO THE WISE

When shopping for a watch, you'll usually find the best discounts (30-44%) on Citizen, Seiko and Movado brands. Expect savings on other brands, including Swiss Army, Cartier, and Tissot, to range from 15-20% off US prices.

Majesty Jewelry, 46 Front Street, ☎ 599-542-2473.
This family-owned store is now run by the second generation, so you can trust them to be around and stand behind anything they sell. And they sell a wide variety of brand name watches, jewelry, and loose or set diamonds. Compare their prices on tanzanite, the exotic blue-to-purple stone from Africa, and alexandrite, a fascinating gem named for a Russian czar that changes from green in daylight to red in incandescent light. (Red and green were the Russian imperial colors.)

Tanzanite International, 71 Front Street, ☎ 599-542-0237.
Before you buy tanzanite anywhere else, check out the prices and large selection here. They have loose stones as well as exquisite earrings, bracelets, and rings. Tanzanite is found only in the state of Tanzania near Mount Kilimanjaro in east Africa, and the spectacular blue stone wasn't discovered until 1967.

Birth Stones

The perfect gift to bring home to someone special is a piece of jewelry designed around their birth stone. Be sure to ask for a certificate of authenticity before you make the purchase.

January . . . . Garnet

February . . . . Amethyst

March . . . . Aquamarine

April . . . . Diamond

May . . . . Emerald

June . . . . Pearl

July . . . . Ruby

August . . . . Peridot

September . . . . Sapphire

October . . . . Opal

November . . . . Topaz

December . . . . Turquoise

Cameras & Video Equipment

There's no shortage of electronic gear and cameras on St. Martin. If you have the tenacity to shop several stores and possess a talent for bargaining, you can get some extraordinary deals. Do a little research before you leave home, so you'll know what you're looking for and what it's worth. Once you're on the island, stop into a couple of stores to check availability and prices. Then go back to your favorite with cash or credit card in hand to make a reasonable offer. Chances are you'll walk away with a super buy.

Both of the stores below are well-stocked with cameras, digital cameras, and video equipment, with brand names such as Nikon, Olympus, JVC, Bose, and Sony.

Boolchand's, 50 Front Street, ☎ 599-542-2245.
Shoppers have been going to Boolchand's since the 1930s for jewelry, watches, and loose diamonds, but the store also has a good selection of electronic, video, and camera equipment.

Caribbean Camera Center, 93 Front Street, ☎ 599-542-5259.
The name just about says it all. If you know what you want, this is the place to compare prices. If you don't have a clue, ask one of the sales

St. Martin

staff to run through the virtues of different brands and help you decide what will work best for you.

Perfume, Cosmetics & Skin Care Products

Lipstick, Polo Ralph Lauren Building, 31 Front Street, ☎ 599-542-6051.

Marigot, the main town on the French side, has three of these popular cosmetic shops, but if you're not going to that side of the island, stop by this boutique inside the Polo Ralph Lauren Building. Look for products by Calvin Klein, Cartier, Dior, Nina Ricci, Estee Lauder, and many brands that are difficult or impossible to find in North America.

Perfume Palace, 48 Front Street, ☎ 599-542-3017.

You'll find more than perfume at this jam-packed shop, but European fragrances are the best buy.

Liquor

Guavaberry Emporium, 8-10 Front Street, ☎ 599-542-2965.

Guavaberry liqueur is made on St. Martin, and sold throughout the islands. You can taste the liqueurs made with this local fruit at the Emporium housed in a colorful 18th-century building that stands on Front Street. If you like the sample, order a Guavaberry Colada to sip as you browse through the shop's other island-made products.

Gift World, 21 and 45 Front Street, ☎ 599-542-0666.

If you want to swoop up all your souvenirs, liquor, and gifts in one shop so that you can hit the beach before noon, this is the store for you. In addition to all the popular brands of liquor, the shelves are filled with sunglasses, T-shirts, post cards, and locally made crafts.

Philipsburg Liquor Store, Point Blanche Cruise Ship Port, ☎ 599-542-3587.

More than 1,000 types of wine and liquor are stocked here, so you're sure to find your favorites. Look for the colorful building located beside the cruise ship dock.

WORD TO THE WISE

*If you're leaving the island by plane, buy your liquor in the airport terminal from **Antillean Liquors**, ☎ 599-545-4267.*

Art

Greenwith Gallery, 33 Front Street, ☎ 599-542-3842.

Possibly the most beautiful shop on the island, Greenwith displays the works of more than 40 Caribbean artists. Choose original paintings, prints, or posters; everything may be purchased framed or unframed. The staff are experts at packing and will even bundle up delicate pottery for the trip back home.

Nanette Bearden Fine Arts Gallery, Promenade Arcade, 44 Front Street, ☎ 599-543-1540.
American Nanette Bearden died in 1996, but she was a great lover of the arts, a former artistic director of her own dance theater, and the wife of internationally acclaimed artist, Romare Bearden, who died 1988. The gallery on the second level of the Promenade Arcade on Front Street remains open as a tribute to its former owners and their passion for promoting the work of young artists. Each month, the shop exhibits the new works of select Caribbean artists.

Mosera, 7 Front Street, ☎ 599-542-0554.
Ras Mosera, a Rasta painter from Saint Lucia, creates and displays his oversized oil and watercolor paintings at this combination studio/gallery.

Tablecloths

Linen Galore, 97 Front Street, ☎ 599-543-0099.
Stock up on tablecloths, place mats, napkins, pillowcases, and other home accessories at one of these two linen boutiques. Choose from Battenburg Lace, embroidered, and crocheted items.

Island-Style Clothing & Stuff

Shipwreck Shop, 34 Front Street, ☎ 599-542-2962.
In addition to T-shirts and beach accessories, you'll find island-made arts and crafts, hammocks, spices, and baskets. Everything is well-priced, so load up that shopping bag.

Last Mango in Paradise, 17 Front Street, ☎ 599-542-2058.
Jimmy Buffett fans must allow plenty of time to look over this large collection of his CDs, books, and Caribbean Soul T-shirts. Shop, then drop into a comfy chair to watch him perform in concert on video.

Boardwalk, 15 Front Street, ☎ 599-542-2737.
You'll be glad you packed light when you spot the great outfits at this shop. Stock up on sun dresses, pants, tops, and accessories to wear while you're on the island and again at summer-time parties back home.

St. Martin

Endless Summer, 27 Front Street, ☎ 599-545-4243.
In a perfect world, summer would last year-round, and you'd be dressed for the beach in the gorgeous designer swim wear and cover-ups sold here. Look for the stylish creations of Gottex, Pilpel, Anne Cole, Calvin Klein, Tara Grinna, and others. Ask the sales people to show you how to tie one of the colorful pareos into a Tahitian-style dress or skirt.

Dalila Boutique, 30 Front Street, ☎ 599-542-3525.
You won't be able to resist the exotic, made-in-Bali batik clothing and handicrafts sold at this small shop.

Del Sol, 23 Front Street, ☎ 599-542-8784.
Ah, technology is terrific. All the casual clothing at this store appears to be decorated with black-and-white designs, but when the fabric is exposed to the sun, the design comes alive with tropical colors. Step back inside, and the picture reverts back to black-and-white. Magic? No, science. The designs are made with organic crystals that react colorfully to ultraviolet light. Great fun, and the perfect gift to bring the kids back home.

Rima Beach World, 95 Pond Fill Road (also called Nisbet Road), ☎ 599-542-1424.
As both a wholesaler and retailer, this factory outlet can offer fantastic prices. It's not on the main drag in Philipsburg, but across from the Heineken Bar (it looks like an airplane) on the road that runs parallel to the salt pond. The store has hundreds of swimsuits, coverups, shirts, towels, and beach bags.

Upscale Clothing & Accessories

The stores listed below sell the clothing and accessories designed by their famous designer namesakes. If you buy these brands at home, you'll recognize the bargains when you see them. Expect to save about 20% over prices in North America; more if you happen to find a sale.

Liz Claiborne, 48 Front Street, ☎ 599-543-0380

Polo Ralph Lauren, 31 Front Street, ☎ 599-543-0195

Tommy Hilfiger, 28 Front Street, ☎ 599-542-6315

United Colors of Benetton, 40 Front Street, ☎ 599-542-2633

This & That

New Amsterdam Store, 66 Front Street, ☎ 599-542-2787.
This three-level store near the courthouse on Wathey Square has been selling everything from designer shoes to fine china since 1925.

Other shops along Front Street sell similar merchandise, but this one-stop outfit puts it all under one roof at competitive prices.

Little Europe, 80 Front Street, ☎ 599-542-4371.
All the pretty little things you love, but never buy for yourself, are nestled into this upscale shop, and you may discover that you can't pass them up at these prices. Hummel figures, Piaget watches, Pasquale Bruni jewels, and other fine items from around the world are duty-free, which makes them 10-15% less pricey than in North America. Go ahead and spoil yourself.

Ashburry's, 79 Front Street, ☎ 599-543-0382.
Only the best is displayed here. Fine leather luggage, exquisite sunglasses, pricey perfume, and fabulous jewelry are all laid out in this pleasant boutique. Plan to spend some time admiring, and perhaps coveting.

■ Best Boutiques in Marigot

In the French capital, shops are spread out among several streets, with the majority of fine boutiques on **Rue de la République** and **Rue de la Liberté**. You'll discover other great buys in stores along **Rue du Président Kennedy**, which borders the Marina Port la Royale, and scattered among the side streets. Vendors set up along the harbor, and a large **public market** takes place at the waterside town square on Wednesdays and Saturdays. If you just want to pick up picnic supplies, sun block, or other everyday necessities, stop at **Match**, the French hypermart, on Rue de Hollande on the far northeast side of town, in the direction of Grand Case.

Park free in front of the Office du Tourisme (☎ 87-57-23) on Rue du Morne, the road leading into town from Sandy Ground to the south, or in the waterfront lot on Blvd. de France. The office has maps and a table with leaflets offering discounts at stores and attractions on the French side.

While Philipsburg is my choice shopping town for bargains on jewelry and Caribbean-style clothes and accessories, Marigot is generally better for European fashions, leather goods, and anything French. Here's a listing of my favorite shops based on merchandise selection, bargain prices, and friendly service:

Most of the stores in Marigot do not display a street number, but the roads are only a few blocks long, so you're never far away. Just stroll until you spot the sign or awning baring the store's name.

Jewelry

Oro de Sol, Rue de la République, ☎ 590-87-56-51.
If you know and love fine things, you'll be impressed with this shop's inventory of imported china, crystal, linens, designer jewelry, and top-name watches.

Chopard, 26 Rue de la République, ☎ 590-51-01-15.
There are those among us who wear only Chopard, the Swiss name made famous in 1860. All others should strive for such heights of luxury. The watches, of course, are absolute perfection, but many are not aware of the excellent Chopard collections of silk scarves and ties, silverware, perfumes, sunglasses, and jewelry. Come. Look. Admire.

Passions, Rue du Général de Gaulle/Plaza Caraïbes, ☎ 590-87-18-00.
Search out a little bauble at this upscale jewelry shop. The collection includes watches by Jaeger-Lecoultre, Chanel, Bell & Ross, Girard-Perregaux, and Chaumet. Unique jewelry designs are by Dinh Van, Pomellato, Hermès, and O.J. Perrin. Browse the luxury, even if you don't buy.

Liquor & Wine

(See sister-store reviews for Vinissimo and Le Goût du Vin under *Top Shops* in the St. Barts section.)

Vinissimo, 1 Rue Low Town, ☎ 590-87-70-78

Le Goût du Vin, Rue de l'Anguill (north of the marina off Rue du Général de Gaulle), ☎ 590-87-25-03

Designer Sunglasses

Optical, Rue du Général de Gaulle, ☎ 590-87-13-08

Optic 2000, 3 Rue du Président Kennedy, ☎ 590-52-97-82

*Don't dismiss **Little Switzerland** on Rue de la République (☎ 590-87-50-03) as a been-there-seen-it-all place. The one in Marigot carries additional French merchandise.*

WORD TO THE WISE

European Fashions & Accessories

Serge Blanco, Rue du Président Kennedy/Marina Port la Royale, ☎ 590-29-65-49.
Named for one of the most talented rugby players in history, this shop carries men's shirts, shorts, and jackets made near Blanco's hometown of Biarritz, France.

Act III, Rue du Général de Gaulle, ☎ 590-29-28-43.
Shop here for the perfect evening gown or cocktail dress. The exquisite fashions carry labels such as Thierry Mugler, Christian Lacroix, and Cerruti.

Hermès, Rue du Général de Gaulle/Plaza Caraïbes, ☎ 590-87-28-48.
Silk scarfs and ties, and luxurious fragrances are best sellers at this renowned shop.

Max Mara, 6 Rue du Président Kennedy, ☎ 590-52-99-75.
Italians can't get enough of the fashions found at Max Mara, and you'll understand why when you see the easy-to-wear designs made of top-quality fabrics.

Perfume, Cosmetics & Skin Care Products

Lipstick, Rue du Président Kennedy/Marina Port la Royale, ☎ 590-87-73-24; Rue de la République, ☎ 590-87-53-92; Rue du Général de Gaulle/Plaza Caraïbes, ☎ 590-87-73-24.
Without question, these shops are the best on the island for skin care products, cosmetics, and perfume. You'll find all your old favorites and discover the latest beauty products from Europe. The Marina Port la Royale location also has a full-service salon.

Beauty and Scents, Rue du Général de Gaulle, ☎ 590-87-58-77.
With many of the same brands as Lipstick, this perfume and cosmetic shop carries exclusive names such as Shiseido and Sisley.

Cameras & Video Equipment

Maneks, Rue de la République, ☎ 590-87-54-9.
Name-brand cameras, such as Nikon, Pentax, and Canon, share space with Swiss Army knives, designer T-shirts, and Cuban cigars at this one-stop shop. You can gather all your gifts and souvenirs right here, then grab some snorkel equipment and sun block and be on your way to the beach.

St. Martin

This & That

L'Occitane en Provence, Marina Port du Royale, ☎ 590-87-79-37.
People live casually and naturally in the Provence region of France.
You can enjoy the same tradition with products manufactured in the
area following scrupulous guidelines. Favorite buys include Shea
Butter Massage Balm, Lavender Hand Cream, Verbena Candles, and
a variety of pure essential oils.

Shipwreck Shop, Marina Port la Royale, ☎ 590-29-50-33; Rue de la
Liberté, ☎ 590-87-92-59.
(See review under *Top Shops in Philipsburg*, page 111.)

L'Epicerie, Marina Port la Royale, ☎ 590-87-17-69.
L'Epicerie means *the grocer's shop* in French, but don't mistake this
elite little market for a common neighborhood food store. Yachtsmen
and residents come here to stock their kitchens with imported caviar,
foie gras, truffles, smoked salmon, chocolates, and fine wines, vodkas,
and champagnes. Stop in to pick up fancy treats for a romantic picnic
on the beach or a party back at your villa.

Where to Stay

■ Private Villas

While private rentals are less common on St. Martin than
on St. Barts, some fabulous properties and a few simple
cottages are available through individual owners and various agencies. Be sure to browse the Internet for homes,
apartments, timeshare units, and bungalows offered by individuals,
but shop carefully and be aware that what's advertised is not always
what you get. If the price seems too low, you're probably looking at an
undesirable location or a rundown shack.

Expect a pleasant, clean, but nothing-special one-bedroom place to
rent for about $100 per night, usually on a weekly basis. A truly out-
standing property with multiple bedrooms and bathrooms may start
at around $300 per bedroom per night on a weekly basis. Some villas
also charge by the number of guests. Some of the most luxurious properties with private swimming pools and great views could top $30,000
per week in high season, but half that during the summer.

Telephoning

Calling to, from, or within St. Martin is confusing. When calling St. Martin from the US or Canada, dial **011** to get international service, then the area code, **590** for the French side and **599** for the Dutch side, plus the on-island number, which will be seven digits on the Dutch side (example: 011-599-xxx-xxxx) and nine digits on the French side, which means dialing 590 twice (011-590-590-xx-xx-xx).

When calling the island from Great Britain, dial **00** to get international service, then the area code, **590** or **599**, plus the on-island number, which means you will dial 590 twice to reach the French side (00-590-590-xx-xx-xx).

To call within the French territory, you must add a **0** to the nine-digit local number (0590-xx-xx-xx).

When calling a French number from Dutch St. Martin, dial 00, then 590, then 590 again, plus the six-digit number (00-590-590-xx-xx-xx).

If you wish to call Dutch St. Martin from the French side, you must dial 1 + 599 + the seven-digit number. To call Dutch St. Martin from St. Barts, dial 00, then 599 plus the seven-digit local number.

St. Martin

Rental Agencies	
WIMCO	☎ 800-932-3222, www.wimco.com
All St. Martin Vacation Rentals	☎ 800-942-6725 (in the US) or 908-832-6655, fax 908-832-6685, www.beachdays.com
MountainWaves	☎ 888-349-7800, www.mountainwaves.com
Villa Lady	☎ 800-338-4552 (in the US), www.villalady.com
Caribbean Way	☎ 877-953-7400 (toll-free in the US), www.caribbeanway.com
French Caribbean International	☎ 800-322-2223, www.frenchcaribbean.com
Heart of the Caribbean	☎ 800-231-5303, www.hotcarib.com
Jennifer's Vacation Villas	☎ 599-544-3107, fax 599-544-3375, www.jennifersvacationvillas.com

Sunshine Properties	☎ 480-515-9136 (in the US) or 599-544-4498, fax 599-544-4544, www.sunshine-properties.com
Island Trips	☎ 800-823-2002 or 410-692-2093 (in the US), fax 410-692-9579, www.islandtrip.com
Island Properties	☎ 800-738-9444 (in the US) or 599-543-6160 (on St. Martin), fax 599-543-6457, www.islandproperties.com
Pierre Caraïbes Rentals & Sales	☎ 590-29-21-46 (phone/fax on St. Martin), www.pierres-caraibes.com

■ Resorts & Hotels

Whether you prefer a sumptuous Dutch high-rise with its own casino or a small French compound with plenty of solitude, look for a package deal which may include airfare, rental car, or discounts at restaurants and watersports centers. Many are offered and you may save a substantial amount of money.

Tour-scan computerizes published package trips to the Caribbean according to season, then selects the best values for each island. You can search for your vacation by destination, cost, hotel rating, and preferred activity. ☎ 800-962-2080, www.tourscan.com.

Vacationpackager.com is an online company that leads you to dozens of other companies offering package vacations to many Caribbean destinations, including St. Martin. Their website also lists toll-free phone numbers and Internet addresses for a variety of travel-related organizations and businesses. Check them out at www.vacationpackager.com.

Both sides of St. Martin have thousands of guest rooms in hundreds of extravagant resorts and simple inns. It's not necessary to spend a great deal on a room if you choose a quaint hotel, rather than a glitzy complex with every imaginable amenity. The differences between staying one side of the island vs. the other are less obvious than they once were, but you'll still find the high-rises on the Dutch side and most of the smaller establishments on French territory.

I've checked out a variety of accommodations to come up with the following list of recommendations. At one time, travel professionals advised "staying on the Dutch side, but playing on the French side." Then, the sages began to advocate staying on the quieter French side, but playing on the livelier Dutch side. We tried both, and can frankly tell you it doesn't matter. The differences between the two sides have become as indistinct as the border that divides them.

If I missed a truly great place or led you to a bad experience, e-mail me (comments@hunterpublishing.com) so we can alert other readers.

Hotel Price Scale	
$	under $100
$$	$100-$200
$$$.	$201-$300
$$$$	over $300

The above scale indicates rates charged per night for a standard double room for two adults during high season. All prices are given in US dollars. A government tax of 8% and a 10-15% service charge will be added to the cost of your room, but may be hidden in the quoted rate. Be sure to ask.

The Timeshare Option

Since the early 1980s, the Dutch side of St. Martin has experienced a timeshare boom and now boasts 16 properties in the 16-square-mile Dutch area. More than 50,000 couples or families (rather than individuals) own a timeshare unit on the island, which makes it one of the most favored markets in the world. All these people can't be wrong.

So, what's the attraction? Owners like the concept of owning a home away from home without actually being responsible for, and paying for, year-round upkeep of an entire property. They simply buy a week or two at a resort, use it if they want to, or trade it for another resort anywhere in the world.

When a timeshare resort finds itself with unused units, they rent them to non-owners, often at very attractive prices. The **St. Maarten Timeshare Association (SMTA)** regulates itself through a code of ethics set up by the American Resort Development Association, and you should not have any terrible experiences with salespeople or the resorts. You will, however, be approached by recruiters on the streets and beaches who hope to lure you to a sales presentation. Just say no if you're not interested.

If you rent a unit in one of the timeshare resorts, or simply stop in to look around, you probably will be offered gifts to entice you to tour the property, which is a thinly veiled sales presentation. Again, just say no if you're not interested. You should never be pressured, but if you are, report the inappropriate conduct to the tourist office, ☎ 599-542-2337.

St. Martin

Timeshare rentals (rather than purchases) can be a good bargain, especially during the off-season, when resorts often have unused units. You can sometimes book by the day, but some resorts rent only on a weekly basis. Choices usually include one- or two-bedroom suites with living areas and full or partial kitchens. You may use all or most of the resort facilities without extra charge.

Resorts Belonging to the SMTA

The Summit Resort, Mullet Bay, ☎ 599-545-2150.

Atrium Beach Resort, Simpson Bay, ☎ 599-544-2126.

Belair Beach Hotel, Cay Hill, ☎ 59-542-3362.

Radisson Oyster Bay, Oyster Pond, ☎ 599-543-6040.

Caravanserai, Burgeaux Bay, ☎ 599-545-4000.

Flamingo Beach Resort, Simpson Bay, ☎ 599-544-3900.

Royal Palm Beach Club, Simpson Bay, ☎ 599-544-3737

Sapphire Beach Club, Lowlands, ☎ 599-545-2179.

Divi Little Bay Beach Resort, Little Bay, ☎ 599-542-2333.

La Vista, Pelican Key, ☎ 599-544-3005.

Princess port de Plaisance, Cole Bay, ☎ 599-544-5222.

Royal Islander Club, Maho Beach, ☎ 599-545-2388.

Pelican Resort, Simpson Bay, ☎ 599-544-2503.

All recommended resorts and hotels are air conditioned, meet average expectations for comfortable furnishings, and are equipped with color cable TV.

Accommodations Directory

The Dutch Side
Atrium Resort, Simpson Bay, ☎ 599-54402125, fax 599-544-2128
Caravanserai Beach Resort, Burgeaux Bay, ☎ 800-616-1154 (in the US), 599-545-4000, fax 599-545-540
Divi Little Bay Beach Resort, Little Bay, ☎ 800-367-3484 (in the US) or 599-542-2333, fax 599-542-5410

Holland House Beach Hotel, Philipsburg, ☎ 800-223-9815 (in the US) or 599-542-2572, fax 599-542-4673
The Horny Toad Guesthouse, Simpson Bay, ☎ 800-417-9361 (in the US) or 599-545-4323, fax 599-545-3316
La Vista Resort, Pelican Key, ☎ 599-544-3005, fax 599-544-3010
Maho Beach Hotel and Casino, Maho Bay, ☎ 800-223–0757 (in the US) or ☎ 99-545-2115, fax 599-545-3180
Mary's Boon Beach Plantation, Simpson Bay, ☎ 599-545-4235, fax 599-545-3403
The Ocean Club, Cupecoy Beach, ☎ 800-942-6725 or 599-545-4362, fax 599-545-4434
Sapphire Beach Club, Cupecoy Beach, ☎ 599-545-2179, fax 599-545-2178
Summit Resort, Mullet Bay, ☎ 599-545-2150, fax 599-545-2615

■ On the Dutch Side

Caravanserai Beach Resort
Burgeaux Bay
☎ 800-616-1154 (in the US), 599-545-4000, fax 599-545-5401
www.caravan-sxm.com
66 units
$$$

Set beside a small beach near Maho Beach and the airport, the Caravanserai just keeps getting better. Part-timeshare, the resort includes one-bedroom apartment-style ocean-view suites, in addition to spacious hotel rooms. On-site attractions include the **Dolphin Casino**, **Bamboo Bernie's Restaurant**, **Bliss** (a nightclub, restaurant, and martini bar), and the popular **Sunset Beach Bar**. A small Asian grocery store/café has a few tables and offers Chinese food to go. A climbing wall was recently built on the landscaped grounds to amuse energetic guests who have tired of the three swimming pools, two tennis courts, and health spa.

Divi Little Bay Beach Resort
Little Bay
☎ 800-367-3484 (in the US) or 599-542-2333, fax 599-542-5410
www.diviresorts.com
245 units
$$$

The beach sand has been refreshed, and Little Bay is a great location; the site of Fort Amsterdam. It sits on a peninsula that juts into the sea southwest of Philipsburg, and the views are fantastic. Sprawled across several landscaped acres, the rooms and suites are in colorful

St. Martin

Dutch-colonial buildings clustered around three pools, two tennis courts, a restaurant, and a well-equipped watersports/dive shop facility. Many of the units have little kitchens and spacious bathrooms with whirlpool tubs and showers. There are scheduled activities, including a weekly barbecue with live music.

Atrium Resort
Simpson Bay
☎ 599-54402125, fax 599-544-2128, www.atrium-resort.com
90 studio, one- , two- , and three-bedroom units
$$
Spacious units in this high-rise have full kitchens and wide balconies with views of the Caribbean. Ceiling fans and tiled floors add a touch of island chic, and a decked pool area is a nice complement to the resort's long white-sand beach. Amenities are scarce, but the **Indiana Restaurant** is located near the pool, and you'll be within walking distance of the eateries and shops along Airport Road.

Sapphire Beach Club
Cupecoy Beach
☎ 599-545-2179, fax 599-545-2178, www.sapphirebeachclub.com
169 studio, one- and two-bedroom units
$$

AUTHOR PICK We think this Wyndham resort is one of the best values on the Dutch side. Even the smallest units have full kitchens with granite countertops and dishwashers, bedrooms with king-size beds and a terrace, a living room with a sleeper sofa, VCR, and Italian marble bathrooms with big tubs. All for less than $100 per person per night during high season. Unlike some timeshare properties, this one even has daily maid service, except on Sundays.

Six people can share a two-bedroom, two-bath, two-level unit, also for about $100 per person per night during high season. These units have private plunge pools, and dining rooms with seating for six that open onto terraces overlooking the sea.

Maho Beach Hotel and Casino
Maho Bay
☎ 800-223-0757 (in the US) or ☎ 99-545-2115, fax 599-545-3180, www.mahobeach.com
600 rooms and suites
$$$
This is by far the largest hotel complex on the island, and one of the best known in the Caribbean. Guests get lost in the twists and turns

of the walkways that connect their room to the casino (the largest on the island), nine restaurants, two pools (one is the largest on the island), nightclub, spa, gym, three bars, four tennis courts, about 40 boutiques, and lovely Maho Beach. But no one minds – it's just too much fun. The only drawback is the darn jumbo jets that fly directly overhead. (Rooms are soundproofed.) Units in two high-rise towers aren't spectacular, but they're fairly spacious and have some nice touches, such as new furnishings, Italian tile, and bidets in the bathrooms.

Mary Boon

Mary's Boon is named after its original owner, Mary Pomeroy, an Englishwoman who left Europe after World War II to settle on the island of Nevis. For years, she ran the elegant Nisbett Plantation, while enraging authorities by publicly criticizing the way they ran the island's government. In the 1970s, while Mary was in Canada visiting a friend, the government seized Nisbett Plantation. When she returned to find she had no home, Mary flew off in her private Piper Cherokee, eventually landing on St. Martin. She found a lovely piece of beachfront property where she could park her plane and built her guesthouse, Mary's Boon. She ran it for about 10 years, until, one day she disappeared while flying her plane.

Mary's Boon Beach Plantation
Simpson Bay
☎ 599-545-4235, fax 599-545-3403, www.marysboon.com
25 rooms, studios, and one- or two-bedroom apartments
$$

AUTHOR PICK

This is a personal favorite – a quiet, well-run inn on three miles of white-sand beach. Owners Mark and Karla Cleveland keep everything running smoothly so guests do nothing but relax. Smaller units have kitchenettes, and the one- and two-bedroom bungalows have full kitchens – perfect for keeping picnic supplies on hand. Ask about the new deluxe studios with four-poster king-size beds and verandahs that face the sea.

Recently, a swim-up bar was added to the lovely pool and Jacuzzi, and you may find yourself spending long afternoons there chatting with other guests. An honor bar is also provided so you can make your own

St. Martin

drinks to enjoy in your room or while lounging in the lush garden. Watersports are available on the beach for the energetic, and there are spa services for those who wish to be pampered. The **Seaside Dining Gallery** serves a delicious fixed-price ($35-$40), family-style West Indies meal every evening, which shouldn't be missed. On Sundays, chef Leona features a superb Champagne Brunch. Reservations are a must.

La Vista Resort
Pelican Key
☎ 599-544-3005, fax 599-544-3010, www.lavistaresort.com
32 suites and cottages
$$

Along with your room at this charming inn, you get full privileges at the tennis courts, watersports center, and spa that belong to neighboring Pelican Resort and Casino. It's really the best of both worlds – the tranquil intimacy of a quaint island-style hotel plus all the goodies that come with a full-service resort.

Every unit, from the junior suite to the oversized one-bedroom penthouse, has a king-size bed, either a patio or balcony, and a kitchenette. The penthouse is cleverly designed with the bedroom and one bathroom on the first floor and the living area with a sleeper sofa and second bathroom on the upper level – ideal for sharing with friends. Our favorite, though, is the private cottage, which looks like a well-tended West Indies home complete with a front porch facing the sea.

La Vista also has its own pool and a small restaurant, **The Hideaway**, which serves hearty well-priced meals throughout the day. In the morning, breakfast includes a variety of egg choices as well as pancakes and French toast – all in the $4-$6 range. Lunch offerings include burgers, sandwiches, and salads priced from $6 to $7. Italian dishes and seafood top the dinner menu, with complete meals ranging from $14 to $28.

The Horny Toad Guesthouse
Simpson Bay
☎ 800-417-9361 (in the US) or 599-545-4323, fax 599-545-3316
www.thehornytoadguesthouse.com
Eight units
$$

After an initial quick glance, we dismissed this inn as too simple to make the recommended list. And, honestly, we were surprised by the rate, $198 per couple per night during the winter, which we thought was too high. Still, we had heard good things about the friendly laid-back mood promoted by owner Betty Vaughan and the fanatic attention to detail of the cleaning staff, so we poked around a bit. Now, we're happy to report a complete change of attitude. Who needs air conditioning, swimming pools, and on-site restaurants when you can have soft breezes straight off the beach and cook your own dinner on a communal gas barbecue grill set up in a covered seaside pavilion?

This place isn't for everyone, but each individually decorated unit in the converted beach house (built in the 1950s by a former governor) is comfortably homey. The beds are king size; the bathrooms are basic, but sparkling; the kitchens are equipped with everything you need, including a full-size refrigerator; and the grounds are landscaped with fragrant flowering bushes. If you think you can't make do with only a ceiling fan, request one of the air-conditioned units.

Holland House Beach Hotel
Philipsburg
☎ 800-223-9815 (in the US) or 599-542-2572, fax 599-542-4673
www.hhbh.com
60 rooms and suites
$$

If you're going to stay in the Dutch capital – and we don't recommend it unless you're on a business or serious shopping trip – check into the Holland House. One side faces Front Street, lined with duty-free shops, and the other faces Great Bay Beach, lined with lounge chairs shaded by yellow umbrellas. The lobby has an old-world appearance with buffed hardwood floors, but the hotel offers modern high-speed Internet access to guests.

Ask for a room facing the water, and request a kitchenette if you want to keep drinks and snacks on hand. Each room is spacious and has a balcony, but the bathrooms are small. Even if you don't stay in the hotel, stop at the open-air **Three Ladies Restaurant** for breakfast, lunch, or dinner. You'll have a view of the bay from your table, and the menu features Dutch, Indonesian, and Continental cuisine.

Summit Resort
Mullet Bay
☎ 599-545-2150, fax 599-545-2615, www.thesummitresort.com
63 suites
$$

AUTHOR
PICK

We couldn't believe the reasonable rental rates, even during the winter, for a garden-view suite at this mostly-timeshare resort. It's a marvelous place, on a cliff above Simpson Bay Lagoon near the French border, about a 10-minute drive from Marigot. It's not on the water, but a van shuttles guests to Cupecoy and Mullet Bay beaches – a two-minute drive away.

St. Martin

Suites are located in green-trimmed coral-colored cottages scattered among mature trees and bushes. The newest units have full kitchens with large refrigerators, living/dining areas, and furnished balconies. Views from the swimming pool are spectacular, and the surrounding sun deck has plenty of lounge chairs and tables under green umbrellas. The adjacent café and bar serve poolside throughout the day.

The Ocean Club
Cupecoy Beach
☎ 800-942-6725 or 599-545-4362, fax 599-545-4434
www.theocesnclub.org
50 villas and suites
$$$

We liked this stunning white village because of its high level of luxury, the gorgeous location, and, most of all, the relaxed atmosphere. Instead of non-stop activities, the resort offers convenient access to one of the island's most popular beaches, a private 45-foot diesel-powered yacht (*Ocean Wave*) that cruises the shoreline and lagoon, a large free-form swimming pool, and a very good restaurant, **The Oasis**.

Owners Barbara and Bob Speranza keep the resort fresh through an ongoing update program. Recent projects added new window treatments, bedspreads, and sleeper sofas in the living areas. Each of the units is nicely furnished and features marble floors and a well-equipped modern kitchen with a full-size fridge and dishwasher. Some units have extra touches: the villas and one-bedroom suites have large Roman-style bathtubs with overhead skylights; ocean-side units have dramatic balconies reaching out toward the sea; the three-bedroom, three-bath penthouse is a two-story unit with a spiral staircase connecting the ground and upper floors.

DID YOU KNOW?

Most resorts and hotels on the French side are assigned between one and four stars according to the French quality-classification system. A property that tops even the four-star rating is designated four-star deluxe ("luxe" in French). Likewise, a hotel that deserves a little more than three stars, but fewer than four, receives a rating of three-star superior ("supérieur" in French). We've included the rating when it's available because it can be helpful when choosing a place to stay.

∎ On the French Side

Accommodations Directory

The French Side
Captain Oliver's Resort, Oyster Pond, ☎ 590-87-40-26, fax 590-87-40-84
Caribbean Princess Condos, Orient Bay, ☎ 590-52-94-94, fax 590-52-95-00
Chez Martine, Grand Case, ☎ 590-87-51-59
Club Orient Resort, Orient Bay, ☎ 590-87-33-85, fax 590-87-33-76
Grand Case Beach Club, Grand Case, ☎ 590-87-51-87, fax 590-87-59-93
Green Cay Village, Orient Bay, ☎ 888-843-4760 (in the US) or 590-87-38-63, fax 590-87-39-27
La Samanna, Baie Longue, ☎ 800/854-2252 or 590-87-64-00, fax 590-87-87-86
L'Esplanade Caraïbes Hotel, Grand Case, ☎ 590-87-06-55, fax 590-87-29-15
Le Petit Hotel, Grand Case, ☎ 590-29-09-65, fax 590-87-09-19
The Mercure Simpson Beach, Baie Nettlé, ☎ 590-87-54-54, fax 590-87-92-11
Le Meridien – L'Habitation Lonvilliers and Le Domaine, L'Anse Marcel, ☎ 800-543-4300 (in the US) or 590-87-67-00, fax 590-87-30-3
Orient Bay Hotel, Orient Bay, ☎ 800-818-5992 (in the US) or 590-87-31-10, fax 590-87-37-66
Palm Court, Orient Bay, ☎ 866-786-2277 (toll-free in the US) or 590-87-41-94, fax 590-29-41-30

St. Martin

La Samanna
Baie Longue
☎ 800/854-2252 or 590-87-64-00, fax 590-87-87-86
www.lasamanna.orient-express.com
83 rooms and suites; four star deluxe
$$$$

AUTHOR PICK

In spite of its reputation as the standard by which all other luxury resorts measure themselves, La Samanna is surprisingly easygoing. The resort puts as much thought and money into making you feel relaxed and pampered as it puts into impressing you with Oriental objets d'art and exquisite Indonesian furniture made of fine mahogany and teak.

The new spa is rated one of the best in the Caribbean and features environmentally serene massage rooms and two hydro-therapy areas where European-trained therapists perform a variety of services using highly effective natural products from France. A new air-conditioned fitness pavilion allows you to gaze at the sea while you work out on Cybex machines under the direction of certified instructors.

After dark, torches light the new floating-edge swimming pool, which seems to overflow toward the sea. Be sure to wear a large pair of dark sunglasses when you lounge here during the day so you can covertly spy on big-name celebrities hiding under nearby umbrellas.

The bathrooms are huge and sumptuous, and the TVs and VCRs are cleverly hidden away in lovely benches when not in use, then pop up in an instant when you want them.

A run down on the amenities reads like a tropical dream: 55 acres of gardens shaded by towering palms set on more than a mile of sandy beach; a gourmet French restaurant serving savory cuisine by candlelight on a lovely patio overlooking the water; watersports for daytime diversion and a disco for dancing the night away.

Chez Martine
Grand Case
☎ 590-87-51-59, www.chez-martine.com
Six rooms
$

This hotel is simple and basic, and we recommend it only for budget travelers who don't plan to spend a lot of time in their room. If you only need a decent bed and a clean shower, read on.

Chez Martine is actually one of many great French restaurants in St. Martin's gourmet capital. The hotel is an afterthought, with just six modest rooms on two floors. Still, there's a little refrigerator for chilling drinks, and an air conditioner to dull street noises and take the heat and humidity out of the air. All the great restaurants and Grand Case Beach are right outside the door.

Palm Court
Orient Bay
☎ 866-786-2277 (toll-free in the US) or 590-87-41-94, fax 590-29-41-30, www.palm-court.net
26 rooms
$$

In the capable hands of manager Elisa Cohen, who also runs the nearby **Bikini Beach Bar and Restaurant** (☎ 590-87-43-25, www.bikinibeach.net), Palm Court is especially popular with watersports enthusiasts because it's just steps from the beach, scuba shops, and watersports centers. Actually, it's a good choice for anyone who wants to be near all the restaurants, shops and activities on Orient Bay.

Rooms have dining/living areas and are outfitted with microwaves, small stoves, and a fridge. Every room has either a king-size bed or two double beds, an ample bathroom, and fans as well as air conditioning. Deluxe rooms on the second floor are particularly pleasant because of their high-beamed ceilings and ocean-view balconies. Ground-floor rooms open onto the lush garden-like grounds, which feature a swimming pool and are shaded by palm and fruit trees.

Club Orient Resort
Orient Bay
☎ 590-87-33-85, fax 590-87-33-76, www.cluborient.com
136 rooms and bungalows
$$$

If you're not accustomed to going about buck naked, this place will take some getting used to. It's called *clothing optional,* but everyone takes the unclothed option rather than look like an out-of-place duffus.

Once you get past the clothing issue, the resort is fairly typical. It sits on high-priced real estate near the water on the powdery white sand lining Orient Bay. Each unit features a kitchen, ceiling fans in addition to air conditioning, and an outdoor shower as well as a full bathroom. Furnishings are comfortable, but rather plain, and there are no TVs or telephones in the rooms. A fully clothed maid cleans daily.

You can join the clothing-optional games that take place on the tennis and volleyball courts, work out in the fitness room, sign up for a cruise to Tintamarre Island at the watersports center, or dine alfresco at **Papagayo Restaurant**. But, don't expect to pick up a date or meet your soul mate here. Most guests are with their family or spouse.

Le Meridien – L'Habitation Lonvilliers and Le Domaine
L'Anse Marcel
☎ 800-543-4300 (in the US) or 590-87-67-00, fax 590-87-30-38
www.lemeridien-ledomaine.com
396 rooms and suites; four stars deluxe
$$$

We have mixed thoughts about this sprawling resort on secluded Marcel Cove. The reception areas are delightfully decorated, and the grounds are stunning – surrounded by a 150-acre nature preserve, and fronting a yacht-filled marina and beautiful 1,600-foot beach. However, many of the rooms suffer from a dank odor, due to inefficient air conditioning that can't handle the tropical humidity. Both

St. Martin

L'Habitation and Le Domaine recently underwent a $3-million reno-
vation, so newly refurbished units are fine for the moment, but the
verdict isn't in on whether or not the air conditioning has been
tweaked enough to make a lasting difference.

L'Habitation, the older hotel, has been spiffed up by French designer
Françoise Robin, who added colorful drapery fabrics, upgraded bed-
ding, and contemporary island-style artwork. Each room has a spacious bathroom with double sinks and an oversized closet. Deluxe
garden units will accommodate four people, and marina suites have
fully equipped kitchens. At Le Domaine, which was built in 1992,
most of the rooms have ocean views from the terrace and all the bathrooms are decked out in marble.

Once you're settled in, there's no need to go off-property. The lavishly
landscaped grounds contain two swimming pools, six tennis courts, a
health club and spa, four restaurants, three bars, a nightclub, and a
watersports center. Since Le Domaine is newer and overlooks the sea,
its rates are higher. L'Habitation has family-sized rooms and a kids'
program, but both resorts share all facilities, and you can participate
in activities scheduled at either hotel.

The Mercure Simpson Beach
Baie Nettlé
☎ 590-87-54-54, fax 590-87-92-11, www.mercure-simson-beach.com
168 suites and apartments; three stars
$$
Located on the French side of Simpson Bay, just a five-minute drive
from Marigot, the Créole-style Mercure is the classiest hotel in its
price bracket. Five three-story buildings surround a large swimming
pool next to an open-air restaurant that serves a huge complimentary
breakfast buffet and a vast patio used for nightly parties featuring is-
land bands.

Each nicely furnished unit has an outdoor kitchenette on the patio or
balcony, ceiling fans, and a basic shower-only bathroom. If you want
more room, ask for a third-floor suite with high ceilings, a sleeping
loft, and an extra bathroom. The landscaped grounds merge with the
palm-shaded white-sand beach, which has a dive shop and
watersports center. A pay-as-you-go shuttle will drop you in Marigot
or Philipsburg for a day of shopping.

Grand Case Beach Club
Grand Case
☎ 590-87-51-87, fax 590-87-59-93, www.gcbc.com
73 studios and one- and two-bedroom suites; three stars
$$$

Located on a quiet stretch of sand east of Grand Case, this popular hotel caters to return guests who enjoy lounging about all day dreaming of the delicacies they will enjoy for dinner at one of the gourmet restaurants down the road. To that end, the resort provides comfortable accommodations in low-rise buildings clustered on landscaped grounds adjacent to a swimming pool, lighted tennis court, well-run watersports center, dive shop, and the casual **Sunset Café**. Each unit has all the amenities you'd expect in a three-star resort, but the furnishings are informal rather than luxurious. Many bedrooms have king-size beds, the kitchenettes have a microwave and small refrigerator, every studio and suite has a patio or balcony, and the sandy beach is no more than a hundred feet from your door.

L'Esplanade Caraïbes Hotel
Grand Case
☎ 590-87-06-55, fax 590-87-29-15, www.lesplanade.com
24 condos
$$$

Views from this resort's hillside perch are truly spectacular. You look out over the sea, the beach, and the row of gourmet restaurants in the quaint village of Grand Case, and ponder the dilemma of what to do next. Walk down to the white-sand beach? Dress for dinner? Simply continue to sit on your private terrace and stare at the hypnotic turquoise water?

We especially liked the spacious loft units on the top floor of this pretty stucco-and-wood resort. They cost a bit more than a studio, but they have a sleeper sofa and half-bath in the living area, and a king-size bed in the upstairs master suite, which includes a full bathroom. Lofts, studios, and one-bedroom suites all have balconies and well-equipped kitchens with standard-sized refrigerators. If you don't have the energy to walk down the hill to the beach, the hotel has a large pool surrounded by flowering bougainvillea and an adjacent bar.

St. Martin

Le Petit Hotel

Grand Case

☎ 590-29-09-65, fax 590-87-09-19, www.lepetithotel.com

Nine studios and one one-bedroom suite

$$$

All accommodations at this little hotel are excellent, but ask for one of the beach-front units with a private terrace facing the sea – one of the best features of the resort. Each suite also features a king-size bed, ceiling fans as well as air conditioning, and a well-equipped kitchen. You may use the pool at sister resort Hôtel L'Esplanade Caraïbes (a short distance away), and walk to Restaurant Row in Grand Case. Manager Kristen Petrelluzi is an expert on the nearby gourmet offerings and will gladly advise you.

Green Cay Village

Orient Bay

☎ 888-843-4760 (in the US) or 590-87-38-63, fax 590-87-39-27

www.greencay.com

16 villas; four stars

$$$

Investigate Green Cay Village if you want the intimacy of a villa and the amenities of a good hotel. The spacious units have one, two, or three bedrooms; a living room with lots of entertainment equipment that opens onto a private deck with a small pool and breathtaking views of the bay; and a full kitchen with a large refrigerator. Designed by French architect Jean-Paul Goergler, each West Indies-style villa is a stand-alone structure set in a landscaped garden so that the pool and deck have total privacy.

Honeymooners will value the extra seclusion of the hilltop cottages. Families and friends traveling together will treasure the private bathrooms adjacent to each bedroom, and the guest bath conveniently located next to the living area. Every detail is carefully planned for your comfort and convenience: most of the bedrooms have king-size beds; the decks have plenty of lounge chairs; the outdoor dining area is covered; the cable TV is equipped with a VCR.

Caribbean Princess Condos

Orient Bay

☎ 590-52-94-94, fax 590-52-95-00

www.cap-caraibes.com/condos.htm

12 two- or three-bedroom condos

$$$$

This is a fairly new complex – expensive, and worth it. Every unit is huge, up to 2,000 square feet, and has two or three bedrooms with one king-size bed or two double beds, large bathrooms connected to each sleeping area, a full kitchen, a living area with a sleeper sofa, and a spacious furnished patio with great views. Skylights, teak, natural stone, and plenty of glass give rooms an airy, contemporary touch. The landscaped grounds have a swimming pool, volleyball court, and a playground for the kids. A tennis club is nearby. If you don't want to cook, there's a restaurant and bar right on the property, and all the bars and bistros on Orient Beach are within walking distance.

Orient Bay Hotel
Orient Bay
☎ 800-818-5992 (in the US) or 590-87-31-10, fax 590-87-37-66
www.orientbayhotel.com
31 one- and two-bedroom villas; three stars
$$

Don't confuse this hotel with the naturalist resort, Club Orient. Here, everyone wears clothes when they swim in one of the two pools or dine in the restaurant. We can't vouch for the attire in the bungalows, which have full kitchens and two terraces. Larger units can accommodate up to five people in two bedrooms, each with an adjoining bathroom. Clothing is, of course, optional at nearby Orient Beach.

Captain Oliver's Resort
Oyster Pond
☎ 590-87-40-26, fax 590-87-40-84, www.captainolivers.com
50 units; four stars
$$$

Popular with both European and American travelers, this attractive resort straddles the French-Dutch border as it crosses Oyster Pond, and is the only hotel grounds in the world that sit partly on French soil and fronting Dutch waters. Staying here is truly an international experience.

More than a hundred luxury yachts are docked at the full-facility marina, and some rooms overlook the wharf. The better view, however, is from one of the spacious ocean-view bungalows. Each unit is in a dusty-rose-colored hillside building and features bathrooms with double sinks and spacious closets. Larger suites have two beds, a sleeper sofa, and a kitchen.

The compound has all sorts of facilities and services. In addition to the marina, there's a glass-walled swimming pool with a deck that extends out into the lagoon and a full-service restaurant serving French and Créole food. The **Dingy Dock bar** has pool tables and serves light meals. The **Iguana Bar** is built over the lagoon and features a two-for-one happy hour from 5-7 pm each evening. You can arrange a

St. Martin

deep-sea fishing trip at the marina or schedule a scuba outing at the on-site dive shop. The resort's taxi boat will shuttle you over to Dawn Beach whenever you like.

Watch where you step. The property is alive with parrots, toucans, turtles, monkeys, iguanas – even an alligator.

Where to Eat

 We probably don't need to tell you that the best restaurants are on the French side. While it's possible to eat quite well on Dutch soil, the most exquisite gourmet meals are prepared in Grand Case, the epicurean capital of St. Martin. Even the waterside open-air *lo-los* serve up tasty island favorites and tender meats grilled on oil-drum barbecue pits. In Marigot, you'll enjoy dining alfresco at one of the bistros facing Marina la Port Royale; at the beach-side restaurants on Orient Bay, your delicious eclectic cuisine will most likely be accompanied by live music.

On the Dutch side, look for delicious international dishes – Indonesian, Indian, and Italian. Philipsburg has a few outstanding eateries, but more variety is found along the main highway between Cole Bay and the airport. Fresh seafood, both locally caught and imported, is the mainstay of these restaurants, but many also serve steaks brought in from the US.

Since food service is a flaky business dependent on the chefs' moods, economic situations, and constantly-changing trends, most of our suggestions are for restaurants that have a longstanding reputation. New places open regularly, so eavesdrop on conversations and ask around to find out where people have recently had a great meal.

WORD TO THE WISE

We've gotten some of our best leads from the folks who run dive shops and watersports facilities. Active people love to eat well, and they'll tell you who makes the best pizza, where to celebrate a special occasion, and which places to skip. They also know all the island gossip, so if a kitchen has some sanitation problems or a top chef just switched restaurants, they'll be happy to pass on the information.

Island Dining

- Make dinner **reservations**, especially during high season.

- **Call ahead** to verify seasonal time changes and closings.

- Shorts and jeans are OK **attire** for most places, but dress up a bit for the finest restaurants: slacks and sport shirts for men; sundresses or slacks for women.

- Unless noted otherwise, restaurant **hours** are noon until 3 pm for lunch and 6 until 10:30 pm for dinner. If breakfast is served, the restaurant typically opens at 7:30 am. French-side restaurants usually close completely between lunch and dinner, while most Dutch-side restaurants stay open throughout the afternoon, though they may serve only a limited menu. If you plan to eat outside these normal hours of operation, call the restaurant to be sure it's open.

- Nearly all restaurants accept major **credit cards**, with the exception of a few small cafés, beach vendors, and fast-food establishments.

- Pick up free copies of *Ti Gourmet* and *Discover* at your hotel or one of the tourist offices. These pocket-sized guides are filled with good restaurant information, including hours of operation and phone numbers, but feature only businesses that pay to be included.

Use the following scale as a guide to what a typical dinner will cost each person, excluding drinks and service charge or tip. Breakfast and lunch prices will be lower.

Dining Price Scale

$	under $15
$$	$16-$25
$$$	$26-$35
$$$$	over $35

No tax is charged on meals, but Dutch-side restaurants often add a 15% service charge. If they do, it's customary to leave a bit more for good service. If they do not, leave the usual 10-20% tip. French-side restaurants include the service charge in the price of the meal, but it's customary to leave an additional 5-10% more on the table as appreciation for good service since the service charge is shared among all employees in the restaurant.

Restaurant Directory

Grand Case
Lo-Lo Fast Food
Sunset Café, Grand Case Beach Resort, north of town, ☎ 590-87-51-87, fax 590-87-17-74
L'Amandier Plage, 28 Boulevard de Grand Case, ☎ 590-87-24-33, fax 590-87-49-78
Auberge Gourmande, 89 Boulevard de Grand Case, ☎ 590-87-73-37, fax 590-29-24-46
Bistrot Caraïbes, 81 Boulevard de Grand Case, ☎ 590-29-08-29, fax 590-29-08-29
Le Tastevin, 86 Boulevard de Grand Case, ☎ 590-87-55-45, fax 590-87-55-45
Le Sébastiano, 234 Boulevard de Grand Case, ☎ 590-87-58-86, fax 590-87-95-29
Le Cottage, 97 Boulevard de Grand Case, ☎ 590-29-03-30
Rainbow, 176 Boulevard de Grand Case, ☎ 590-87-55–80, fax 590-29-07-76
Il Nettuno, 70 Boulevard de Grand Case, ☎ 590-87-77-38, fax 590-87-77-38
Le Pressoir, 30 Boulevard de Grand Case, ☎ 590-87-76-62

■ In Grand Case

Lo-Lo Fast Food

If you're on a tight budget, or just want to have a tasty meal while hangin' with the locals, stop at one of the half-dozen *lo-los* set up along the main drag south of the fishing pier. These outdoor eateries run by local cooks are such an important part of the town's culinary scene that the government financed their rebirth after Hurricane Luis wrecked them several years ago.

You don't need a map to find them. Just follow your nose and the smoke wafting skyward from the makeshift barbecue pits. Menus are handwritten on blackboards, but don't bother reading the selections. Everything is laid out before you on a blazing oil-drum grill.

Ribs are popular, and the half-chickens are always tempting, but we suggest grilled fish or lobster. You won't find it fresher or cheaper anywhere else on the island. Patrons walk away carrying Styrofoam plates piled high with mixed grill and side-dishes for well under $10.

Sunset Café
Grand Case Beach Resort, north of town
☎ 590-87-51-87, fax 590-87-17-74
American, French $$
Open all day for breakfast, lunch, and dinner
Buzz at the front gate and announce your intention to dine in order to gain entry to the resort grounds. During the day, this is a fine way to gain access to the resort's stretch of fine sand that separates Grand Case Beach from Petite Plage and overlooks Creole Rock. Order a croissant or full American breakfast, then settle yourself on the beach. The lounge chairs have flags that you raise whenever you want something from the bar. At lunchtime, order a burger or salad, stay on for happy hour drinks, then linger over a candlelight French dinner prepared by chef Jean-Pierre.

(Don't confuse this with Sunset Beach Bar near the Dutch-side airport on Maho Beach.)

L'Amandier Plage
28 Boulevard de Grand Case
☎ 590-87-24-33, fax 590-87-49-78
French $$$
Open all day for breakfast, lunch, and dinner
Closed Tuesdays during off-season
This beautifully laid-out beachfront compound includes a pool, bar, lounge, spa, and boutique, in addition to the lovely open-air restaurant. The main dining room faces the bay and glows with candlelight after dark. During the day, you can lounge on beach chairs under green umbrellas, take a swim, and order breakfast, lunch, and drinks. The dinner menu features French and Creole dishes, with many grilled specialties, including lobster from the live tank. The wine list is extensive, and desserts are worth every calorie. Servings are large, so plan to share the salads and appetizers.

St. Martin

Auberge Gourmande
89 Boulevard de Grand Case
☎ 590-87-73-37, fax 590-29-24-46
French $$$
Dinner only
Set in a lovely refurbished old Creole house, the romantic surround-ings alone are worth the price of dinner, especially if you sit at one of the tables on the tiny porch. The waitresses wear halter tops and shorts, so the atmosphere is casual and unassuming. Take your time and enjoy each beautiful presentation as it comes to your table from chef Didier Rochat's kitchen. An apricot champagne cocktail. Warm foie gras. Pumpkin and crab bisque. A bit of smoked salmon. Perfectly grilled inch-thick tuna steak with a pink center and a sun-dried to-mato crust, accompanied by pesto mashed potatoes. Or, perhaps the veal sweetbreads. You won't find them prepared as well, or at all, back home. Finish with a rich dessert. The friendly staff will help you choose the perfect wine from their well-stocked cellar, without a hint of intimidation.

Bistrot Caraïbes
81 Boulevard de Grand Case
☎ 590-29-08-29, fax 590-29-08-29
French/Creole $$$
Dinner only
You walk past the live lobster pool when you enter this cozy bistro on your way to a candlelit table. Thibault and Amaury, brother chefs from Lyon, France, personally oversee the kitchen and dining room, so you are guaranteed a wonderful meal. If you don't order lobster, consider the scallops drizzled with garlic butter, grilled rack of lamb, or one of the nightly specials. The highlight for dessert is homemade ice cream.

Le Tastevin
86 Boulevard de Grand Case
☎ 590-87-55-45, fax 590-87-55-45
French $$$
Reserve a table overlooking the beach. The view will add to your din-ing experience, especially at lunch, when there's plenty of activity to watch. At lunch, order one of the creative salads or rich soups. In the evening, ask about the chef's specials – you can't go wrong with roasted duck or grilled fish. Almost every entrée is dressed with a col-orful, tangy sauce and matched with perfectly grilled vegetables. The restaurant's name hints at a well-stocked wine cellar, so ask the staff for suggestions.

Le Sébastiano
234 Boulevard de Grand Case
☎ 590-87-58-86, fax 590-87-95-29
Northern Italian $$$
Dinner only
Closed Sundays during low season and for vacation from September to mid-October
Owner Christine Janot was recently inducted into the prestigious association of French restaurateurs, *Chaine des Rotisseurs*. Her renowned restaurant opened in Grand Case in 1981, and many celebrities have enjoyed her hospitality and cooking talents over the years. Chef Sergio Cussighn works with her in the kitchen to create tempting offerings for the huge menu, which includes several pastas, a variety of delicately sauced meats, and homemade fruit sorbets. You'll need to nibble a nourishing piece of freshly-baked focaccia in order to read through all the standard dishes and nightly specials. If you want a shortcut, just order the lobster-filled ravioli and the stuffed baked chicken breast. Select something light and white from the long French-Italian wine list. You can't beat the tiramisu for dessert.

Le Cottage
97 Boulevard de Grand Case
☎ 590-29-03-30
French $$$
Dinner only
Closed Sundays during off-season and for vacation from mid-September to mid-October
There's no view of the sea from this lovely white stucco restaurant, but you won't miss it. The yellow and blue plates and dining room décor will remind you of sunny Provence; the colorfully tiled lobster tank is strikingly Caribbean. Creative dishes from the kitchen include pumpkin soup, foie gras with unusual sauces (even chocolate), duck confit, almond-crusted beef tenderloin, and homemade sorbet. Ask Stéphane, the sommelier, to help you select a different glass of wine to go with each course of your dinner. The restaurant claims to have the most extensive wine list on the island, and offers the most wines by the glass, so take this opportunity to try several different vintages.

St. Martin

Rainbow

176 Boulevard de Grand Case
☎ 590-87-55–80, fax 590-29-07-76
French $$$
Dinner only
Rainbow has been a popular dinner spot for more than 20 years and has recently remodeled and added an upstairs terrace serving drinks and desserts. Views of the sea are fabulous. The menu is best described as eclectic French. Tandoori swordfish. Italian-Japanese sesame-crusted tuna with spinach ravioli. Scallops with curried fruit salsa. Side-dishes are equally creative and delicious: asparagus in raspberry vinegar; vegetable rolls with ginger sauce; garlicky mashed potatoes. We could go on, but you get the idea. Owners David and Fleur are members of the prestigious association of French restaurateurs, *Chaine des Rotisseurs*.

Il Nettuno

70 Boulevard de Grand Case
☎ 590-87-77-38, fax 590-87-77-38
Italian $$$
Closed for vacation in September
The owner, Ramon, is from the US, and the chefs are from various parts of Europe, but the cuisine is mouth-watering Italian. Hunger-spiking aromas coming from the kitchen indicate a liberal use of garlic and spices, and may cause you to be impatient, but take your time mulling over the large menu as you nibble the bruschetta delivered to your table by the friendly staff. On a recent visit with Italian-American friends, the tender fried calamari appetizer was a big hit. Next time, we plan to try the house specialty, sautéed shrimp in white wine and garlic. The much-acclaimed Saltimbocca alla Romana (veal scallops and prosciuto ham rolled around fresh herbs) lived up to its superb reputation, and the vegetarian in our group raved about the homemade pasta. Terrific Italian wines are available by the glass.

Le Pressoir

30 Boulevard de Grand Case
☎ 590-87-76-62
French $$$
Dinner only
Closed Sundays during low season, July 15-July 31 and in September
Located in one of the oldest houses on the island, this charming country-French restaurant is on many visitors' must-do list because of the flawless service and superb cuisine. Stephane Mabille, the owner-chef, is quite proud of his well-stocked wine cellar and will suggest a

great vintage to accompany your meal. (We were pleasantly surprised to find that his recommended bottle was priced at less than
$30.) On a recent visit, our group sampled traditional scallops St-
Jacques (sweet and tender), roasted duck in ginger sauce (moist without being oily), and a vegetable tart. We thought we had been transported to France – or heaven. Things only improved when we savored
warm chocolate cake topped with vanilla ice cream for dessert.

Restaurant Directory

Marigot
Don Carmello, Marina Royale ☎ 590-87-52-88
La Belle Epoque, Marina Royale, ☎ 590-87-87-70
La Main à la Pâte, Marina Royale, ☎ 590-87-71-19
Le Chanteclair, Marina Royale, ☎ 590-87-94-60
La Petite Auberge des Îles, Marina Royale, ☎ 590-87-56-31
Jean Dupont, ☎ 590-87-71-13
La Brasserie de la Gare, ☎ 590-87-20-64
The Foufounes from Paris, ☎ 590-87-55-20
Le Galion, ☎ 590-87-28-73
Le Saint Germain, ☎ 590-87-92-87
Le Bar de la Mer, Waterfront, ☎ 590-29-03-82
La Vie en Rose, Boulevard de France, ☎ 590-87-54-42

■ In Marigot

Marina Royale

It's a lot of fun to eat at one of the open-air restaurants lining the
boardwalk of Marina Royale in Marigot. The atmosphere is casual,
and the food is wonderful. If you're a true gourmet, you will want to
stick to the two dozen restaurants lining the main boulevard in
Grand Case, but the average palate won't be able to discern a great
difference between the fare offered in these two towns.

As in France, all the restaurants post their menus and nightly specials outside the dining room, so you can spend a leisurely half-hour
strolling along the waterfront comparing dishes and prices. Many of
the postings will seem to be similar, which may make your decision
difficult. We always choose the eatery with the biggest crowd. Below
are a few of our favorites, followed by the name and phone number of
others along the boardwalk.

St. Martin

WORD TO THE WISE

During high season, Marina Royale sponsors a mini-festival on Thursday nights, featuring live bands, clowns, and dance lessons. Make your dinner reservation well in advance.

La Petite Auberge des Îles
☎ 590-87-56-31
French and Créole $$
Monday-Saturday, 11:30 am-11 pm

This is one of the smallest cafés around the marina, and tables spill out of the tiny dining area onto the boardwalk. Just wiggle into any smidgen of space that's available and prepare for a fantastic treat. Owners Françoise and Bruno Darricarrere will make you feel like old friends almost immediately, with Bruno hustling around tending bar and waiting tables, while Françoise periodically dashes out of the kitchen to chat. You won't go wrong ordering the nightly special, but start with the escargot drenched in garlic butter and finish with profiteroles. On one of our many visits, we met a charming English woman digging into the chocolate-drenched ice cream-filled cream puffs with great gusto, while her much younger companion dined on salad. We commented that she seemed to be enjoying herself, and she told us that she came over from Saba once a month to shop and eat profiteroles at La Petite Auberge des Îles, which reminded her of past indulgences in France. She never bothered with a proper meal first, and said at her age, she ate whatever she pleased and nothing pleased her more than profiteroles.

La Belle Epoque
☎ 590-87-87-70
French $$
Monday-Saturday, 7:30 am-11 pm

When this bistro is crowded, the service suffers a bit, but your meal will be excellent when it arrives. Everything from pizza to steak is popular, but we especially like the French onion soup and the salmon with basil sauce. Diners nearby said the lobster was delicious, and friends from Chicago (where everyone is a pizza expert) voted the Roquefort-chèvre-mozzarella pizza the best they'd ever tasted.

La Main à la Pâte
☎ 590-87-71-19
French $$
Monday-Saturday, 11:30 am-11 pm

The name translates *hand in the dough*, but loosely means the chef makes everything from scratch. We sampled several things and found the Caribbean Seafood Pot (pasta, clams, shrimp, and mahi-mahi in tomato sauce) and the red snapper in passion sauce outstanding. Our French waiter was friendly and gave good advice about ordering from the extensive menu. Prices are very reasonable.

Le Chanteclair
☎ 590-87-94-60
French $$$
Daily, 6-10:30 pm
Chef Cécile's *No Name* dessert is famous, the foie gras is a superb specialty and the grilled tuna is wonderful. The prices are on the high side, but well worth it.

Don Carmello
☎ 590-87-52-88
Italian $$
Monday-Saturday, 6:30-10:30 pm
We heard about this fantastic restaurant from Vinny, the dive master at Dive Adventures. He isn't the only one impressed by the food and friendly ambiance. Letters and post cards written by dozens of happy, well-fed patrons cover one wall and part of several windows. It takes a truly extraordinary meal to inspire such poetic praise. Enzo, the gracious Sicilian owner and host, sees to your every need and will make suggestions if you find the menu overwhelming. The tomato and mozzarella salad is large enough to share, portions of homemade pasta are generous, and the homemade bread topped with an anchovy-enhanced spread is addictive. Try the fruit tart for dessert.

Jean Dupont
☎ 590-87-71-13
French $$$
Daily, 11:30 am-11 pm
Jean Dupont also owns Le Santal, the famous St. Martin restaurant commended by international food magazines for many years, and this more casual sister restaurant is expected to collect its own share of rave reviews. The menu offers many temptations, but we especially enjoyed the fish soup, followed by tender filet mignon. There's nothing stuffy or intimidating about this waterside café, but the décor is classy, and you can dine on Dupont-quality fare at bistro prices.

Other Restaurants at the Marina

In addition to the above recommendations, the following restaurants face the marina and offer great views and a festive ambiance. Call for

St. Martin

a reservation, especially on Thursdays during high season, or arrive early enough to browse the posted menus before booking a table.

La Brasserie de la Gare
☎ 590-87-20-64
French $$
Daily, 11:30 am-1 am

The Foufounes from Paris
☎ 590-87-55-20
Créole and French $$
Monday-Saturday, 11:30 am-11 pm

Le Galion
☎ 590-87-28-73
French $$
Daily, 11 am-11 pm

Le Saint Germain
☎ 590-87-92-87
Crêpes and French $$
Daily, 8 am-11 pm

Restaurants Elsewhere in Marigot

Le Bar de la Mer
Waterfront – near the public market
☎ 590-29-03-82
Varied menu $$
Daily, 8 am-1 am
Everyone eventually comes to Le Bar, and it may seem that they all arrive just when you want to eat. Nudge your way through the crowd around the downstairs bar and make your way up to the dining room on the second floor. At lunch, you can't go wrong with the pizza. Its tantalizing aroma will seduce you as soon as you arrive. For dinner, go for the highly-acclaimed Caribbean barbecue served on the spacious terrace. All kinds of fish and meats are basted with a spicy marinade and grilled to perfection. Fantastic flavors.

La Vie en Rose
Boulevard de France
☎ 590-87-54-42
French $$$$
Daily, 11:30 am-2:30 pm and 6:30-10 pm
This is one of the oldest and most popular restaurants on St. Martin. Prices are high, but you should try it. Year after year, it ranks among

the best restaurants on the island. It's located in a colonial-style house with a patio that opens out to the street and a second-floor balcony, which is great for people watching. When we arrived during the busy lunchtime, we thought the servers had a bit of a snooty attitude, but on a return visit, this time for dinner, the service was relaxed and gracious. Stick to reasonably priced salads and sandwiches at lunch, but splurge on dinner. Each elegant course will be served slowly to allow you time to enjoy and digest. Choices are fairly typical – roasted duck, rack of lamb, fresh fish – but the sauces and other embellishments are out of this world. Think puff pastry surrounding some type of meat and drizzled with herb-spiked butter, warm raspberry sauce poured over a poultry breast, goat cheese sprinkled over lightly grilled filets. Your surroundings will be as remarkable as the meal – coffered ceilings and candlelight.

Restaurant Directory

Philipsburg
Antoine, Front Street, ☎ 599-542-2964
Taloula Mango, Hendrickstraat, ☎ 599-542-4278

Simpson Bay
Hot Tomatoes, Airport Road, ☎ 599-545-4176
Ric's Place, Airport Road, ☎ 599-545-3630
Saratoga, Simpson Bay Yacht Club, Airport Road, ☎ 599-544-2421
Turtle Pier, Simpson Bay Lagoon Marina/Airport Road, ☎ 599-545-2562

St. Martin

■ In Philipsburg

Taloula Mango
Hendrickstraat
☎ 599-542-4278
Eclectic $
Daily, 7:30 am-6:30 pm

As **Kangaroo Court Café**, this was our favorite restaurant in Philipsburg. Owner Norman Wathey changed its name and menu late in 2002, and preliminary reports on the new place are favorable. Norman is a coffee connoisseur, and the restaurant now features a variety of gourmet coffees and coffee drinks. The menu is also bigger, but freshly baked pastries, big salads, and meal-size sandwiches are still available. Stop in early for a shot of espresso to get you in the shopping mood, then return for lunch on the shaded patio. Look for the new sign on a side-street near the courthouse off Front Street.

Antoine
Front Street
☎ 599-542-2964
Italian, Créole, French $$$
Daily, 11:30 am-10 pm
Owners Jean-Pierre Pomarico and Pierre-Louis Kesner oversee this wonderful restaurant, with splendid views of Great Bay. Skip over the Italian dishes, you can find better elsewhere, but the French and Créole meals are as good as any you'll find on the island. Start with freshly made pâté or one of the soups, then ask for guidance on the entrée. Seafood, veal, and beef are on the menu, and Pierre-Louis often prepares a daily special. You can't go wrong with the veal scallopini or steak au poivre, and a *New York Times'* food critic says the lobster thermidor is outstanding.

■ In Simpson Bay

Ric's Place
Airport Road
☎ 599-545-3630
Tex-Mex and American $
Daily, 8 am-11 pm
If you visited St. Martin some time ago, you may remember Ric's location on Front Street in Philipsburg. He and wife Kathy have moved the restaurant to this larger place near the drawbridge, east of the airport. This is the place to come for familiar North American fare and Tex-Mex food in a sports bar setting. Start your day with French toast, come back for a jumbo-sized burger around lunch time, then dig into a plate of tacos for dinner. If a game's on, order a plate of nachos to share with fellow fans. The only downside to this popular place is that it doesn't accept credit cards.

Hot Tomatoes
Airport Road
☎ 599-545-4176
Pizza and Italian $
Daily, 11 am-midnight
Brad and Neil, the previous owners of the popular Sunset Beach Bar, opened this chic, casual bar and bistro in the summer of 2002. The build-your-own pizza, cooked in a wood-fire oven, is excellent. We also tried the daily special, which was mussels flown in from Nova Scotia and steamed in a spicy red sauce. Fabulous. Chef Ron makes his own whimsical sauces, which vary according to his mood. Try them on one

of the pastas. You watch everything being cooked in the open kitchen that faces the dining room. Call ahead for a table on the patio.

Turtle Pier
Simpson Bay Lagoon Marina/Airport Road
☎ 599-545-2562
Eclectic and seafood $$
Breakfast, lunch, and dinner daily
The all-you-can-eat chicken and rib barbecue held on Monday nights draws a big crowd, and we've heard good things about the lobster specials on Wednesday nights. We didn't make it there for either, but we were delighted with the coconut shrimp that we ordered on another night. Jumbo shrimp were coated in beer batter, dipped in coconut and fried to a crispy golden brown. Yummy. Later, we returned for a sandwich lunch, mostly so that we could enjoy a waterside table and look out at the lagoon. Things were a little slow coming out of the kitchen, but we didn't mind since it gave us a chance to wander out to the entrance path to visit with the caged monkeys and parrots. Happy hour runs from 5 to 7 pm every day, and this is the perfect spot to watch the sunset over the lagoon. Live music plays several nights each week during high season.

Saratoga
Simpson Bay Yacht Club, Airport Road
☎ 599-544-2421
Seafood $$
Daily, 6:30-10:30 pm
Call ahead for a table near the water – you'll enjoy your meal even more. The menu changes frequently, and always features fresh seafood. Chef John Jackson (from Saratoga Springs, New York) cooks with an Asian flair, which tends to be lower in fat. If you've had your fill of seafood, look for steaks, chicken, duck, and pork dishes. Everything is well prepared, so you can't make a bad choice.

Nightlife

 St. Martin is not an island that goes dark after the sun sets. Dutch-side casinos, bars, and clubs go strong until the early morning hours, and frequently changing hot spots draw a sleek party crowd. You'll have to ask around to find out where the best bands are playing and the best drinks are being poured while you're on the island, but we've listed a

few of the always-popular places. Also, check the entertainment listings in free publications such as *St. Maarten Nights, Discover St.
Martin/St. Maarten* and *Ti Gourmet*. You'll find copies in hotel lob-
bies, restaurants, and at the tourist office.

If there's a full moon, you must go to **Kali's Beach Bar** on Friar's
Bay, ☎ 590-51-07-44. There will be a big bonfire on the beach and
dancing to a live reggae band until the sun comes up. **Waterfront
Wednesdays** take place at the public market in Marigot, beginning
at 7 pm. Caribbean bands play and locals turn out to sell their wares.
On Thursday evenings, **Marina Royale** in Marigot features live
bands, clowns, jugglers, and other entertainers along the boardwalk.
Stores stay open for late-night shopping. Call for a restaurant reservation if you hope to have dinner.

*From May through November, the island is
quieter and many residents leave for their own
vacation. Call ahead or check with the tourist
office to verify that specific activities will be
taking place before you make plans.*

**WORD TO
THE WISE**

■ Popular Dance/Music Clubs

The Q Club, Maho Beach Resort, ☎ 599-545-2115,
Wednesday-Sunday

Club One, Marigot, ☎ 590-87-98-41, Tuesday-Sunday

Pasha, Marigot, ☎ 590-51-08-03, Monday-Sunday

Cohibar, Baie Nettlé, ☎ 590-29-65-22. Currently the number-one
place to party on Monday nights, beginning after 10 pm.

The Green House, Bobby's Marina, Philipsburg, ☎ 599-542-2941.
Now the best place for live music, dancing, and happy hour on Tuesday nights.

DID YOU KNOW?

*Listen to **Bulldog**, St. Martin's number-one
music junkie and party animal, on the radio at
101.1 FM on weekday mornings to find out
where it's happenin'.*

The Boathouse, Airport Road, Simpson Bay, ☎ 599-544-5409. This
is the Friday night rockin' place to be. *Iguana Soup* begins playing
around 11 pm.

The Hideaway, La Vista Resort, ☎ 599-544-3005, ext. 1132. Thursday and Saturday nights, this restaurant hosts a one-man band. You can join in with karaoke.

Cheri's Café, Maho, ☎ 599-545-3361. See an American-style musical stage show here on Saturday nights.

Captain Oliver's, Oyster Pond, ☎ 590-87-40-26. Call for a reservation for the Saturday night lobster buffet and dance party with live music.

Friar's Beach Club, Friar's Bay, ☎ 590-49-16-87. Drop by on Sunday nights for dancing to music provided by a local band.

■ Casinos

 On any night of the week, you can try your luck at the casinos on the Dutch side. The dealers are friendly and laid back, so you won't have the pressure common at serious Las Vegas game tables.

Slots take US currency, and entertainment is scheduled most nights of the week.

Atlantis, Cupecoy, ☎ 599-545-4601, www.atlantiscasino.com

Casino Royale, Maho Reef, ☎ 599-545-2590

Coliseum, Front Street, Philipsburg, ☎ 599-543-2101

Diamond Casino, Front Street, Philipsburg, ☎ 599-543-2565

Dolphin Casino, Caravanserai Beach Resort, ☎ 599-545-3707, www.stmaarten.org/Casinos/Dolphin.html

Golden Casino, Little Bay, ☎ 599-542-2446, www.casinocity.com/an/philipsburg/smgreatb

Hollywood Casino, Simpson Bay, ☎ 599-544-4463, www.casinocity.com/an/philipsburg/pelicanr

Lightning Casino, Cole Bay, ☎ 599-544-3293

Princess Casino, Cole Bay, ☎ 599-544-5222, www.twinroom.com/hd_st_maarten/SXMPRIN.shtml

Paradise Plaza, Front Street, Philipsburg, ☎ 599-543-2721, www.aboutthecaribbean.com/stmartin/listing.jsp;jsessionid=jkiq7dare1?listingId=021127.2c&categoryId=010724.1

St. Martin

Rouge and Noir Casino, Front Street, Philipsburg, ☎ 599-542-2952, www.casinocity.com/an/philipsburg/stmrouge

Tropicana Casino, Cole Bay, ☎ 599-544-5654, www.casinocity.com/an/colebay/tropcole

Island Facts & Numbers

 AIRPORTS: **Princess Juliana** on the Dutch side, ☎ 599-545-4211. The airport code is SMX. (Juliana became Queen of the Netherlands after the airport was built.) Most international flights arrive at this larger airport. **L'Espérance** is on the French side, ☎ 590-87-53-03. The airport code is SFG. This airport accepts only small aircraft.

AREA CODES: 590 on the French side; 599 on the Dutch side. (See *Telephone* below.)

ATMS & BANKS: Cash machines are scattered in convenient locations throughout both the French and Dutch sides of St. Martin.

ABN-Amro Bank ATMs accept **MasterCard** and **Cirrus** on Emmaplein in Philipsburg, in front of Port de Plaisance Resort in Cole Bay, at the Shell Station on Airport Road in Simpson Bay, and at Food Fair in Madame Estate.

Barclays Bank ATM on Front Street, Philipsburg, accepts **Visa**.

Windward Islands Bank ATMs accept **Cirrus**, **Plus**, **MasterCard** and **American Express** at the cruise ship terminal, Bobby's Marina, and Captain Hodge Pier, as well as on Front Street in Philipsburg, at the Shell Station in Madame Estate, at Food Center in Cole Bay and on Bush Road, at the bank on Airport Road in Simpson Bay, at Maho's Casino Royale, and in the airport arrival area.

Scotiabank ATMs accept **Cirrus** at the main bank on Back Street in Philipsburg, Ram's Food World in Cay Hill, and at the bank at the Simpson Bay Yacht Club.

BFC Bank ATMs accept **MasterCard** and **Visa** at the main office in Bellevue, the Match Supermarket in Margot, and the Trio gas station in La Savane.

BDAF Bank ATM on Rue de la République in Marigot accepts **Visa**, **MasterCard** and **EuroCard**.

Crédit Mutuel ATM on Rue de la République in Marigot accepts **Visa**, **Euro MasterCard**, **Maestro**, **Plus** and **Cirrus**.

ATMs on the Dutch side dispense US dollars; those on the French side dispense euros. Some machines give you a choice.

BUSES: Private mini-buses and vans travel the main roads between Philipsburg, Marigot, Grand Case, and the large residential areas. Fares are inexpensive, around $1 or $2, depending on the distance, but you may have to change vehicles several times to reach your destination. Buses/vans, which are meant for local workers, are crowded during morning and afternoon rush hours. Few or no vehicles provide service at night.

CAPITALS: Philipsburg (Dutch) and **Marigot** (French).

CELL PHONES: Eastern Caribbean Cellular (☎ 599-542-2100, fax 599-542-5678, www.eastcaribbeancellular.com) and **Cellular One** (☎ 599-545-2430 in Simpson Bay and ☎ 599-543-0222 in Philipsburg) will program your personal cell phone for use on the island at a reasonable price. Consider bringing and activating two phones if you want to keep in touch with friends or family who are also on the island. (If you don't own a cell phone, you can rent one while on the island.)

You may be able to have your home phone programmed with an international calling plan which allows people at home to call you on the island for less than 50¢ a minute – a great savings and particularly convenient if you need to stay in touch with kids or elderly relatives. Not all telephone services offer this option, and AT&T charges their customers a small monthly fee for the international calling plan.

CREDIT CARDS: Most large restaurants, hotels, businesses, and shops accept major credit cards. Ask before you shop, if the credit card symbols are not displayed in the window. Small establishments deal mainly in cash, especially on the French side.

DRINKING WATER: Most people drink bottled water, and it is sold everywhere throughout the island. However, water served in restaurants and used in hotel bathrooms is collected rain water or desalinated sea water. It's safe to drink, but you may not care for the taste. Children, elderly people, and anyone with a sensitive stomach or immune problem should stick to bottled water.

DRESS: Wear swimsuits and other skimpy clothing only on the beaches and around the pools. Otherwise, shorts and other casual wear are appropriate during the day. People dress up a bit for restaurant dinners, casinos, and nightclubs, but there's no need for a jacket or tie, unless you go someplace really elegant. You may need a light sweater in the evening, especially if the wind is blowing.

St. Martin

ELECTRICITY: 220 volts on the French side and plugs must fit French outlets. Appliances made for use in North America require a converter and a plug adapter. Those made for European use may run hot. It's 110 volts on the Dutch side and appliances made for use in North America do not need a converter or plug adapter. Those made for European use require a converter and adapter.

EMERGENCY NUMBERS:

Dutch

Fire, ☎ 542-6001; **Police**, ☎ 542–2111 or 542-2112; **Police patrol** or **sea rescue**, ☎ 542-2222; **Ambulance**, ☎ 542-2111; **Hospital**, ☎ 543-1111.

French

Fire, **Police**, **Medical Emergency**, ☎ 18.

Non-emergency calls: **Police**, ☎ 590-87-73-84; **Fire**, ☎ 590-87-50-08; **Ambulance**, ☎ 590-87-86-25 (daytime) or 590-87-72-00 (at night); **Hospital**, ☎ 590-29-57-57.

HIGHEST POINT: Paradise Peak (Pic Paradis) at 1,391 feet.

INTERNET: Many of the large resorts have Internet kiosks for their guests, usually at a charge. If your hotel doesn't offer access, ask where the nearest Internet station or cyber café is located.

LAND AREA: 36 square miles total. French side = 20 square miles; Dutch side = 16 square miles.

LANGUAGE: Most residents on the Dutch side and many on the French side speak English. Many residents also speak a French-based patois, and perhaps some Spanish.

However, the official language of Dutch St. Martin is Dutch, and some people speak Papiamento, the language spoken on Aruba and other Dutch Caribbean islands. The official language of French St. Martin is French, and a large number of residents speak little or nothing else.

MONEY: On the Dutch side, the official currency is the **Netherlands Antilles florin** (1.75 NAF = $1), but US dollars are accepted almost everywhere. If prices are quoted in florins, the quick math is to divide the total by two then add 10%.

On the French side, the official currency is the **euro**, which is within a few pennies of equaling $1. US dollars are widely accepted, but not as welcome as on the Dutch side. If you pay in dollars, expect change back in euros.

NEWSPAPERS: The English-language *The Daily Herald,* ☎ 599-542-5253; in French, *Saint Martin's Week,* ☎ 590-87-78-67.

PHARMACIES: **Central Drugstore**, ☎ 599-542-5576 (in Philipsburg); **The Druggist**, ☎ 599-545-2777 (in Simpson Bay); **Caraïbes**, ☎ 590-87-47-27 (in Cul-de-Sac); **Chartus**, ☎ 590-87-99-46 (near Match Supermarket in Marigot); **Grand Case**, ☎ 590-87-77-46 (in Grand Case).

POLITICAL STATUS: Dutch St. Martin is politically tied to the Kingdom of the Netherlands and is part of the six-island group known as The Netherlands Antilles. The island of Curaçao serves as the seat of government. French St. Martin is politically tied to the island of Guadeloupe, which is an Overseas Region of France. (For more details, see page 58.)

POPULATION: Approximately 69,000.

POST OFFICE: The main post office is on Cannegieter Street, near the intersection with Schoolsteeg, in Philipsburg, ☎ 599-542-2298.

RADIO STATIONS: **Radio Transat**, 106.1 FM, ☎ 590-87-55-55. **PJD-1 Mix FM**, 94.7 FM, ☎ 599-543-1133.

TAXIS: Taxis are plentiful at the airport and ferry docks. Drivers are licensed by either the French or Dutch government and carry a published rate sheet, which lists authorized fares between many common destinations, such as from the airport to major hotels. Ask to see it. Daytime rates apply from 7 am to 9 pm. An additional 25% is added to the base fare from 9 until midnight; 50% is added from midnight to 7 am. If your destination isn't listed, negotiate a price before you get into the cab, and confirm whether the rate quoted is per-trip or per-passenger.

Unless the driver overcharges, is rude, or takes you out of your way, add at least a 10% tip to the fare. Tip a little extra if the driver gives information about the island as you travel or helps you with your luggage (50¢ to $1 per bag is standard, depending on the size and weight of each piece). US dollars and euros are accepted, but don't expect the driver to have change for large-denomination bills.

Taxi Dispatch Hotline, ☎ 147. You can also call the individual taxi stands: in **Philipsburg**, Dutch St. Martin, ☎ 599-542-2359; at the **airport** on Dutch St. Martin, ☎ 599-5435-4317; in **Marigot**, French St. Martin, ☎ 0590-87-56-54; at the airport in **Grand Case**, French St. Martin, ☎ 0590-87-75-79.

St. Martin

TELEPHONE:

- The area code for **French** St. Martin is 590.

- The area code for **Dutch** St. Martin is 599.

- When calling within the French system, add a 0 to the nine-digit local number (0590-xx-xx-xx).

- When calling from the Dutch side to the French side, dial 00, then 590, then 590 again, plus the six-digit number (00-590-590-xx-xx-xx).

- When calling from the French side to the Dutch side, dial 00 + 599 + the seven-digit number.

- When dialing St. Martin from the US or Canada, dial 011 to get international service, then the area code, 590 for the French side or 599 for the Dutch side, plus the on-island number. When calling a number on the French side, you must dial 590 twice (011-590-590-xx-xx-xx).

- When calling the islands from Great Britain, dial 00 to get international service, then the area code, 590 or 599, plus the on-island number, which means you will dial 590 twice when calling the French side (00-590-590-xx-xx-xx).

TELEPHONE CARDS: Public phone booths don't accept coins. Buy a *Télécarte*, which looks like a credit card, to make local and international calls when you're on the **French** side and a similar-looking **TELCard,** when you're on **Dutch** soil. This is less expensive than phoning from your hotel. TELCards are readily available at convenience stores, gas stations, and hotel desks on the Dutch side. A *Télécarte* may be harder to find on the French side, but most resorts and many shops in the larger towns have them.

Major credit cards can be used from some phone booths on both sides of the island for long distance calls, but the rates are higher than with a prepaid calling card.

TELEPHONE OPERATOR: ☎ 599-542-2211 on the Dutch side; ☎ 12 on the French side.

TEMPERATURE RANGE: Year-round average low is 72°F and the average high is 86°F.

TIME: Both sides of St. Martin are on Atlantic Standard Time and do not observe Daylight Savings Time. During the summer months, island time is the same as Eastern Daylight Time; in the winter, island time is one hour ahead. St. Martin's time is five hours behind England and six hours behind France and the rest of western Europe during the summer; four hours behind England and five hours behind western Europe in the winter.

TIPPING IN RESTAURANTS: On the Dutch side, a service charge may or may not be added to the bill's total. If one is added, most people leave another 5-10% on the table for the server, since anything added to the bill is split among all the employees.

On the French side, as in France, the service charge is added (hidden) to the price of each item on the menu and divided among the restaurant's employees. Most people leave an additional 5-10% for the waiter in appreciation for good service.

If service is poor, tell the manager or owner as you leave the restaurant. Simply not leaving a tip will do nothing to correct the problem.

TOURIST OFFICES:

Dutch side: Sint Maarten Tourism Office, ☎ 800-786-2278 (in North America), located at W.G. Buncamper Road 33, in the Vineyard Park Building near the Police station on the northeast end of Philipsburg. Local contact, ☎ 599-542-2337, fax 599-542-2734, www.st-maarten. com.

French side: Office du Tourisme de Saint-Martin, located on Route de Sandy-Ground, near the Saint Martin Arawak Museum on the south side of Marigot, ☎ 590-87-57-21, fax 590-87-56-43, www.st-martin.org.

WEBSITES:

Dutch

www.st-maarten.com; www.stmaarten.org
www.jmbcommunications.com/sxm.html

French

www.saintmartinsintmaarten.com
www.frenchcaribbean.com/StMartinFrenchCaribbean.html

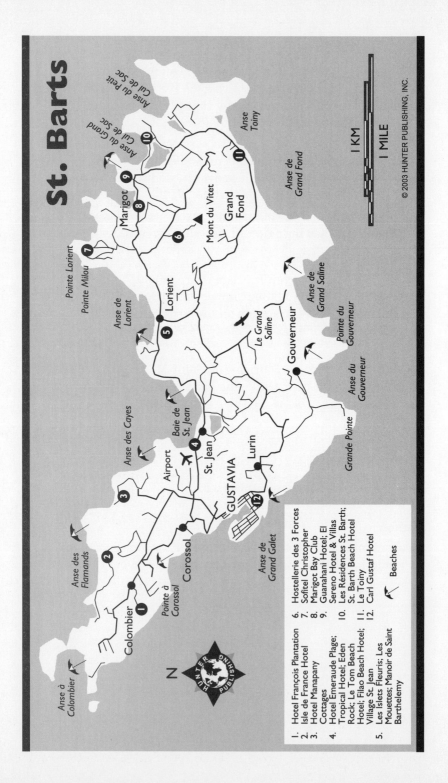

St. Barts

1. Hotel François Plantation
2. Isle de France Hotel
3. Hotel Manapany
   Cottages
4. Hotel Emeraude Plage;
   Tropical Hotel; Eden
   Rock; Le Tom Beach
   Hotel; Filao Beach Hotel;
   Village St. Jean
5. Les Islets Fleuris; Les
   Mouettes; Manoir de Saint
   Barthelemy

6. Hostellerie des 3 Forces
7. Softel Christopher
8. Marigot Bay Club
9. Guanahani Hotel; El
   Sereno Hotel & Villas
10. Les Résidences St. Barth;
    St. Barth Beach Hotel
11. Le Toiny
12. Carl Gustaf Hotel

↗ Beaches

1 KM
1 MILE

© 2003 HUNTER PUBLISHING, INC.

St. Barts

For such a tiny island, measuring only eight square miles, **Saint Barthélemy** (say *sain bar tay leh MEE*) has a mighty reputation and enormous appeal. Fans call it by its diminutive nicknames, St. Barts or St. Barth, which fit its sleek prestigious image better than its long official French name, and are vastly better than its Columbus-given Italian name, St. Bartoloméo.

The island is probably the least Caribbean of all the Caribbean islands. Since it has little history, it has few remnants of colonial architecture, few residents who trace their ancestry back to African slaves, and few deeply entrenched West Indian traditions. All in all, it's an attractive little enclave that takes great care to protect its privacy and doesn't try in the least to be anything that it is not.

The Top Temptations

- **Fabulous little hotels** with distinct personalities.
- **Privacy**, even for celebrities.
- Magnificent **gourmet restaurants**.
- **Chic boutiques**.
- More than 20 **beaches**, some among the best in the Caribbean.
- **Hiking** to hidden coves.
- Villa spying while **cruising** the coast.

Before the late 1960s, St. Barts was an isolated hideaway for the ultra-rich. Fewer than 400 people lived full-time on the island as recently as 1967. Today, the permanent population numbers around

7,000, and the island draws thousands of visitors year-round. Promoters have begun courting a wider range of travelers to fill the expanding number of hotel rooms, but the majority of visitors still are wealthy North Americans, and many of those hold celebrity status.

Don't let St. Barts elitist reputation keep you away. The tiny isle is really quite affable, and while prices are among the highest in the Caribbean, they aren't wildly outside the budget of many travelers, especially during the off-season. You won't have a non-stop schedule of things to do and places to see, but if you're seeking peace, relaxation, and hedonist pleasures, St. Barts offers the best that money can buy.

A Small Island Long Ignored

Historians presume a few **Ciboney Indians** lived on St. Barts for a short time as early as 1000 BC, but they didn't stay long, and may have been the island's first seasonal visitors. There was no fresh water and very little fertile land – very little land at all, in fact. So, they couldn't grow crops, had nothing to drink with their fresh-catch of the day, and were limited on decent hiding spots when enemy tribes canoed over from other islands. Before long, they moved on, leaving little trace of their stay.

Later, around 100 AD, **Arawak Indians** arrived, and may have stayed longer if they hadn't been invaded by the nasty **Caribs** around 800 AD. Both tribes left behind some interesting stuff. Pottery shards and crude tools have been discovered by amateur archeologists at various spots around the island, including a site at the base of a huge boulder near today's airport. Nothing scientific has been written specifically about these two tribes, but experts assume they were related to and similar to Indians that inhabited nearby islands in greater numbers during this time period. (See *A Shared History*, page 19, in the *Introduction*.)

Christopher Columbus takes official credit for "discovering" St. Barts during his second voyage in 1493. But, like the Indians before him, he wasn't too interested in a tiny spit of land with no fresh water. When he sailed by, he didn't notice any natives wearing gold, figured the place was worthless, and moved on after naming it honor of his brother, Bartoloméo.

For years, nothing happened. The Spanish didn't want to settle, even though they technically owned the place. Other Europeans were more intrigued with larger, more valuable islands. Only a few Indians lived or temporarily camped along the shores. Finally, in 1648, a small group of French citizens from nearby St. Kitts moved over to St. Barts, but they couldn't generate much interest from their king or entice other settlers to join them, and the island was sold to the **Knights of Malta** in 1651. As each group of settlers arrived, the hostile Caribs attacked and, within five years, all Europeans were wiped out.

During the remainder of the 17th century, the French government tried to set up a thriving colony on St. Barts, but the island proved to be more valuable as a hideout for pirates. In 1784, King Louis XVI traded the island to King Gustaf III of Sweden for duty-free trading rights at the port in Gothenburg.

With great enthusiasm, the Swedish king renamed the harbor Gustavia, began laying out roads, and put up warehouses and homes around the port. The city grew and thrived as a free trade zone, which made it an attractive target for the British, who attacked and took over in 1801-1802. Sweden was back in control when slavery was abolished in 1847, and, although very few slaves were held on St. Barts, the entire region suffered an economic blow. Then, a massive hurricane hit in 1852, followed by a devastating fire. Most residents fled, and the island became an undesirable economic burden. In 1878, Sweden agreed to sell St. Barts back to France, with the agreement that the island would remain duty-free and the residents would never pay taxes.

You can see a collection of documents, photographs, and artifacts from St. Barts' history at the **Musée Municipal,** located in Wall House on Rue Schoelcher at the far end of La Pointe on the south side of Gustavia's harbor, ☎ 590-29-71-55. Admission is $5 and the museum is open Tuesday-Friday, 8:30 am-12:30 pm and 2:30-6 pm, Monday, 2:30-6 pm, and Saturday 9 am-1 pm.

St. Barts

Official Business

Like French St. Martin, St. Barts is part of the *sous-préfecture* which is overseen by Guadeloupe, a *département français d'outremer.* Four elected representatives speak for this overseas de-

partment in the French *Assemblée Nationale,* and two elected senators hold seats in the *Sénat.* Residents enjoy all the social programs
available to French citizens living on the continent, but are heavily
dependent on France economically and politically. Residents of
Guadeloupe regularly lobby for autonomy, but French St. Martin and
St. Barts appear content with their status as French possessions.

DID YOU KNOW?

*Citizens of St. Barts are French nationals and
carry passports issued by the European Union.*

Getting There

■ By Air

Most travelers get to St. Barts via St. Martin. Several major airlines have direct flights to **Queen Juliana International Airport** (SXM) on the Dutch side. You can also
take a direct flight to San Juan, Puerto Rico, then hop
over to St. Martin on a connecting flight before taking a 15-minute
ride on a regional carrier to St. Barts. In addition, **Air St. Thomas**
flies to St. Barts from St. Thomas, and **Air Caraïbes** has service from
Guadeloupe.

**WORD TO
THE WISE**

*After you land on St. Martin and go through
customs, claim your bags, then walk through
the courtyard to the departure terminal, where
you will find the check-in counter for all the
regional airlines. Get a boarding pass from the
airline taking you to St. Barts, then take it and
your passport to the brown booth, where you
can get a departure tax waiver. You can't get the
tax waiver without a boarding pass, and you
can't get into the boarding area without your
passport, tax waiver, and boarding pass.*

St. Barts' Airport (SBH), near St. Jean Bay on the north coast, has
one short runway and accepts nothing larger than 20-seat planes.

Since there are no runway lights, flights can't land after dark. The recently-enlarged terminal has car rental booths, a small store, and a bar. **La Savane Commercial Center**, just across a narrow road, has a pharmacy, supermarket, and a couple of shops.

WORD TO THE WISE

Be sure to confirm your return flight well in advance since the small airlines juggle their schedules to meet passenger demand and flight times may change. Allow yourself plenty of time to get to St. Martin for your return flight home, and remember that most airlines now require passengers to check in at least three hours prior to departure in order to clear security. Also, remember that you must check in and get a boarding pass before you go to the booth to pay your departure tax.

Flying to St. Barts is a thrill. Pilots are required to have special training, and you'll understand why once you've seen the landing approach. After takeoff out of St. Martin, your little plane climbs, soars, and almost immediately begins its descent. You get a great low-level view of St. Barts as you approach, but unfortunately it's spoiled by an ugly incinerator plant and junkyard. Then, about the time you begin to wonder why you don't see the airport, the pilot shoves the plane's nose sharply towards the ground, you glimpse the tops of cars on the road below as you glide by, much too close, then plunge below a mountaintop directly onto the landing strip. Just when you think the plane will hit the ocean at the end of the short runway, you stop.

Wow!

Pilots perform this magic flawlessly several times a day, so the experience is a thrill, not a danger. Later, take a walk along the beach beside the airport and watch this amazing feat from the ground.

You must phone the airport in St. Martin at the following numbers for information.

Airline Contact Information	
International Carriers	
Air Canada	☎ 800-776-3000 (US), 888-247-2262 (Canada), 599-542-3316 (St. Martin), www.aircanada.ca
Air France	☎ 800-237-2747 (US/Canada), 599-545-4212 (St. Martin), www.airfrance.com

St. Barts

American Airlines/ American Eagle	☎ 800-433-7300 (US/Canada), 599-545-2040 (St. Martin), www.aa.com
Continental Airlines	☎ 800-523-3273 (US), 599-545-3444 (St. Martin), www.flycontinental.com
Delta Air Lines	☎ 800-325-1999 (US/Canada), 599-545-3085 (St. Martin), www.delta-air.com
KLM	☎ 599-545-4747 (St. Martin), 800-447-4747 (US/Canada), www.klmuk.com
US Airways	☎ 800-428-4322 (US), 599-545-4344 (St. Martin), www.usairways.com

Local Airlines & Air Taxis

Air Caraïbes	☎ 590-87-10-36 (SFG St. Martin), www.aircaraibes.com
Air Mango	☎ 590-27-88-81 (St. Barts), www.st-barths.com/air-mango
Air St. Barth	☎ 590-27-61-90, fax 590-27-67-03
Air St. Thomas	☎ 590-27-71-76, fax 590-27-21-26 (St. Barts), www.airstthomas.com
Caribbean Star Airlines	☎ 800-744-7827 (in the Caribbean), www.flycaribbeanstar.com
LIAT	☎ 800-468-0482 (US), 599-545-5428 (St. Martin), www.liat.com
St. Barth Commuter	☎ 590-27-54-54, fax 590-27-54-58 (St. Barts), www.st-barths.com/stbarth-commuter/index.html
Winair	☎ 590-27-61-01 (St. Barts), 599-545-2568 (SMX St. Martin), www.fly-winair.com
Windward Island Air	☎ 599-545-4230, fax 599-545-4229 (St. Martin)

■ By Inter-Island Ferry

Voyager I and *Voyager II*, ☎ 599-542-4096 (Philipsburg), 059-87-10-68 (Marigot), 0590-27-54-10 (Gustavia).

The Oyster Line, ☎ 0590-87-46-13

The Edge, ☎ 599-544-2640

Marine Service, ☎ 0590-27-70-34

You can find additional information about inter-island ferry service on page 53.

Getting Around

There's no public transportation on St. Barts, so you'll be getting around by **taxi** or **rental car**. The beaches, hotels, and restaurants are scattered from one end of the island to the other, so walking the entire thing is not an option. If you're an experienced motor biker, or a daredevil, take to the narrow mountain roads on a motorcycle or scooter.

■ By Taxi

Taxis are plentiful, and fares are generally low, since it's impossible to go very far. They wait at the airport and harbor side in Gustavia, or you can call the offices in either Gustavia (☎ 590-27-66-31) or St. Jean (☎ 590-27-75-81). Drivers offer sightseeing tours, and most will agree to drop you at a beach and return for you at an appointed time.

Taxis are privately owned and do not have meters, so always agree on a rate before you get into the cab. Drivers are allowed to charge more on holidays, Sundays, and after dark.

WORD TO THE WISE

■ By Rental Car

The best way to get around, even if you're just a day-visitor, is by rental car. The roads are narrow (but in good shape), and you will have to tackle steep inclines and sharp curves. Otherwise, conditions are great: driving is on the right; there's very little traffic outside Gustavia; the island has no traffic lights; the speed limit is 28 mph (45 kph), so nothing very bad can happen.

St. Barts

The tiny but chic Smart Car is a popular rental, and many people enjoy driving the jeep-like no-doors mini moke, but you can also request a larger car with automatic transmission and air conditioning. Don't bother with a four-wheel-drive vehicle. All you need is a valid driver's license and a credit card.

Daily rates run about $60 per day during high season, but drop to around $40 during the off-season. Weekly rates are a better deal at approximately $350 in high season, $245 in low season, depending on the size and condition of the vehicle.

Gas is priced about like European fuel, which at publication time was a bit over $1 per liter (that's about $3 per gallon). Cars are fuel-efficient, and distances are short, so you won't fill up often, which is good, since there are only **two gas stations** on the island. One is across from the airport in St. Jean, ☎ 590-27-50-50. It's open Monday-Saturday, 7:30 am-noon and 2:30-5 pm; closed Sunday. You can buy a special gas card that will operate the 24-hour automatic pump for about $10. You must purchase the card during regular business hours. The other gas station is in Lorient, ☎ 590-27-62-30. It's open daily, 7:30 am-5 pm, except Thursdays, when it closes at noon, and Sundays, when it's closed all day.

WORD TO THE WISE

Reserve your rental car in advance, especially during high season.

Decline insurance coverage offered by the rental-car agency only if the credit card you will be using covers you for an accident or damage to the car. American Express and Visa Gold Card customers are not covered when they rent a sports car or four-wheel-drive vehicle.

Following are local contact numbers. For toll-free numbers and websites, see page 52.

International Car Rental Companies	
Alamo/National	St. Jean Airport, ☎ 590-29-60-12, fax 590-29-60-12
Avis	St. Jean Airport, ☎ 590-27-71-43, fax 590-27-69-32
Budget	St. Jean Airport, ☎ 590-27-66-30, fax 590-27-83-93; Gustavia, ☎ 590-27-67-43, fax 590-27-83-93

Europcar	St. Jean Airport, ☎ 590-27-74-34, fax 590-27-80-77
Hertz	St. Jean Airport, ☎ 590-27-71-14, fax 590-27-90-63
Local Car Rental Companies	
Island	St. Jean Airport, ☎ 590-27-70-01, fax 590-27-62-55
Tropic'All	Gustavia, ☎ 590-27-64-76, fax 590-27-86-47
TopLoc	St. Jean Airport, ☎ 590-29-02-02, fax 590-29-03-03
Smart of Saint Barth	St. Jean, ☎ 590-29-71-31, fax 590-29-70-27
Barth'loc	Gustavia, ☎ 590-27-52-81, fax 590-27-52-41
Chez Béranger	Gustavia, ☎ 590-27-89-00, fax 590-27-80-28
Gumbs	St. Jean Airport, ☎ 590-27-75-32, fax 590-27-78-99
Questel	St. Jean Airport, ☎ 590-27-73-22, fax 590-27-89-54
Soleil Caraïbes	St. Jean Airport, ☎ 590-27-67-18, fax 590-27-65-06
Ti l'Auto	Vitet, ☎ 590-27-85-39
Maurice	St. Jean Airport, ☎ 590-27-73-22, fax 590-29-63-60
Turbe	St. Jean Airport, ☎ 590-27-71-42

St. Barts

DID YOU KNOW?

If you do not arrive by plane, most major and local companies will deliver your rental car to you at the ferry dock or at your hotel.

■ By Scooter or Motorcycle

Rates run about $30 per day to rent a motorcycle or scooter and are higher for a Harley. You'll be required to wear a helmet, which is included in the rental price, and you must hold a valid motorcycle permit or driver's license.

Several car rental companies offer scooters and motorcycles as well, including **Barthloc**, **Chez Béranger**, and **Tropic'All**.

Motorcycle Rental Companies	
Dufau (Honda and Peugeot)	St. Jean, ☎ 590-27-54-83, fax 590-27-83-05
Meca Moto (Harley Davidson)	Gustavia, ☎ 590-52-92-49, fax 590-29-85-33

Getting Married

Honeymooning on St. Bart is fabulous. Getting legally married on the island is a French horror story. Unless you're a citizen of France, forget about it. The requirements, waiting period, and paperwork are just too difficult. But, if you're determined, contact **The French Government Tourist Office** in New York, ☎ 202-659-7779, or the **Office du Tourisme** on St. Barts, ☎ 590-27-87-27, well in advance for advice. Then contact Melanie Smith Vitelli, ☎ 590-29-84-54, fax 590-29-76-04. She's an American citizen who lives in the islands and can help you with all the plans.

Exploring St. Barts

■ Organized Tours

The **Office du Tourisme** (☎ 590-27-87-27) sponsors three sightseeing tours of the island. They leave by minibus from the pier near the tourist office on Quai du Général de Gaulle, on the southeast side of the harbor parking lot.

The 90-minute trip is the best deal and covers the most ground. It takes you over the hill to St. Jean, hits many of the prime sites on both the eastern and western ends of the island and makes three stops. The cost for up to three people is about $45. The hour-long tour is the same as the 90-minute trip, but skips everything west of St. Jean and Gustavia, which means you miss the villages of Colombier and Corossol. It makes two stops and costs approximately $35 for up to three people. The shortest tour is a 45-minute ride west of Gustavia with a glimpse of Colombier, Flamands, Corossol, and Public. This one-stop mini-tour is priced at around $25 for up to three people.

WORD TO THE WISE

*If you're going to take the group tour, sign on for the 90-minute route. You miss too much with anything shorter. Contact the **Office du Tourisme** (☎ 590-27-87-27) for times, which change seasonally.*

■ Taxi Tours

You'll get more individual attention and be able to make more stops if you take a guided tour with one of the island's delightful taxi drivers. Request an English-speaking driver who knows the island well, and agree on a fee before you start out. You'll pay about $40-$50 for two people on a two-hour tour. Drivers usually charge less during the off-season, and more during the winter months. Make a couple of calls and compare the itineraries before you decide on a guide, and be sure you understand his accent.

Check with the Office du Tourisme for a current list of recommended guides, or contact one of the following:

Raymond Gréaux, ☎ 590-27-66-32

Denis Gumbs, ☎ 590-27-65-61

René Bernier, ☎ 590-27-63-75

On a recent visit, a sign posted at the gazebo in the harborside parking lot in Gustavia offered a taxi tour of the island for $10 per person. At that time, anyone who was interested could simply show up at 4 pm to meet J.C., the driver.

■ Independent Touring

The very best way to see St. Barts is on your own. Set your own pace, stop when something interests you, and linger as long as you like at outstanding sites. The island is not physically gorgeous overall, as some travel guides would lead you to believe, but it has many, many beautiful places.

St. Barts is shaped like a flaky croissant with both ends pointing north, a puffy middle, and mouse-size bites all along the edges. **Gustavia** is on the southwest outward curve; **St. Jean** is directly over the hilly mid-section, nestled into the northwest inward curve. More than 20 coves and beaches are nibbled into the shoreline. Steep, winding roads criss-cross the entire island, and even ace navigators get lost. But, you'll easily find your way again, and you'll discover incredible vistas and sites along the way. St. Barts is no more than two miles across at its widest point and 11 miles long tip-to-tip, so you can't drive far without spotting water. Friendly locals will point you in the right direction, if you become hopelessly confused.

A Walking Tour of Gustavia

Start your tour in the capital and largest town on St. Barts. It's built around a lovely horseshoe-shaped harbor filled with elegant yachts from around the world. Unlike most port cities, Gustavia is seldom overrun by cruise ship passengers. For a brief time during the late 1990s, large ships were encouraged to unload the masses, but the resulting commercialism horrified the locals and offended longtime visitors. Now, the government charges ships a hefty per-person entrance fee for all tourists coming ashore, so most of the lower-budget ocean liners visit elsewhere.

WORD TO THE WISE

If you want to avoid the cruise-ship passengers that shuttle in from big ships anchored offshore, check with the tourist office for a port schedule, ☎ 590-27-87-27.

Stop at the **Office du Tourisme** when you come into town to pick up maps and brochures. It's located on the harborfront at Quai du Général de Gaulle and is open Monday-Friday, 8 am-12:30 pm, and Saturdays, 9-11 am.

You can park in the free lot at Quai du Général de Gaulle, then explore on foot. Everything is laid out on a half-dozen main streets running parallel to the three-sided harbor, and you can easily walk to the shops, sidewalk cafés, a couple of historic sites, and Shell Beach.

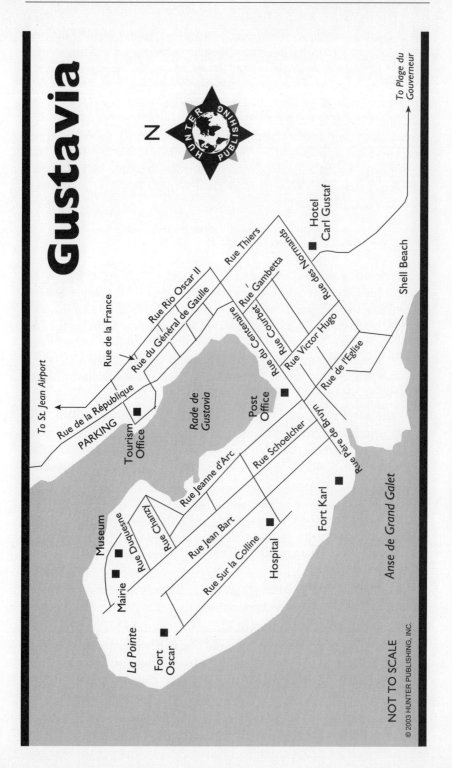

Gustavia

N

St. Barts

NOT TO SCALE

© 2003 HUNTER PUBLISHING, INC.

To St. Jean Airport

Rue de la France

Rue Rio Oscar II

Rue du Général de Gaulle

Rue Thiers

Rue de la République

PARKING

Tourism Office

Rade de Gustavia

Rue Jeanne d'Arc

Museum

Mairie

Rue Duquesne

Rue Chanzy

Rue Jean Bart

Rue Sur la Colline

La Pointe

Fort Oscar

Rue du Centenaire

Rue Gambetta

Rue des Normands

Rue Courbet

Rue Victor Hugo

Rue de l'Eglise

Post Office

Rue Schoelcher

Rue Père de Bruyn

Hospital

Fort Karl

Hotel Carl Gustaf

Shell Beach

To Plage du Gouverneur

Anse de Grand Galet

Picture Gustavia as a squared-off capital "U," with the top opening facing northwest. Standing at the bottom of the "U" and facing the harbor, the landside ferry dock and tourist office are on your right. On your left, the waterside arm of the "U" is a peninsula that juts out into the sea. Its far tip is known as La Pointe, location of Wall House and Fort Oscar. Rue Jeanne d'Arc parallels the waterside arm, Rue de la République runs along the landside arm, and Rue du Centenaire connects the two at the bottom of the "U." All of the town's other streets run parallel and perpendicular to these three main roads.

The parking lot and its adjoining gazebo are on tree-lined Rue de la République. Attractive two-story colonial-style buildings line the inland side of the road and house some of the island's classy boutiques. Most of the town's original architecture was destroyed during a 1744 British invasion. New structures were built around Le Carénage (as the port was called) and the Swedes added their own styles when they took over in 1785, but most of that was reduced to ashes and rubble by a hurricane and fire in 1852.

Nevertheless, a few lovely old buildings still stand in the capital. The former Swedish governor's home is now the **Mairie**, or town hall, and you can see the green and white *maison* on Rue Auguste Nejman (also spelled Nyman), which is a straight walk inland from the harbor along Rue Couturier.

The **Vieux Clocher** (old bell tower) doesn't have a bell any more, but the picturesque structure is probably the oldest in town. It was built in 1799 as part of a church on Rue du Presbytère at the southeast end of town, and the elevated bell notified residents as each hour passed throughout the day. A large clock has replaced the original bell, and the church was destroyed long ago, but the lovely stone tower stands as a reminder of the town's colonial past.

On Rue du Centenaire, a handsome street that runs along the harbor's shortest side, you'll find the old **Saint-Barthélemew Anglican church**, topped by a bell tower and surrounded by a low rock wall. It was built in 1885 with stone from St. Eustatius and France. Services are held here every Sunday at 9 am, ☎ 590-27-89-44.

The **Catholic church**, between Rue du Presbytère and Rue de l'Eglise, is even older. It was built in 1822 in a style similar to the island's oldest Catholic church in Lorient. The bell tower is detached from and taller than the austere main building, which allows the bell to peal more intensely. Masses are held at either the Lorient or Gustavia church on Sundays, 8 am, and Saturdays, 5:30 pm. If you want to attend, call to find out which church will be having services, ☎ 590-27-61-08.

St. Barts Municipal Museum (also called *Musée Municipal, Musée Saint-Barthélemy,* and *Wall House Museum)* is located in an old gray-stone warehouse known locally as **Wall House** on Rue Schoelcher at the far end of La Pointe. It's topped by colorful flags; old cannons sit outside. Inside, you can browse among the photographs, ancient maps, paintings, and artifacts spanning the island's French, British, and Swedish history. Director Eddy Galvani has done a terrific job of recreating the island's past through fascinating displays of ancestral costumes, antique tools, model Créole homes, and traditional fishing boats. Admission is $5 and the museum is open Tuesday-Friday, 8:30 am-12:30 pm, and 2:30-6 pm, Monday, 2:30-6 pm, and Saturday, 9 am-1 pm, ☎ 590-29-71-55.

The Swedes built three defensive forts around the harbor. **Fort Oscar**, which is closed to the public, stands facing the sea on the far side of La Pointe at the end of Rue Jean Bart. Fort Karl has long-since disappeared.

The ruins of **Fort Gustav** are scattered next to the weather station and lighthouse (built in 1961) on the hill at the north end of town. You won't see much history at Fort Gustav, but you can drive there as you leave Gustavia going toward Public. A panoramic tableau identifies neighbor islands and the main buildings in Gustavia. Visit late in the day, and enjoy the glorious view of the town as the sun sets over the ocean.

DID YOU KNOW?

"Anse" is French for cove or bay. It also means handle, like the anse of a frying pan, which is what many deep bays look like.

Anse de Grand Galet (*galet* is French for pebble), commonly known as **Shell Beach**, is a short walk from Gustavia. Follow Rue Jeanne d'Arc away from town to find the beach, which is covered with thousands of small sea shells brought in by waves. Hurricane Lenny, which made a nasty pass over the island in 1999, caused a lot of damage here, but new sand was brought in to rebuild the beach in the spring of 2000, and shells are washing ashore again. There are better places to sun or swim, but the shells make a nice surface for strolling and jogging. You can see the islands of St. Eustatius and Saba in the distance.

WORD TO THE WISE

*Sunsets are fantastic from Shell Beach. Stop by at the end of the day, then have dinner at **Dō Brazil Restaurant**, right on the beach. They specialize in Brazilian and French food, and serve breakfast, lunch, and dinner during high season (call for limited low-season hours), ☎ 590-29-06-60.*

Before you leave Gustavia, wander along the streets and stop at a few of the town's many shops, art galleries, bars, and restaurants. A little **produce market** (*ti marché*) is set up on Rue du Roi Oscar, where ladies from Guadeloupe (locally known as *Doudous*) sell fruits, vegetables and spices from their fertile island. If you've lingered long enough for happy hour, stop for a *ti punch* at one of the well-known people-watching spots such as **Le Select** or **L'Oubli**.

See Where to Eat, *page 205, for restaurant recommendations and* Shopping, *page 183, for information on stores and galleries.*

Along the North Coast

St. Jean is the island's number two town and its main tourist center. Its spectacular crescent-shaped **Baie de Saint-Jean** is divided by a cliff supporting Eden Rock Resort and has a calm reef-sheltered eastern area and a larger western stretch with more surf. Airplanes take off over the western beach, which is located at the end of the airport's short runway. Watersports operators, restaurants, resorts, and bars line up along the length of the bay.

A favorite pastime is standing on **La Tourmente**, the central hill that separates St. Jean from Gustavia, to watch the planes approach, glide low overhead, then dive below the rise to land. Five shopping malls are home to ritzy boutiques, excellent restaurants, and the only gas station on the island that accepts credit cards; lovely homes dot the surrounding hillsides.

Lorient, just east of St. Jean, is a quiet village full of history. The first French settlement was built here in 1648, and the town has two charming cemeteries decorated with crosses and flowers at each grave. It's also home to the island's oldest **Catholic church**, Notre Dame de l'Assomption, where St. Barts Music Festival holds annual performances each January. One of the island's two gas stations is located here, along with a couple of mini-marts, and a petite post office.

Just past the most eastern cemetery, a road leads to the long white-sand beach, **Anse de Lorient** – popular with surfers. (The annual St. Barth Festival of Caribbean Cinema is held on the tennis courts of the AJOE Surf Club each April.)

WORD TO THE WISE

*Look for **Le Manoir** de St. Barthélemy (☎ 590-27-79-27) on Route de Saline near the Ligne St. Barth boutique. It is a Norman house built in 1610 and brought in pieces to St. Barts in 1984 by Jeanne Audy Rowland, author of* Fils de Vikings *(Viking Sons), a history of St. Barts written in French. The rustic structure was reconstructed on the island and now serves as the centerpiece for the low-budget hotel near Lorient Beach.*

East of Lorient, the main road veers off toward **Pointe Milou** and **Mont Jean** and becomes dramatic. It winds up the hillsides in this isolated residential area past some of the island's most beautiful homes, villas, and resorts. The coast has no beaches and is covered with rocks that are battered by the pounding surf. Overlooks on top of the sheer cliffs offer spectacular views of nearby islets and faraway St. Martin. Stop for a drink at the **Sofitel Christopher Hotel**, located at the bottom of the steep road leading to Pointe Milou. The bar sits beside an infinity pool that appears to merge with the sea. If the conditions are right, local surfers will be riding the waves offshore.

Anse de Marigot and **Anse du Grand Cul-de-Sac** are attractive lagoons on the far eastern tip of the north coast. The main road climbs, dips, and winds through the hills east of the village of Marigot and passes the calm bays, which are lined with golden sand and surrounded by protective cliffs. Windsurfers take advantage of the steady breeze, swimmers float in the deep blue placid water, and snorkelers enjoy exploring the close-in reefs.

Watersports operators rent all types of equipment (including the popular kitesurfers) and restaurants, bars, and resorts provide all the creature comforts. The terrain in this area is quite arid, but the hotels have planted palms and bushes along their stretches of beach, and the resorts' gardens are colorful and lush.

Morne du Vitet is the island's highest peak at 922 feet. Its steep slopes are criss-crossed by low stone walls that once imprisoned sheep and goats. Drive up the mountain's winding narrow road that goes south from Grand Cul-de-Sac for panoramic views of the rugged coastline.

St. Barts

Anse des Cayes, Anse des Lézards, Anse des Flamands and **Petite Anse** line up along the northern shore west of the town of St. Jean. Surfers favor Cayes and Lézards, while swimmers and snorkelers prefer Flamands and Petite Anse. Each is worth a visit. Although the beaches are adjacent to one another, they are separated by rocky outcroppings, which prevent you from walking from one to the other.

Ile Fourchue

This uninhabited island off the western coast is a popular day-trip from St. Barts. Visitors like to go out to the tiny isle to get away from civilization, explore the rocky desert-like terrain, and climb to the top of the hills for extraordinary views. The entire place is a nature preserve and underwater life is protected by the St. Bart Marine Reserve. Forty-two of the 54 coral species known to thrive in the Lesser Antilles grow offshore, and a vast number of sea creatures live around the reefs. If you decide to visit, you'll have only wild goats for company, and there's no shade, so plan accordingly. Expect to pay about $100 per person for a scheduled day cruise, snorkeling equipment, open bar, and a gourmet lunch with wine. Contact the following for information: **Marine Service**, Quai du Yacht Club, Gustavia, ☎ 590-27-70-34; **Yacht Charter Agency**, Rue Jeanne d'Arc, Gustavia, ☎ 590-27-62-38; **Océan Must**, La Pointe, near Wall House, Gustavia, ☎ 590-27-62-25. Beware of seasickness if the ocean is rough or you're prone to that type of malady.

West of Gustavia

Anse de Colombier is one of the most spectacular sites on the island, and the only way to get there is by boat or on foot. Two hiking paths lead to the secluded beach; one begins at the top of the hill above the waterfront; the other begins near Petite Anse, on the Atlantic coast northwest of Anse des Flamands. Either trek will take about 20 to 30 minutes.

The hilltop path starts near a rock lookout point in a parking lot at the end of a paved road west of the tiny village of **Colombier**. (An orientation tableau points out little nearby isles and St. Martin in the distance.) The trail is steep, rocky, lined with cactus, and a real challenge for anyone in less than top physical shape. If you can make it down, you'll find it less difficult going back up, since you'll have better traction, thus less slipping.

The path from Petite Anse is lovely and less taxing. It's nothing more than an old goat path at the end of the paved road from Flamands that goes all the way to the west end of the island, then curves southward. Steps lead down to Anse du Colombier. You won't have much climbing, since there are only gradual changes in elevation, and several points along the rocky, winding trail have spectacular views.

No matter which trail you take, wear closed-toe shoes and bring water. There's no shade and no facilities once you reach the sand at Anse de Colombier. And don't expect to be alone. Private yachts and tour boats from Gustavia stop here, and you will probably not be the only one to hike in. The water is usually calm and ideal for swimming and snorkeling; the long crescent-shaped beach has deep white sand and a view of St. Martin.

Colombier is nothing more than a small village with a chapel built in 1918, a school, a few shops, and hillside homes for about 300 residents. Visit for the dramatic views of Anse Colombier and Anse des Flamands.

*You can drive to the village of **Colombier** on a very steep paved road that begins in the center of the little village of **Flamands**.*

Corossol, on the south coast west of Gustavia, is a traditional fishing village with fewer than 300 residents living in colorful houses topped by orange-red roofs. Some of the local women still weave hats and baskets from the leaves of palm trees and sell them from their little wooden cottages, which are called *cases* (say *caz*).

Traditional houses on St. Barts are either les cases à vent *(wind houses), which are built to withstand hurricane-force gales, or* les cases Créoles *(Créole houses), which are constructed to provide shade and ventilation. Both types have freestanding kitchens so heat from cooking won't come into the living areas and an accidental fire won't burn down the entire home.*

Brightly painted fishing boats float on the calm turquoise waters of **Anse de Corossol**, and lobster traps lie along the beige-sand beach. Nearby, **The Inter-Ocean Museum** displays 9,000 seashells from around the world, including 1,600 from the Caribbean. Ingénu

St. Barts

Magras owns the private collection and welcomes visitors Tuesday-Sunday, 9 am-12:30 pm and 2-5 pm, ☎ 590-27-62-97. Admission is $5 for adults.

Along the Southeastern Coast

The beaches at this end of the island are fabulous, but not good for swimming.

Anse du Gouverneur is a long, uncrowded, U-shaped beach at the bottom of an exhilarating mountain road that leads from the small residential village of **Lurin**. The sand is wide, deep, and white, and there's just enough surf to make things interesting. Snorkeling is good around the cliffs at each end, but there are no facilities, and little shade.

DID YOU KNOW?

It's rumored that the pirate known as **Montbars the Exterminator** *buried treasure here and never returned for it. Wouldn't hurt to bring a metal detector.*

Go back to the main road and head east, following the signs for **Grande Saline**. You'll pass the old salt pond, which is now a huge murky basin surrounded by a mangrove swamp that attracts a lot of tropical birds. Park near the salt pond and walk up the rough trail that leads to a sand dune, where you'll have an awesome view of the sea and Anse de Grande Saline.

Anse de Grande Saline is as lovely as Gouverneur and popular with locals as well as tourists. The white-sand beach is long; rocky cliffs on each end draw a variety of fish, which makes for good snorkeling. Since there are no facilities, you won't have to share your space with a crowd, just a few nude sunbathers.

Anse à Toiny and **Anse Grand Fond** are part of St. Barts' craggy, wild southern coast. Steep cliffs surround both coral beaches and the currents and waves are often too rough for swimmers. Visit for the breathtaking views and rustic tranquility. You'll probably be entertained by experienced surfers riding the waves.

The Washing Machine is a natural pool hidden in the hills. Get there on foot by following a path from the beach at Grand Fond; about a 10-minute walk. Local surfers favor this secret spot because the swirling agitation caused by seawater pouring into the basin creates impressive breakers.

Anse du Petit Cul-de-Sac is lined with seagrape trees, which provide some shade, and has no development. It's perfect for beach bums who want to get away from it all. The shore is rocky, so not a good place for swimming, but the views are nice, and you'll probably have the whole place to yourself, especially on weekdays. Explore the little caves among the boulders.

Adventures on Water

■ Best Beaches

 The folks who do the official counting say St. Barts has 22 beaches; 15 are suitable for swimming. Even the mathematically challenged can understand that this is an amazing number for an eight-square-mile island.

In the Caribbean, trade winds blow from east to west and on St. Barts the beaches are divided into those on the eastern windward side (*côte au vent*), and those on the western leeward side (*côte sous le vent*). Some of the windward beaches are protected by hills or reefs, so their waters are still ideal for swimming, even though the wind is strong enough for windsurfing. The leeward beaches are protected by the island itself, so their waters are typically calm. Sunset watchers, boaters, and strollers gravitate toward secluded coves where boulders, pebbles, and seashells frustrate swimmers and watersports enthusiasts.

So, which beaches are best? That depends on your intent.

All beaches are public and free, even if a resort is hogging most of the sand. None are officially nude, but topless swimming and sunbathing is common on all of them, and some are known as popular spots for naturalists. We haven't heard of officials hassling anyone for being naked on a public beach here, but it could happen, so best stick to remote spots if you want to strip bare.

Best Beaches on the Windward Side

St. Jean Beach is extremely popular and offers watersports (**Eden Rock Sea Sport Club**, ☎ 590-27-74-77), and several bars and restaurants. Nice resorts open directly onto the sand. You can find some natural shade or rent an umbrella. The water is typically calm enough for swimming, and the wind blows strongly enough for wind-surfing on the east side of Eden Rock Resort.

Lorient Beach is long and wide and offers some shade. Surfers with their own equipment gather at the eastern end, but families with kids find calm swimming conditions west of mid-beach. You'll have less company here than at St. Jean. The nearby village has restaurants and shops.

Grand Cul-de-Sac has a watersports outfitter (**Wind Wave Power**, ☎ 590-27-82-57) and several places to eat. The long stretch of sand is narrow and protected by an offshore reef.

Anse Toiny is for the experienced surfer and beach stroller. The currents are too strong for swimming, but you'll love this wild, remote part of the island.

Anse de Grande Saline is dazzling. Do not miss its unspoiled grandeur. The only drawback is the lack of shade, which doesn't seem to bother the nude sunbathers.

Best Beaches on the Leeward Side

Anse du Gouverneur has tons of great sand, calm water, and no facilities. It's perfect for lounging, swimming, and snorkeling. You may have a lot of company, but it's just as likely you'll have the whole place to yourself. Bring sunblock or an umbrella because there's no natural shade.

Anse de Colombier is a fabulous off-the-beaten-track beach that can be reached only by boat or on foot. Two old goat paths lead to the gorgeous sand surrounded by green hills. One begins from a parking lot at the end of the main road that cuts through the village of Colombier; the other leaves from Petite Anse, at the end of the paved road from Flamands. The trail from Petite Anse is less difficult. Bring drinks and snacks, since you'll want to stay awhile. The water is ideal for swimming and snorkeling.

Anse des Flamands is a long, wide, lovely beach with fine sand. Palms provide shade for afternoon naps, and sometimes the waves kick up enough for body surfing. Park in the lot beside the Grande Saline salt pond (a smelly, marshy place favored by tropical birds) and walk down a dirt road, over a rocky rise and a sand dune, to the gorgeous turquoise water. Ile Chevreaux, a small offshore isle, is straight out from the white sand beach.

■ Jet Skiing & Water-Skiing

 The following organize Jet Ski tours of the coast and rent equipment to individuals. Tour costs are in the $45-$75 range, depending on the length of the trip. Jet skis rent for about $40 per half-hour. **Master Ski Pilou** and **Marine Services** also offer water-skiing trips priced in the $50 range.

Use of motorized watersports equipment is prohibited within 300 yards of the shore.

WORD TO THE WISE

F.W.I (French West Indies) Watersports, Quai du Yacht Club, Gustavia, ☎ 590-27-52-06, cell 690-49-54-72

Master Ski Pilou, Carl Gustaf Resort, Gustavia, ☎ 590-27-91-79, cell 690-27-38-33

Wind Wave Power, Saint-Barth Beach Hotel, Grand Cul-de-Sac, ☎ 590-27-82-57, fax 590-27-72-76

Marine Service, Quai du Yacht Club, Gustavia, ☎ 590-27-70-34, fax 590-27-70-36. Ask for Stéphan Jouany, an expert water-skier.

■ Surfboarding & Windsurfing

 When the surf's up, all the surfer dudes head for Lorient, Toiny, St. Jean, Pointe Milou, or Grand Cul-de-Sac. Rent a board from one of the following outfitters for about $20 per hour.

Water Play, St. Jean Beach, ☎ cell 690-27-32-62, fax 590-27-87-18

Sea Sports Club, Eden Rock Resort, St. Jean, ☎ 590-27-74-77, fax 590-27-88-37

Wind Wave Power, Saint-Barth Beach Hotel, Grand Cul-de-Sac, ☎ 590-27-82-57, fax 590-27-72-76

Surf Life Creation, Pointe Milou, ☎ 590-27-94-64

■ Boating

 St. Barts is a yacht haven. If you don't own your own boat, rent one for the day or week, or join a scheduled sightseeing/snorkeling/sunset cruise. Prices vary according the

St. Barts

type of boat, length of trip, and included extras, so check with a couple of companies listed below to compare your options. We found full-day cruises running about $100 per person, including snorkeling, open bar, lunch, and two beach stops.

Several boating events take place on the island each year, including the **Saint-Barth Regatta** in February, the **Saint-Barth's Cup** in April, and the **International Regatta** in May. Contact the Office du Tourisme, ☎ 590-27-87-27, or the Saint Barth Yacht Club, ☎ 590-27-70-41, for exact dates and information.

Marine Service, Quai du Yacht Club, Gustavia, ☎ 590-27-70-34, fax 590-27-70-36

Nautica, Rue de la République, Gustavia, ☎ 590-27-56-50, fax 590-27-56-52

Caraïbes Yachting, Rue Jeanne d'Arc, Gustavia, ☎ 590-590-27-52-48, fax 590-27-52-06

Océan Must, La Pointe, Gustavia, ☎ 590-27-62-25; 590-27-95-17

Saint Barth Sea Cursion, Marigot, ☎ 590-27-61-76, fax 590-27-61-76

■ Deep-Sea Fishing

Anglers head to the waters off Lorient, Flamands, and Corossol to reel in tuna, marlin, bonito, barracuda, and wahoo. Several local big-game anglers will take your party out on a private excursion or hook you up with another group. Costs are about $450 per day or $300 per half-day for a group of four, but the prices vary widely depending on the number in your group, size of the boat, and type of gear, food, and drinks supplied.

Ocean Must, La Pointe, Gustavia, ☎ 590-27-62-25, fax 590-27-95-17

Marine Service, Quai du Yacht Club, Gustavia, ☎ 590-27-70-34, fax 590-27-70-36

Capitaine Jérome Lefort, Anse des Cayes, ☎ 590-27-62-65

Capitaine Fernand Pineau, Lorient, ☎ 590-27-66-40, fax 590-27-74-88

Adventures Underwater

The ocean surrounding St. Barts is full of marine life and pristine coral reefs protected as a marine park since 1996. Most guides take divers to sites near Gustavia where caves and a wreck provide interesting swim-throughs. Anemones, urchins, sea cucumbers and eels live on the reefs along with turtles, conch and many species of tropical fish. Most of the reefs are in fairly shallow water and offer good visibility.

Contact one of the following dive operators to schedule a scuba trip. Costs range from $50 for a one-tank dive to $90 for a two-tank dive. Multi-day packages are also available.

West Indies Dive recently added the *Apollo AV-1* submarine scooters for experienced divers. The high-speed machine allows you to get more places faster and they rent for about $90 per dive. If you aren't interested in or skilled enough for a scooter dive, the multilingual PADI-certified guides will take you on a regular slow-speed tour. They are classified as a Gold Palm Resort by PADI and enjoy showing the sites to divers at all skill levels. If you plan to do a lot of diving, ask about their vacation package with La Banane Resort. The shop is open daily, 8:30 am-1 pm and 3-6 pm. They're located at Marine Service, Quai du Yacht Club, Gustavia, ☎ 590-27-70-34, fax 590-27-91-80; www.west-indies-dive.com.

La Bulle, which is associated with *Ocean Must*, is another major dive operation in Gustavia. Laurence and Fred are PADI-certified instructor/guides who take divers out at 8:30 am, 10:30 am, and 2:30 pm. Their expertise ranges from instructing new students to leading experienced divers on personalized trips to the most challenging sites. Give them a call at the office on La Pointe in the capital (the phone is answered 24 hours a day), ☎ 590-27-62-25 or 590-27-68-93.

Plongée Caraïbes is run by Marion, Franck, and Vincent, three of the friendliest scuba guides on the island. They dive from a huge 46-foot customized catamaran that allows plenty of room, easy-in/easy-out water access, and shade for those who want it. There's even a toilet and hot-water shower. An onboard compressor allows the crew to refill tanks without returning to the dock. The boat goes out at 9:30 am and 2:30 pm daily and every Thursday at 6:30 pm for a night dive. Look for them near the tourist office at the harbor in Gustavia or contact them at ☎ 690-54-66-14 (cell), fax 590-27-55-94, www. plongee-caraibes.com

Ocean Master Dive has a full menu of diving opportunities, including night dives and drift dives. Dive masters Olivier Domage and Philippe Berneron also give instruction on using underwater scooters and guide experienced adventurers. Their custom-outfitted boat leaves Gustavia Harbor three times each day at 9 am, 11 am and 2 pm. Drop by the shop on Rue Jeanne d'Arc or call ☎ 690-63-74-34 (cell), fax 590-27-61-26.

St. Barts joined other Caribbean islands in an attempt to protect their marine resources by creating the St. Barths' Marine Reserve on October 10, 1996.

If you're staying in the Grand Cul-de-Sac area (or want to dive from there), call **Mermaid Diving Center** at the Sereno Beach Hotel, ☎ 690-58-79-29 (cell).

Adventures on Land

■ Horseback Riding

Seeing the island on horseback is fun, even if you don't know anything about riding. Laure Nicolas at Ranch des Flamands, located on a hill above Anse des Flamands beach, organizes two-hour beach and countryside rides each morning at nine o'clock and every afternoon at three o'clock for novice and experienced riders. The cost is $35 per person. **Ranch des Flamands**, Main Road, Flamands, ☎ 590-27-80-72 or 690-62-99-30 (cell), fax 590-52-05-58.

■ Hiking

Most of St. Barts is hilly, but there are no high mountains to climb, so most hiking is moderately strenuous. If you're in relatively good physical shape, you will enjoy walking along the sandy beaches and hiking the trails that cut across the island's interior countryside.

If you want to trek over some interesting terrain to get to a secluded beach, check with the tourist office (☎ 590-27-87-27) on the Gustavia harbor for trail suggestions.

Le Chemin Douanier (the customs officer's road) is one of the most popular routes. It begins on the pebbly beach at Anse de Grand Fond on the southeast coast and continues into the surrounding hills. You'll see the path at the east end of the beach and follow it past the surfers' favored spot, Washing Machine, until the trail becomes overgrown as it goes uphill. Count on about 45 minutes to walk the path one-way without stopping. You'll probably want to take breaks in the most scenic areas, so allow an additional two or three hours for exploring and resting.

The walk to **Colombier Beach** is spectacular. There are two paths, one from the end of the road that cuts through the village of Colombier and one from the end of the road that goes through the hamlet of Flamands. See directions for both routes in the listing for Anse de Colombier on page 178.

■ Tennis

Tennis buffs will want to stay at one of the resorts with courts, but if you just want to play a couple of times during your vacation, you can pay a guest fee and play at one of the island's tennis clubs. Resorts with courts include Hotel St. Barth Isle de France, Hotel Guanahani, and Hotel Manapany. See *Where to Stay*, page 190, for information and contact numbers for the resorts.

The following tennis clubs welcome visitors and have lighted courts for night play.

Tennis Club du Flamboyant, Grand Cul-de-Sac, ☎ 590-27-69-82

AJOE Tennis Club, Orient, ☎ 590-27-67-63

ASCCO, Colombier, ☎ 590-27-61-07

Shopping

Ardent shoppers will want to stop in Marigot or Philipsburg on St. Martin for the best variety of duty-free merchandise, but St. Barts has many lovely shops. As with everything else on the island, the boutiques are upscale and carry top-quality goods. Most of the best stores are located in Gustavia along Rue du Général de Gaulle and Rue de la République, but St. Jean also has its share of treasures. Since there are more than 200 retail shops on St. Barts, you probably won't get to all of them, so we've sorted through the offerings and present our personal favorites below.

WORD TO THE WISE

Store hours on St. Barts are similar to those in France, with most opening from 8 am until noon, closing during midday for a leisurely déjeuner, then reopening from 2 until 6 pm. Most shops are closed all day Sunday, and some reduce their hours during low season and close for several weeks during the late summer. Call the stores directly to check their hours.

■ Top Shops

AUTHOR'S PICK

Jewelry

Fabienne Miot, Rue de la République, Gustavia, ☎ 590-27-63-31

Stop in to see Fabienne's fabulous creations, including the ultimate souvenir, her limited-edition 18-karat gold Medallion of St-Barts. You can watch the artist as she crafts unusually shaped rings, bracelets, and necklaces from pearls, precious stones, and gold. The shop also carries individually selected pieces by French designer Alain Roure and American artisans Michael Good and Kabana.

Diamond Genesis, 12 Rue du Général de Gaulle, ☎ 590-27-66-94
As at Fabienne Miot's shop, jewelry is made right on the premises at Diamond Genesis. There's a little bit of everything here, including big-dollar European-style necklaces and rings, but you can also find some well-priced pieces. Diamonds are, of course, hot sellers, but the shop also sells a huge assortment of watches by international companies such as Jaeger Lecoultre, Tag Heuer, Corum, and Ikepod.

Donna del Sol, Rue de la République, Gustavia, ☎ 590-27-90-53
Even if you don't buy anything, stop by this shop in the Carre d'Or shopping plaza across from the harbor to see the collection of stretch 18K gold bracelets. Each bracelet is made up of three to six rows of thin flexible gold set with diamonds and other precious or semi-precious stones.

Goldfinger, Rue de la France, Gustavia, ☎ 590-27-64-66
The first floor is full of fabulous Roberto Coin, Torrente, Dimodolo, and Baraka jewelry, as well as high-fashion watches, such as Gucci,

Rado, and Corum. The second floor is laid out in luxury crystal and porcelain. You could spend hours admiring all the lovely goods here, and, if you decide to buy, you'll pay about 20% less than retail in the US. During the off- and shoulder-season, the store holds good sales, and you could save even more.

> Le Carré d'Or *(Gold Square) is a multi-level complex on Rue de la République across from the harbor in Gustavia. It houses some of the well-known designer boutiques such as Cartier, Hermès, and Polo.*

Perfume & Cosmetics

Parfums de France, Rue du Général de Gaulle, Gustavia, ☎ 590-27-60-29

There's more to this store than perfume. You'll also find a good selection of French cosmetics intermingled with dollar-store type trash and treasures. Pick up a few top quality Ligne St. Barth products, a T-shirt to wear over your swimsuit, and maybe a ball cap to keep the Caribbean sun out of your eyes. And, don't forget the reason you came in, French perfume.

Beauty Cocktail

New Yorkers may know about a line of products called **Belou's P**, which are sold at Boutique Calypso St-Barth stores. The products are custom-designed by Helene Muntal from natural ingredients according to traditional Mediterranean formulas. Used together, the soaps, oils, and exfoliating glove are touted as a *beauty cocktail* for the skin. Each of the oils is named for a place on St. Barts – Colombier, Lorient, and Chauvette – and make a nice souvenir of your vacation. You will find the products at various boutiques throughout the island. For more information, phone the headquarters in Petit Cul-de-Sac, ☎ 590-27-55-23.

Privilège, Rue de la République, Gustavia, ☎ 590-27-67-43; Les Galeries du Commerce, St. Jean, ☎ 590-27-72-08

These sister stores stock so many brand name cosmetics and perfumes, you're sure to find your favorites. Bring an extra bag to tote home your tax-free Chanel, Valmont, Clarins, Christian Dior, Calvin Klein, Hermès....

Skin Care

The Brins family owns and operates **Ligne St. Barth**, the renowned skin care company whose products are used by women throughout the world. Their ancestors came to St. Barts from France in the 1600s, and today the family formulates and manufactures beauty products in the village of Lorient for international distribution. You can visit the store on Route de Saline to purchase skin creams, sun screens, body lotions, and bath oils.

To pamper your skin while you're on the island, consider using their sun screen made from ground *roucou* seeds, which contain a form of vitamin A that stimulates melanin to accelerate tanning. In addition to this ingredient that was first used by the island's Indian inhabitants, the product contains micro-fine zinc oxide to protect your skin from the intense Caribbean sun. Their other products are great island-made gifts for the folks back home. For more information, ☎ 590-27-82-63.

Clothing

Iléna, Villa Créole, St. Jean, ☎ 590-29-84-05
If you're looking for stunning lingerie or a sexy swimsuit, this is the store. It's full of fabulous, provocative creations from international designers such as Andrés Sardá (Spain), Naory (Italy) and Verde Veronica (Italy).

Villa Créole is located on St. Jean's main road east of Eden Rock Resort, going in the direction of Grande Saline. **Les Galeries du Commerce** *is located on the main road between the airport and St. Jean Beach.* **La Savanne** *is a small complex across the main road from the airport.*

Pati de Saint Barth, Rue du Général de Gaulle, Gustavia, ☎ 590-27-78-04; Villa Créole, St. Jean, ☎ 590-27-59-06

The shops are full of items displaying the popular "St Barth French West Indies" logo designed by artist Pati Guyot.

Terre St. Barths, St. Jean Beach, ☎ 590-27-57-50
Wonderful accessories make this clothing store unique. It's located next to the popular beach, so stop in to browse through the hats, bags, and colorful jewelry. The lightweight shawls are perfect for throwing over your shoulders on a balmy St. Barts evening.

Saint-Barth Stock Exchange is a consign-ment store that sells clothing for men, women, and children. Look for it on La Pointe one block south and one block east of Wall House on Rue Shoelcher ☎ 590-27-68-12.

Mandarine, Rue de la République, Gustavia, ☎ 590-29-74-77
Sister shop to Terre St. Barths in St. Jean, Mandarine is stocked with accessories you'll love (squishy hats that roll up for packing, big bags to hold all your stuff when you go to the beach, colorful pareos that you can wear as a skirt, dress, or shawl), and beautiful silk, cotton, and linen dresses for day or evening wear.

Laurent Eiffel, Rue du Général de Gaulle, Gustavia, ☎ 590-27-54-02
Faux is a far more civilized word than fake, but, whatever you call it, it's done oh so well at this sophisticated shop. Even if you're suave enough to discern the difference, who can walk away from knock-off versions of Prada, Hermès, Gucci, et cetera at a fraction of the cost of the real thing?

Blue Coast, 5 Rue du Bord de Mer, Gustavia, ☎ 590-29-60-18
Owner Marine has filled her little shop with shirts made of fine Irish linen and available in 20 tropical colors. Women have limited selec-tion here, but there's no rule that prohibits them from wearing these soft, pastel men's shirts.

If you forgot your swimsuit, or need a new one, head over to one of the KiWi St-Tropez shops in Gustavia (at the Carré d'Or complex across from the harbor on Rue de la République, ☎ 590-27-68-97) or in St. Jean (in the Villa Créole, ☎ 590-27-57-08).

Paradoxe St Barth, Villa Créole, St. Jean, ☎ 590-27-84-98
Catherine is the footloose talent behind Shoe Bizz women's shoes, a line of comfy fashionable shoes sold in her Paradoxe store. Styles change several times each year, and you'll find good sale prices dur-ing the off season.

Human Steps, Rue de la France, Gustavia, ☎ 590-52-04-03
Both men and women can pick up the latest styles of their favorite shoes here. Look for name brands such as Prada, Miu Miu, Sergio Rossi, Charles Jourdan, Robert Clergerie, and Paul Smith.

Liquor & Wine

Vinissimo, Rue du Bord de Mer, Gustavia, ☎ 590-27-74-48
With sister shops in St. Martin and Anguilla, Vinissimo is a well-known name among wine connoisseurs. They offer about 400,000 bottles of wine, from simple table varieties to distinguished vintages. The wine waiters are friendly, knowledgeable and eager to help you select the proper bottle for any meal or occasion.

Le Goût du Vin, Rue du Roi Oscar II, Gustavia, ☎ 590-27-88-02
Residents have become accustomed to shopping at this wine and spirit store over the past few years. It's the exclusive distributor of Laurent Perrier Champagnes and wine produced by Bouchard Père et Fils Burgundy, but also stocks an impressive list of Italian, Chilean, Australian, and Spanish wines. Prices range from $5 to $700 per bottle. If you're overwhelmed by the choices, just ask one of the amicable sales staff for help.

La Cave de Saint Barthélemy, Marigot, ☎ 590-27-63-21
The largest (in area) wine cellar on St. Barts (and probably the largest anywhere in the Caribbean), isn't in Gustavia, but in the little town of Marigot. It has 300 varieties of French wine among its 250,000 bottles stored in a 6,000-square-foot climate-controlled area. Drop by when you tour the island, but don't come on Sunday or Monday (closed) or during the two-hour lunch break from noon until 2 pm, Tuesday-Saturday. Call ahead for directions.

Gifts & Home Decor

The House, Rue du Général de Gaulle, ☎ 590-27-88-04
Walking through the door of this fabulously decorated showroom is like visiting a luxurious private home, only better. Everything is paired up and arranged so that you can see how each piece of furniture and accent object works in a room. Whatever your style, you'll find antiques, replicas, and exquisite accent pieces to carry back to your own house.

Goldfinger, Rue de la France, Gustavia, ☎ 590-27-64-66 (see *Jewelry*, page 184).

Made in St. Barth, Villa Créole, St. Jean, ☎ 590-27-56-57

You can't walk past this red-roofed shop in St. Jean without looking through the window and being drawn into the wonderland of hand-made crafts, jewelry, and paintings. Pick up a straw hat made by the women who live in the little village of Corossol, and buy a few Made in St-Barth logo T-shirts for friends back home.

Groceries

Match Supermarché, La Savane, St. Jean, ☎ 590-27-68-16

Health Products

Pharmacie St. Barth, Rue de la République, Gustavia, ☎ 590-27-61-82
Conveniently located diagonally across from the ferry dock, this drug-store carries all sorts of medicines, over-the-counter cures, herbs, and beauty potions. The friendly staff will help you find exactly what you need, whether you're ill or just hoping to block the damaging rays of the Caribbean sun.

Art

The Caribbean can make an artist out of almost anyone, and St. Barts draws new talent every year. Many display and sell their art from their home studios or one of the island's galleries. It's impossible to name all the current artists and locations where you can see their work because new names are added constantly while others move on.

If you're an artist or photographer yourself, set up an easel or roam with camera in hand and create your own masterpieces. It's not un-usual to see professional and amateur painters and photographers here and there taking advantage of St. Barts' enchanting light and in-spiring turquoise sea.

Look for the following galleries and home studios as you tour the is-land:

L'Atelier de Peinture, Artist, Jane Fabas, Rue de la Paix, Gustavia, ☎ 590-27-80-55

Les Artisans, Artist, Alain le Chatelier, Rue du Roi Oscar II, Gustavia, ☎ 590-27-50-40

Galerie Sur Le Port, Artist, Paul Elliott Thuleau, Rue du Centenaire, Gustavia, ☎ 590-27-51-33, www.thuleau.com

Galerie Christian Mas, Rue Jeanne d'Arc, Gustavia, ☎ 590-52-93-66

St. Barts

Cargo, Various artists, Villa Créole, St. Jean, ☎ 590-29-84-91; Carré d'Or Complex, Rue de la République, Gustavia, ☎ 590- 27-50-45

L'Espace 21, Artist, Kay Quattrochi, Carré d'Or Complex, Rue de la République, Gustavia, ☎ 590-27-57-01

Nomads Gallery, Artists, Jean-Michel Lengrand and Marion Vinot, Carré d'Or Complex, Rue de la République, Gustavia, ☎ 590-27-71-00

Bank of Bhagdad Gallery, Artist, Loulou Magras, Rue du Général de Gaulle, Gustavia, (no phone)

La Vieille Case, Artists, Catherine Theodose, Christian Vannier, and Stanislas Defize, Rue du Général de Gaulle, Gustavia, ☎ 590-27-89-33

M-A Gallery , Artist, Marie-Anne Chaygneaud Dupuis, Main Road, Colombier, ☎ 590-52-46-06

Hannah Moser, Main Road, Petit Cul-de-Sac, ☎ 590-27-78-71

Chez Pompi, Artist, Pompi, Main Road, Petit Cul-de-Sac, ☎ 590-27-75-67

Cecile Robinet, Résidence Sea Horse, Marigot, ☎ 590-52-02-57

Pascal Ledee, La Savane, St. Jean, ☎ 590-27-75-67

Indigo Boutique, Various artists, including Aline from Lurin and Denis Hermenge, St. Jean Beach (near Eden Rock Resort), ☎ 590-27-59-40

Robert Danet, Carénage, St. Jean, ☎ 590-27-66-05

Where to Stay

■ Private Villas

 If you really want to do St. Barts right, rent a private villa. All the celebrities do, and you can find exquisite places that are just a bit of a splurge, especially if you share the space and cost with friends. Of course, the most divine abodes are quite pricey, but you can save a little by preparing your own meals and having happy hour on the terrace.

Many rentals include daily maid service, as well as pool and garden maintenance. You can even arrange for a local chef to create scrumptious meals right in your own kitchen. (One to try: **Bruno Benedetti**, ☎ 590-27-86-71.) The best amenity is total privacy. The biggest drawback is that few villas are on a beach, although most have a private pool.

If you decide that villa life is for you, you won't have any problem finding a place. Wee St. Barts has about 400 rentals, and most have more than one bedroom. Expect a just-ok one-bedroom to run about $1,000 per week and a super-luxurious three-or-more-bedroom to top out at around $26,000 per week. Between these extremes, you'll find many choices that average $4,000 per week per bedroom during high season and about $2,500 per week per bedroom during low season.

WORD TO THE WISE

Whether you're reserving a villa or resort room, be aware that everything books up early for the Christmas season. A year is not too early to make reservations; six months is probably too late.

Rental Agencies

St. Barth Properties
☎ 800-421-3396 or 508-528-7727, fax 508-528-7789, www.stbarth.com
American owner Peg Walsh and her staff personally inspect all the villas and select hotels that they represent on St. Barts.

MountainWaves
☎ 888-349-7800, www.mountainwaves.com
Luxury private villas on St. Martin and St. Barts. Each property is personally visited and inspected.

French Caribbean International
☎ 800-322-2223, www.frenchcaribbean.com
Based in California, this rental agency handles hundreds of private villas on all the French Caribbean islands.

Sibarth
☎ 590-29-88-90, fax 590-27-60-52, www.st-barths.com/sibarth/
Sibarth is owned and operated by islander Brook Lacour, who started the international rental agency, WIMCO, with her husband Roger.

WIMCO
☎ 800-932-3222, www.wimco.com
Although it's run by the same owners, WIMCO and Sibarth offer different properties and services. Check out both (and notice small details such as service fees and credit card policies) before you make a reservation.

St. Barts

Ici et La

☎ 590-27-78-78, fax 590-27-78-28, www.icilastbart.com
Director Patrick Catalan operates out of an office above the Cartier jewelry store in Gustavia. He and his staff manage properties for absent owners and arrange a variety of services for their villa renters.

WORD TO THE WISE

Island-based real estate agencies may have smaller (less expensive) homes in their rental inventory, which may work better for you if you want to save money or rent for the season rather than the week. But, don't expect the same level of prestige service offered by villa-only agencies. Contact several companies to compare their offerings before you decide.

New Agency

Quai de la République, Gustavia
☎ 590-27-81-14, fax 590-27-87-67, www.st-barth-newagency.com
This local real estate agency also handles vacation rentals.

Saint Barth V.I.P

Rue de la République, Gustavia
☎ 590-27-94-86, fax 590-27-56-52, www.st-barth-vip.com
V.I.P. stands for Villas in Paradise, and this local realtor will sell or rent one to you.

■ Resorts & Hotels

St. Barts has some of the most stunning resorts in all of the Caribbean. You won't find high-rise compounds with glitzy casinos and non-stop activities. Rather, you will be nestled into a petit retreat with a dozen or so rooms. (The largest hotel on the island, Hotel Guanahani, has 75 rooms.)

The island has a handful of hotels offering *less expensive* rooms, but don't expect *inexpensive* accommodations. You'll pay a minimum of $200 per room per night during "the season" (mid-December through mid-April) and a bit more than half that during the summer and fall. For this amount, you get personal attention and chic surroundings. The island is Frenchly blunt about its desire to keep out the undesirable and locals have no plans to compromise their standards in order to draw more tourists.

All but the smallest hotels are assigned between one and four stars according to the French quality-classification system. A property that tops even the four-star rating is designated **four-star deluxe** (luxe in French). Likewise, a hotel that deserves a little more than three stars, but fewer than four, receives a rating of **three-star supérieur**.

We've found the ratings to be helpful, but not the final word, when choosing a place to stay. Likewise, being a member of a distinguished group, such as Relais & Chateaux or Small Luxury Hotels of the World, doesn't always mean the property lives up to group expectations. Use the stars and groups as a preliminary guide only.

We've checked out a variety of accommodations to come up with the following list of recommendations, but we feel safe in saying that you won't find a bad room on St. Barts. If you uncover a bargain, go for it. If you have a bad experience, please tell us about it (comments@hunterpublishing.com) so we can warn others.

WORD TO THE WISE

Many hotels, restaurants, and shops close annually during late summer and early fall. You may be able to wrangle a great rate at a hotel or private villa during this time, but remember that the island will be very quiet and you will have limited services.

The following scale indicates rates charged per night for a standard double room with two adults during high season. All prices are given in US dollars. Most hotels do not add service charges and there is no hotel tax on St. Barts.

Hotel Price Scale	
$	under $100
$$	$100-$200
$$$.	$201-$300
$$$$	over $300

Calling for Reservations

When dialing St. Barts from the US or Canada, dial 011 to get international service, then the area code, **590**, plus the on-island nine-digit number, which means dialing 590 twice (011-590-590-xx-xx-xx).

When calling the islands from Great Britain, dial **00** to get international service, then the area code, **590**, plus the on-island nine-digit number; so you dial 590 twice (00-590-590-xx-xx-xx). On St. Barts or from French St. Martin, you add a **0** to the nine-digit local number (0590-xx-xx-xx).

Accommodations Directory

Gustavia

Carl Gustaf, Rue des Normands, ☎ 800-322-2223 (in the US) or 590-29-79-00, fax 590-27-82-37

Sunset Hôtel, Rue de la République, ☎ 590-27-77-21, fax 590-27-01-59

St. Jean

Eden Rock, St. Jean Beach, ☎ 590-29-79-89, fax 590-27-88-37

Filao Beach Hotel, St. Jean Beach, ☎ 590-27-64-84, fax 590-27-62-24

Hôtel Emeraude Plage, St. Jean Beach, ☎ 590-27-64-78; fax 590-27-83-08

Hôtel les Islets de la Plage, St. Jean Beach, ☎ 590-27-88-57, fax 590-27-88-58

Le Village St. Jean, Hillside above St. Jean Bay, ☎ 590-27-61-39, fax 590-27-77-96

Tom Beach Hôtel, St. Jean Beach, ☎ 800-322-2223 (in the US), 590-27-53-13, fax 590-27-53-15

Tropical Hotel, Hillside above St. Jean Bay, ☎ 590-27-64-87, fax 590-27-81-74

Anse du Grand Cul-de-Sac

Hôtel les Ondines sur la Plage, ☎ 800-421-3396 or 508-528-7727, fax 508-528-7789

Le Guanahani, ☎ 590-27-66-60, fax 590-27-70-70

Sereno Beach Hotel, ☎ 590-27-64-80, fax 590-27-75-47

St. Barth Beach Hotel, ☎ 590-27-60-70, fax 590-27-75-57

Around the Island

Auberge de la Petite Anse, Petite Anse, ☎ 590-27-64-89, fax 590-27-83-09

La Banane, Lorient Hills, ☎ 590-27-68-25, fax 590-27-68-44

François Plantation Hôtel, Colombier, ☎ 590-29-80-22, fax 800-207-8071 (from the US) or 590-27-61-26

Hostellerie des Trois Forces, Morne Vivet, ☎ 590-27-61-25, fax 590-27-81-38

Hôtel Manapany, Anse des Cayes, ☎ 800-888-4747 (in the US and Canada) or 590-27-66-55, fax 590-27-75-28

Hôtel St. Barth Isle de France, Baie des Flamands, ☎ 590-27-61-81, fax 590-27-86-83

Le Toiny, Anse de Toiny, ☎ 800-421-3396 (in the US) or 590-29-77-50, fax 590-27-89-30

Sofitel Christopher, Pointe Milou, ☎ 590-27-63-63, fax 590-27-92-92

In Gustavia

Sunset Hôtel
Rue de la République
☎ 590-27-77-21, fax 590-27-01-59
10 rooms; two stars
$

AUTHOR PICK

This is probably the best deal on the island. For around $100 you can check into a superior double with air conditioning, TV, mini-bar, and a direct-dial telephone. The three-story West Indian-style hotel has recently renovated all the rooms, and the front balcony overlooks the town and harbor. Rooms are pretty basic, but the oversized bathrooms are beautifully tiled and have a huge open shower. Owner Jean Pierre Chabrier will treat you like an invited guest, see to all your needs, and tell you what's new in town. Be sure to ask him for a front room facing the harbor; otherwise, you may get stuck with a dreary view.

Carl Gustaf
Rue des Normands
☎ 800-322-2223 (in the US) or 590-29-79-00, fax 590-27-82-37
www.carlgustaf.com
14 one- and two-bedroom suites; four-star deluxe
$$$$
Set in a hillside garden overlooking the town, this ultra-chic hotel is elegant enough for the Swedish king whose name it bears. We're talking Italian marble, Greek columns, private plunge pools, and priceless sunset views. Each room is decked out in exquisite furniture and opens onto a private terrace with a small dipping pool. Guests receive special rates on sightseeing outings aboard the hotel's two cabin cruisers, and Shell Beach is within walking distance. Because of its wonderful restaurant, the hotel is a member of Gourmet Hotels of St. Barts, an eight-member group with outstanding chefs who promote classic French cooking.

In St. Jean

Eden Rock
St. Jean Beach
☎ 590-29-79-89, fax 590-27-88-37, www.edenrockhotel.com
16 suites, cottages, and cabins; four-star deluxe
$$$$
Eden Rock was St. Barts' first hotel (six rooms in the 1950s) and is still one of its finest, thanks to new owners, David and Jane

St. Barts

Matthews. It sits on the rock promontory that juts into St. Jean Bay midway down the powdery beach. All the suites are unique, filled with antiques, and feature rock-wall bathrooms. Magnificent Harbour House is the top accommodation, with a mosaic-tile plunge pool in the private garden. A waterside spa offers personal health and beauty treatments, and watersports are just steps away on the beach. The resort is a member of the prestigious Relais & Chateaux (recently merged with Leading Hotels of the World) and Gourmet Hotels of St. Barth.

Tom Beach Hôtel

St. Jean Beach
☎ 800-322-2223 (in the US), 590-27-53-13, fax 590-27-53-15, www.tombeach.com
12 rooms; four stars
$$$$
You know when you walk into the quaint little lobby that you are going to have an awesome time. This Créole-style boutique hotel is painted in fire-engine reds, sunburst yellows, and lollipop blues, which makes it stand out on the main road running through St. Jean. Out back, across the bridge that spans the freeform swimming pool, the open-air restaurant (**La Plage**) extends onto the beach (some tables actually sit in the sand), where an energetic young Frenchman tends bar. Each of the spacious rooms has a king-size four-poster bed, a big bathroom with a hair dryer and thick towels, and a private garden patio with a hammock, wet bar, and lounge chairs. Ask for unit eight or nine, which face the beach.

Hôtel Emeraude Plage

St. Jean Beach
☎ 590-27-64-78; fax 590-27-83-08
24 bungalows, three suites, one villa; three stars
$$$
You'll be near the airport at this seaside resort, but only small planes go in and out during the day, and all aviation ceases after dark, so you won't be unduly bothered by the noise. The sound of waves breaking on the beach blocks everything else anyway. All units are air conditioned and have ceiling fans, king-size beds and large patios. Each duplex bungalow has a small kitchenette and the villa and cottages have full kitchens, which makes this a great place if you're planning a long stay or want to eat in to save a little money.

Filao Beach Hotel
St. Jean Beach
☎ 590-27-64-84, fax 590-27-62-24, www.st-barths.com/filao-beach
30 rooms; three stars
$$$$

Excellent service, fabulous beachfront location, and updated rooms make this one of the most popular resorts in the Caribbean. Thirty nice-sized rooms in duplex bungalows face either the beach or lush garden and feature a shady patio. You'll have all the standard amenities, including a mini-fridge, but it's really the easy-going hospitality and impeccable housekeeping that will impress you most. The hotel is a member of the Relais & Chateaux, as well as Small Luxury Hotels of the World. Because of its superb pool-side/ocean-view restaurant, it is also part of the Gourmet Hotels of St. Barts. Repeat guests book rooms early, so the hotel sells out quickly during high season. It's closed annually from the end of August until mid-October.

Hôtel les Islets de la Plage
St. Jean Beach
☎ 590-27-88-57, fax 590-27-88-58
11 one- and two-bedroom bungalows
$$$$

Adorable is the word that best sums up these colorful mini-villas on the beach. All units have lovely teak furniture, even on the covered terrace, which features a well-equipped kitchenette. One-bedroom bungalows have a single spacious bathroom, ceiling fans, and an air-conditioned sleeping area with a queen-size bed. The two-bedroom units have separate bathrooms for each of the air-conditioned bedrooms – one with twin beds, the other with a queen-size bed. Palm trees and flowing bushes extend up the rise from the beach and surround each villa and the swimming pool. Rentals are by the week.

Le Village St. Jean
Hillside above St. Jean Bay
☎ 590-27-61-39, fax 590-27-77-96, www.west-indies-online.com/Village-St-Jean/rooms.html
Four rooms, 20 cottages; three stars
$$

We think this is among the best bargains on the island. It's not on the beach, but you can walk downhill to the sand in a couple of minutes (going back up takes a tad longer), and the quaint duplex cottages and large infinity pool (no ledge) have great sea views. Inside, everything is sleek with teak and tile throughout. The Charneau family started the village during the 1950s and continue to manage the property,

St. Barts

turning first-time visitors into repeaters and friends. Whether you stay in one of the standard hotel rooms outfitted with twin beds and a mini-fridge, or one of the large two-bedroom units with a full kitchen and private patio, you'll enjoy the hospitality as well as the terrific pool and gourmet restaurant, **Le Patio**.

Tropical Hotel

Hillside above St. Jean Bay
☎ 590-27-64-87, fax 590-27-81-74, www.st-barths.com/tropical-hotel
21 rooms; three stars
$$

You won't be directly on the beach if you stay here, but you'll be only about 50 yards up a steep road, and nine of the rooms have a view of the sea from their patios. Both the sea-view and garden rooms have king-size beds draped with totally unnecessary, but romantic, mosquito netting. Every room is air conditioned and furnished with a TV and small refrigerator. A French-style continental breakfast is served pool side every morning, where you'll enjoy a marvelous view of St. Jean Beach. Manager Marithe Weber and her friendly staff go out of their way to make your stay comfortable. The hotel is closed annually from the first of June through mid-July.

On Anse du Grand Cul-de-Sac

Le Guanahani

Grand Cul-de-Sac Beach
☎ 590-27-66-60, fax 590-27-70-70; www.leguanahani.com
75 rooms and suites; four stars deluxe
$$$$

AUTHOR PICK

The Guanahani is unquestionably *magnifique*. In addition to flaunting the highest French star rating, the resort now holds the impressive Five Star Diamond Award, given to only a few exceptional hotels around the world by the American Academy of Hospitality Sciences for extraordinary quality of service and hospitality. The accolade is not given frivolously and is one of the most coveted international titles. (The Ritz and Le Crillon in Paris, as well as Mar a Lago in Palm Beach, are a few of the 105 hotels that brandish the honor.) The hotel's restaurant and its chef, Philippe Masseglia, are also recognized as Five Star Diamond champions.

So, what does that mean to you, the guest who is spending no less than $500 a night for a prime-time garden-view room? Understated indulgence, *mon cher*.

The oversized compound (75 rooms spread over 16 acres) is huge by St. Barts' standards. But, the resort manages to make every guest feel special in intimate Créole-style cottages, each painted a different tropical color and decorated in white fabrics with soft pastel accents and casual furniture made of fine woods. The reception area feels more like a friend's seaside cabin than a deluxe resort's lobby, and the wooden decking around the pools lends a rustic quality.

But, make no mistake, this is a high-priced top-notch property and you get plenty of bang for your buck. The beach area is outstanding, spruced up with sculptures, thatched shade umbrellas, plenty of lounge chairs, and a variety of free watersports. When you tire of the beach, you can enjoy complimentary use of the lighted tennis courts and air-conditioned fitness center. The concierge takes care of tedious little details, such as car rental and sunset cruises, and, back in your cottage, room service arrives promptly 24 hours a day.

You'll have little need to leave the property, since **Indigo**, the poolside café that overlooks the beach, serves a tropical breakfast buffet and marvelous lunches, while the **Bartolomeo Restaurant** serves Provencal-style French dishes for dinner. In the evening, you'll be entertained at the piano bar by the music of Charles Darden, an American who graduated from the renowned Curtis School of Music in Philadelphia and formerly worked in New York and Cannes. Or, you can simply wander the starlit paths that wind through the landscaped acres of Guanahani's award-winning paradise.

DID YOU KNOW?

Guanahani *means welcome in the Arawak language.*

Sereno Beach Hotel

Grand Cul-de-Sac Beach
☎ 590-27-64-80, fax 590-27-75-47, www.serenobeach.com
32 rooms and suites; three stars superior
$$$

Long-time visitors say this hotel was once a quiet retreat with nothing going on, but that's certainly not the case now. A four-poster king-size bed sits in the sand between the outdoor bar and water's edge. Nap, anyone? Nearby, a giant wooden sculpture of a hand invites you to have a seat on the palm while you sip an icy drink. Out in the bay, people are kitesurfing, sailing colorful Hobie Cats, and playing in the gentle waves. Pelicans diving around the protective reef mark the best spot for snorkelers. Almost as much activity is taking place at the

St. Barts

pool, which is built above the sand and shares deck space with the open-air **West Indies Café**.

Accommodations include 14 suites with sea views and 18 rooms that open onto garden patios. Each air-conditioned unit is furnished with comfortable chairs, a four-poster bed (similar to the one on the beach), a mini-fridge, and color TV. If you can tear yourself away from the beach and pool, you can work out in the health club or play a couple of sets on the lighted tennis courts.

A major sprucing up is planned at the end of the 2003 high season, so things should be in top form by the time you visit. (The resort closes annually in September and October.)

St. Barth Beach Hotel
Grand Cul-de-Sac Beach
☎ 590-27-60-70, fax 590-27-75-57, www.saintbarthbeachhotel.com
36 rooms, eight one- and two-bedroom villas
$$$$
Located just south of Sereno Beach Hotel, facing the lagoon, this quiet little complex offers something for everyone. Hotel rooms are small and basic, but have king-size beds, air conditioning, TVs, refrigerators, and doors opening onto a covered terrace with a view of the sea. The villas are large, with the same number of baths as bedrooms. Each air-conditioned unit has a full kitchen, a TV with VCR, and a sea-view patio with a barbecue grill. The hotel is separated from the villas by a large beach-side pool and well-equipped gym. Whether you book a room or a villa, you'll enjoy complimentary airport pickup, a discount on windsurf and scuba diving gear, and free use of lounge chairs and snorkeling equipment on the beach.

Hôtel les Ondines sur la Plage
Grand Cul-de-Sac Beach
☎ 800-421-3396 or 508-528-7727, fax 508-528-7789 (St. Barth Properties)
Six suites
$$
To stay in the $200 price range (high season), you'll have to settle for a one-bedroom pond-view unit, but that's half the price of a beach-view suite, so it's a real bargain. This is a new property, so everything is right-out-of-the-box fresh, and the sleek furnishings lend a modern, minimalist theme. Kitchens are fully equipped, with a built-in dishwasher and French-style clothes washer. Terra cotta tile floors in the living area and bedroom continue right out to furnished patios, which are directly on the sand in beach-side units. Every detail was care-

fully planned to suit guests who enjoy staying home, and all the facilities of Grand Cul-de-Sac are within walking distance.

Around on the Island

Hôtel St. Barth Isle de France
Baie des Flamands
☎ 590-27-61-81, fax 590-27-86-83, www.isle-de-france.com
33 rooms and cottages; four-star deluxe
$$$$

AUTHOR PICK

The view of stunning Flamands Beach framed by white columns, as you walk into the reception area, will take your breath away. After you recover, you'll realize the rest of the resort lives up to the view.

From the wide beach, an array of hotel rooms and cottages spread up a landscaped hillside. Nine rooms are in the main building, each a spacious air-conditioned sanctuary with fans in the high ceilings, a king-size bed, comfortable chairs, a small refrigerator with complimentary drinks (bottles of cognac, rum, and champagne are set out on a table, along with a price list), and a lovely cabinet filled with all types of audio/video gadgets, including a DVD. The bathrooms feature double marble sinks, a tub and separate shower, as well as hair dryers. French doors open out to a furnished terrace overlooking the pool and beach. Three suites, also in the main building, offer more living area and a Jacuzzi tub in the bathroom.

Next to the main hotel, a few bungalows face the beach and others continue up the palm-studded hillside. At the top of the rise, the Fisherman's Cottage flaunts its own interior courtyard, an outdoor garden, and more than 1,000 square feet of space that contains two bedrooms, two bathrooms, and a kitchenette. The premier accommodation is the ocean-side suite, with almost 1,500 square feet. This jumbo-sized gem has two bedrooms and a living area that sprawls out to an ocean-view deck with a hot tub.

If you can coax yourself out of your lovely embroidered robe (provided in every room) and out onto the grounds, you'll find a great gourmet French beach-side restaurant (**La Case de l'Île**), two swimming pools, a lighted tennis court, a well-equipped fitness center, and an upscale boutique filled with fashion labels such as Calvin Klein and Fendi. On the beach, there are lounge chairs under green canvas umbrellas and a fantastic watersports facility.

Readers of Conde Nast Traveler *magazine recently voted Hôtel St. Barth Isle de France the top resort on St. Barts.*

Auberge de la Petite Anse
Petite Anse
☎ 590-27-64-89, fax 590-27-83-09
16 bungalows
$$

We think this little string of cottages sitting on the rocks above Petite Anse is a good bargain, especially off-season. The property's open year-round, so you can get a cottage when most everything else is closed, and all units have a little kitchenette, so you can stay in for dinner and save your money for shopping. Rooms are basic, but clean and comfortable. You'll have to walk down the road to reach stairs leading to the tiny beach, where you'll find good snorkeling around the rocks.

François Plantation Hôtel
Colombier
☎ 590-29-80-22, fax 800-207-8071 (from the US) or 590-27-61-26, www.francois-plantation.com
12 bungalows; four stars
$$$$

Owner François Beret has an impressive stack of great media reviews for his restaurant and wine cellar, and his resort shares the same demanding standards. It sits on a hill in Colombier surrounded by lush landscaping and with fantastic views of the island and sea. The colorful cottages have queen-size beds made of fine mahogany, marble bathrooms with double sinks and a bidet, satellite TVs, and covered terraces (most have views of the water). Linens are changed daily, a robe hangs near the bed, refreshments wait in the mini-bar, and complimentary breakfast is served each morning in the garden restaurant. The main building is a colonial-style manor house with a large comfortable lobby decorated in dark woods, potted plants, and tropical prints. An equally inviting furnished deck surrounds the house, offering a cool breeze, wonderful vistas, and quiet spots for reading or just sitting with no agenda. You feel right at home in these classy but informal surroundings, and suspect that you could quite easily become used to this good life.

Hôtel Manapany

Anse des Cayes

☎ 800-888-4747 (in the US and Canada) or 590-27-66-55, fax 590-27-75-28, www.lemanapany.com

32 cottages; four stars deluxe

$$$$

Manapany has a legendary reputation as the first luxury hotel on St. Barts. Some say it's showing its age, but style never goes out of style, and Manapany just keeps getting better. Six newer apartments have more room, but every unit is air conditioned and furnished in fine dark woods, and equipped with a large TV and VCR and either a kitchenette or small refrigerator. The main building and **Le Fellini Restaurant** wrap around a lovely pool and deck, and the beach is just steps away. Be aware that some of the cottages are located up the hill from the beach, so don't book one if you don't want to do a little aerobic climbing.

Le Toiny

Anse de Toiny

☎ 800-421-3396 (in the US) or 590-29-77-50, fax 590-27-89-30, www.letoiny.com

12 villas; four stars deluxe

$$$$

AUTHOR PICK For the past decade, Le Toiny has been known as one of the priciest resorts in the Caribbean, and repeat guests believe it's well worth every dollar (about $1,500 per night during season and half that in the summer). We enjoyed a marvelous lunch at the pool-side restaurant and snooped around a bit afterwards. We can honestly sum up the resort in one word – WOW.

If you win the lottery, run immediately to the phone and book a room. Any one will do nicely. They all have a private 10 x 20-foot pool, four-poster beds in oversized bedrooms, rich mahogany furniture hand-crafted in Martinique, luxurious bathrooms, and a well-equipped kitchenette. While you're hanging out *chez vous,* you can enjoy two satellite TVs, a VCR, DVD, and a CD player. The only bummer here is that the beach at Anse de Toiny is about a 10-minute walk from the resort, and, once you get there, the water is too rough for swimming.

La Banane

Lorient Hills

☎ 590-27-68-25, fax 590-27-68-44, www.labanane.com

Nine bungalows

$$$$

The thing that impresses most when you first arrive is all the shade. A palm tree even stands on an island in the middle of the swimming pool. Bungalows are secluded in thick tropical vegetation topped by towering trees. Owner Jean-Marie Riviere has recently refurbished each air-conditioned unit with up-to-date furniture (including four-poster beds), and added DVD players for the TVs. Bathrooms are uniquely designed with open walls onto a private garden or patio and an open-air shower. Two swimming pools are tucked into the landscaping; a tennis court and restaurant are nearby. You'll have a short walk to Lorient Beach.

Sofitel Christopher

Pointe Milou

☎ 590-27-63-63, fax 590-27-92-92

41 rooms; four stars.

$$$$

There's really no beach at Pointe Milou; the coast is rocky, and the water is too rough for swimming, but don't let that stop you from checking in at this dynamic hotel. You will get all the water and sun time you need at the huge interconnected double-oval swimming pool – the largest on the island at 4,500 square feet. If you must have a proper beach, Lorient is 10 minutes away by car.

Rooms in this sprawling complex are located in two-story hillside buildings, each with a view of the sea, and each nicely furnished in island-style with TVs, mini-bars, plus patios or balconies. Since Christopher is part of the Sofitel hotel chain (the luxury division of the French ACCOR group), it doesn't have the unique personality of the independent properties. However, the staff is as friendly and hospitable as if they owned the place themselves, and the resort offers some extra frills (such as Nini Ricci bath products and complimentary massages) that are usually available only at higher-priced resorts.

Hostellerie des Trois Forces

Morne Vivet (the island's highest hill)

☎ 590-27-61-25, fax 590-27-81-38, www.3forces.net

Seven rooms

$$$

Owner/chef/astrologer Hubert Delamotte and his wife, Ginette, run this 20-year-old New Age resort with love, and they vow that you will leave their hillside retreat refreshed, transformed, and renewed.

Each room is named for and individually designed around a sign of the zodiac, and Hubert will help you choose the unit that will suit you best. All are air conditioned (but you may not need it, since you'll have cooling trade winds), comfortably furnished with four-poster beds, and outfitted with hammocks on a private terrace. If you want to prepare snacks or simple meals in your unit, ask for one with a kitchenette. The rooms are in individual and attached bungalows, and each has a spectacular view of the ocean. Beaches are a five- to 10-minute drive away, but you can relax beside the lovely pool, which is surrounded by a natural-rock deck and padded lounge chairs.

As you would expect, the **restaurant** is gourmet and outstanding. Hubert is an award-winning master chef who puts so much creative spirit into his dishes that he gives *soul food* a whole new meaning. He has been recognized twice by France's prestigious *Confrérie de la Marmite d'Or*, which honors exceptional restaurants and chefs throughout the world. You should devote the entire evening to dining. Hubert doesn't rush, and everything is prepared from scratch, often with organic produce. The menu changes and may include Châteaubriand or veal flambée, and vegetarian dishes are always available. Desserts are invariably works of art. Don't be surprised when your *profiterole au chocolat* (pastry filled with crême or ice cream and topped with chocolate sauce) arrives shaped in the form of a long-necked swan.

Where to Eat

 Allocate a large part of your St. Barts' vacation budget for restaurant meals. The French believe that eating well is the key to living well, and they refuse to live any other way.

Of course, fine dining is rarely inexpensive, and on St. Barts you will be paying for imported foods prepared with great care by talented European-trained chefs. Such meals are improved by the addition of a choice bottle of wine, followed by dessert and a steaming cup of espresso. By the time you purr *L'addition, s'il vous plaît*, your bill will be *très grand*, and worth every euro.

Realizing that your credit card and your waistline may need an occasional change from the typical rich fare, we've also included a few budget-friendly cafés. There are no American-style fast-food joints on St. Barts. Cheap eats are limited to what the French call *les snacks* or *les petits creux* (*creux* means hollow or empty – the state of your stomach, which is remedied by a small meal). These include such things as sandwiches, pizzas, salads and crêpes.

Island Dining

- You can eat as well on St. Barts as in France. Even little out-of-the-way **cafés** take tremendous pride in serving exquisite cuisine, whether it's French or Créole.

- Make dinner **reservations**, especially during high season.

- Call ahead to verify **seasonal** time changes and closings.

- People dress up a bit for dinner, but shorts and jeans are acceptable at most places during the day. Even the finest restaurants don't require men to wear a jacket or tie, and resort wear is standard at even the finest restaurants.

- **West Indian** food is typically local vegetables served with fresh seafood. **Créole** adds a spicy mix of African and Caribbean seasonings – and perhaps a slice of grilled goat.

- Traditional French favorites such as crêpes, quiche, and soupe à l'oignon can be found at some of the small open-air cafés, and *cuisine gastronomique* (a creative mix of French and Créole) is popular in many restaurants.

- Unless noted otherwise, **restaurant hours** are noon until 3 pm for lunch and 6 until 10:30 pm for dinner. If breakfast is served, the restaurant typically opens at 7 am and serves until 10 am.

- Nearly all restaurants accept major **credit cards**, with the exception of a few small cafés.

- Pick up a free copy of *Ti Gourmet* at your hotel or the tourist office. This pocket-sized guide is filled with good restaurant information, including hours of operation and phone numbers, but features only businesses that pay to be included.

Use the following scale as a guide to what a typical dinner will cost each person, excluding drinks and service charge or tip. Breakfast and lunch prices will be lower.

Dining Price Scale
$ . . . . under $15
$$. . . . . $16-$25
$$$ . . . . $26-$35
$$$$ . . . . over $35

No tax is charged on meals. As in France, service is included in the price of the meal, but it is customary to leave a small tip. French people usually leave between five and 10% as a *pourboir* ("for drink" in French).

Calling for Reservations

When dialing St. Barts from the US or Canada, dial **011** to get international service, then the area code, **590**, plus the on-island nine-digit number, which means dialing 590 twice (011-590-590-xx-xx-xx).

When calling the islands from Great Britain, dial **00** to get international service first, then follow the above procedure.

On St. Barts or from French St. Martin, you must add a **0** to the nine-digit local number (0590-xx-xx-xx).

Restaurant Directory

Gustavia
Dõ Brazil, Shell Beach, ☎ 590-29-06-66
Le Select, Rue du Général de Gaulle, ☎ 590-27-86-87
Chez Domi, Rue du Général de Gaulle, ☎ 590-29-85-10
La Sapotillier, Rue de Centenaire, ☎ 590-27-60-28
Le Repaire, Quai de la République, ☎ 590-27-72-48
La Mandala, Rue Courbet (Rue de la Sous-Préfecture), ☎ 590-27-96-96
Au Port, Rue du Centenaire, ☎ 590-27-62-36, fax 590-27-97-12
L'Iguane, Rue de la République, ☎ 590-27-88-46

St. Barts

La Marine, Rue Jeanne d'Arc, ☎ 590-27-68-91
St. Jean
La Plage, Tom Beach Hotel, ☎ 590-27-53-13
Terrazza, Le Village St. Jean Hôtel, ☎ 590-27-70-67
Lorient
K'fé Massaï, Oasis Shopping Center, ☎ 590-29-76-78
Pointe Milou
Le Ti St-Barth, Pointe Milou Hills, ☎ 590-27-97-71
Anse des Cayes
Chez Yvon, Main Road, ☎ 590-29-86-81
New Born, Main Road, ☎ 590-27-67-07, fax 590-27-55-79
Anse des Flamands
La Langouste, Baie des Anges Hotel, ☎ 590-27-63-61, fax 590-27-83-44
Grande Saline Beach
Le Gommier, ☎ 590-27-70-57, fax 590-27-54-32
Le Grain de Sel, ☎ 590-52-46-05, fax 590-27-71-03
Grand Cul-de-Sac
La Gloriette, ☎ 590-27-75-66, fax 590-27-56-32
La Lafayette Club, ☎ 590-27-62-51

■ In Gustavia

St. Barts' main town has several excellent upscale restaurants and a couple of popular bistros where those in the know hang out and enjoy a good meal.

Dõ Brazil
Shell Beach
☎ 590-29-06-66
French and Brazilian $$$$
Lunch and dinner daily
Steps lead up from the sand to the open-air dining room that offers a knock-out view of the ocean. Try one of the Brazilian drinks as you watch the sun set, then stay for dinner. Owned by Christophe Barjetta (nicknamed Boubou), a Parisian who also owns La Mandala Restaurant, Dõ Brazil adds South American zip to French cuisine. You'll find lamb with sweet spices, grilled Brazilian lobster, and, of course, Brazilian-style beef.

Le Select
Rue du Général de Gaulle
☎ 590-27-86-87
Burgers and snacks $
Lunch and dinner, Monday-Saturday

Said to be the inspiration for Jimmy Buffet's song, *Cheeseburger in Paradise,* this ultra-casual joint is actually more like a gathering spot for locals and savvy visitors than a restaurant. Still, you can get a beer or cold drink and a cheeseburger (all the sandwiches are very good) and hang out in the shady courtyard while you're waiting for the stores to open for the afternoon. It's also a good place to hear local gossip, find out about new restaurant openings, and perhaps get invited to a party. Most of the patrons will be speaking French, but you won't feel out of place. Activity runs non-stop Monday through Saturday from 10 am until 11 pm.

Chez Domi
Rue du Général de Gaulle
☎ 590-29-85-10
Pizza and snacks $
Lunch and dinner, Monday-Saturday

You can pick up sandwiches for the beach, but we suggest the pizza. Several unusual toppings are available, and the crust is so good that even plain cheese is delicious.

La Sapotillier
Rue de Centenaire
☎ 590-27-60-28
French/Seafood $$$
Dinner daily
Closed May-October and on Mondays in November and April

Look for this island-style house at the end of the street by Rue du Général de Gaulle. Owner/chef Adam Rajner runs his small restaurant with critical attention to every detail, which wins him many repeat customers. You'll have to call well in advance to get a table under the sapotillier tree (sarsparilla) that dominates the romantic patio.

Outdoor seating is our preference, but you can also dine inside the little cottage, which was moved to the city from the quaint village of Corossol. On our visit, we started by nibbling a superb pâté, moved on to garlicky fish soup, then shared plates of perfectly prepared veal and huge shrimp. Other offerings on the menu included young pigeon flown in from France, frog legs *à la provençale*, and several types of fish served with various sauces. The dishes reminded us of those found in a typical restaurant in Provence.

After lingering over a glass of wine, we had dessert, and highly recommend the apple tart.

Le Repaire
Quai de la République
☎ 590-27-72-48
French and Créole $$
Breakfast, lunch, and dinner daily

You can always get a good meal or refreshing drink at Le Repaire, which means *the den*. The restaurant's complete name is Le Repaire des Rebelles et des Emigrés, but we saw no protesters or exiles in the den on our visits, only some folks playing pool in the back. Everyone else seemed to be there for the well-priced food. We sat facing the marina, people-watching and enjoying mahi mahi and salads. One evening, the menu featured fresh mussels, a personal favorite, and we found them as delicious as those we've had on the French Atlantic coast. The cocktails looked exotic, with lots of fruit and flowers around the glass rim, but we stuck to bottled water, then indulged in ice cream for dessert. If you're in town late at night, the bar and pool tables are open at Le Repaire until midnight.

La Mandala
Rue Courbet (Rue de la Sous-Préfecture)
☎ 590-27-96-96
Asian and French $$$
Bar opens daily at 5 pm for tapas
The restaurant serves dinner daily beginning at 7 pm

A mandala is an Oriental design, basically a square inside a circle, that serves as the Buddhist symbol of compassion and universal harmony. The design and concept is reflected throughout the restaurant in clever ways that incorporate Feng Shui design principles. Tall plants in huge pots. Wind chimes. Asian furniture. High beamed ceilings with fans.

Make reservations for a table on the terrace and arrive before dusk so you can enjoy tapas and drinks while you watch the sun set over the harbor. Stay on for dinner, which may include jumbo shrimp in ginger sauce, curried fish, conch in puff pasty, or chicken in peanut sauce. The menu changes to take advantage of the freshest products and showcase the chef's talents.

This is a Boubou creation. He's Christophe Barjetta, the well-known restaurateur, who owns several exotic eateries on St. Barts, including his nick-namesake at Sereno Beach Hotel on Grand Cul-de-Sac. He and partner Olivier Megnin, known as Kiki, have vast experience with some top French restaurants, and their expertise combined with whimsical ideas is a boon for St. Barts.

Au Port
Rue du Centenaire
☎ 590-27-62-36, fax 590-27-97-12
French and Créole $$$
Dinner only
Closed Sundays and annually July-August

On the top floor of a two-story Créole-style building, Au Port claims to be the oldest restaurant on the island. You may think that means out of date and ragged, but Alain Bunel and his congenial staff keep it fresh and welcoming with plants and fresh flowers. The dining area opens onto a lovely balcony overlooking the town, and chef Eric France serves generous portions to keep patrons coming back. The nightly $30 fixed-price Créole meal, which includes wine, is a good choice. Duck is prepared several ways, but we ordered fish and chicken dishes – both were excellent.

L'Iguane
Rue de la République
☎ 590-27-88-46
Japanese $$$
Breakfast, lunch, and dinner daily during high season
Closed Sundays off-season. Closed annually September-October

When you come into town early to shop, stop at the L'Iguane's café for a full American-style breakfast. It's located in the Carré d'Or shopping complex across from the harbor, near many of the best stores.

Sushi and sashimi are the draw during lunch, when everyone wants something cool and light to eat, and the menu includes salads and sandwiches, as well. At dinner, sushi still dominates, but more people order grilled fish, fried rice, and other Asian favorites.

La Marine
Rue Jeanne d'Arc
☎ 590-27-68-91
Seafood $$
Lunch and dinner Monday-Saturday
Closed from September to mid-October

We probably wouldn't have stopped at this restaurant on La Pointe if locals hadn't told us about the mussel feast held every Thursday. Be sure to make a reservation, because it seems everyone shows up. Other menu choices at this casual dock-side spot include grilled fish, burgers, and steaks.

The Gourmet Hotels of St. Barts

Eight of St. Barts' top hotels have organized the Gourmet Hotels program. It may be of interest to you, if you stay at one of the hotels for a at least five nights and want to try several of the best hotel-based French restaurants. The program offers gourmet gifts and a membership card that entitles you to a free aperitif with every lunch or dinner at the participating restaurants. Just mention the program to your travel agent or the hotel when you reserve your room.

If you aren't staying at one of the participating hotels, or don't want to get involved with the program, it still helps to know who belongs, so you can make educated choices when you book a table for special nights out. The following restaurants are not individually reviewed in this guide, but each has a reputation for excellent French cuisine prepared by a master chef (usually trained in Europe's finest kitchens) and served in elegant surroundings. Prices are high, but you expect that. Most of the hotels also have more casual cafés that offer equally fine food at more moderate prices.

Bartoloméo, Hôtel Guanahani, Grand Cul-de-Sac, ☎ 590-27-66-60, fax 590-27-70-70.

La Case de l'Île, Hôtel St. Barth Isle de France, Anse des Flamands, ☎ 590-27-61-81, fax 590-27-86-83.

Le Gaïac, Hôtel le Toiny, Anse de Toiny, ☎ 590-29-77-47, fax 590-27-89-30.

L'Orchidée, Hôtel Sofitel Christopher, Pointe Milou, ☎ 590-52-06-19.

Carl Gustaf Restaurant, Hôtel Carl Gustaf, Gustavia, ☎ 590-27-79-00, fax 590-27-82-37.

Filao Beach Restaurant, Filao Beach, St. Jean, ☎ 590-27-64-84, fax 590-27-62-24. (In addition to its gourmet French dinner menu, the restaurant serves breakfast and lunch in an informal setting overlooking St. Jean Bay.)

The Rock Restaurant, Eden Rock Hotel, St. Jean, ☎ 590-27-72-94, fax 590-27-88-37. (**On the Rock's** serves tapas and splendid cocktails; **The Sand Bar** serves lunch on the beach.)

La Route des Epices, François Plantation, Colombier, ☎ 590-29-80-22, fax 590-27-61-26.

■ St. Jean

La Plage
Tom Beach Hotel
☎ 590-27-53-13
Créole, French, Eclectic $$$
Breakfast, lunch and dinner served daily
Tables spill out of this brilliantly decorated open-air restaurant onto the beach, where you can start your day with fresh-squeezed orange juice and thick French toast. After a morning of watersports, stop back in for a meal-size salad or a hearty sandwich. Créole dishes are the star in the evening, and we suggest you try one of the fresh fish offerings. If you're a guest of the hotel or stop by a couple of times, the friendly staff will know you by name, and the bartender will start mixing your favorite drink before you have time to order.

Terrazza
Le Village St. Jean Hôtel
☎ 590-27-70-67
Italian $$
Dinner Thursday-Tuesday
Closed annually in September
We stopped in for pizza one evening and were impressed with the ambitious menu at this indoor/outdoor hotel restaurant. A new chef, Franco Romeao, from Courchevel, France, has taken over the kitchen, which still turns out fragrant homemade breads to accompany every meal. His Italian specialties have been added to the menu, including pan-fried foie gras (good, even if you don't usually care for it pâté-style) and arugula-stuffed veal filet. Expect the menu to change regularly as Romeao adds new dishes, but be assured you can't make a poor selection.

AUTHOR
PICK

*Casual, inexpensive meals in St. Jean include sandwiches, fried or grilled fish, and large salads from various cafés in or near the **Villa Créole** shopping center across the main road from the bay, east of Eden Rock. Our favorites include: **Le Pélican**, ☎ 590-27-64-64; **Le Piment**, ☎ 590-27-53-88; **Kiki-é-Mo**, ☎ 590-27-90-65.*

■ Lorient

K'fé Massaï
Oasis Shopping Center
☎ 590-29-76-78
French Contemporary $$$
Dinner daily
No credit cards

AUTHOR PICK

Put this African-themed café and bar on your list. It's currently one of the island's hot spots for trendy locals. Co-owners Pascal Vallon (everyone calls him Pinpin) and Hervé Chovet put special emphasis on high quality at an affordable price, and we give them four stars for succeeding. K'fé Massaï serves matchless nouveau-French cuisine with Asian and Caribbean accents. The décor features dark wood and captivating African sculpture, designed to draw you in and entice you to stay. Comfortable lounge areas open onto a lush garden, and custom-designed tables and chairs add to the ethnic ambience of the dining room. Still, it's the intriguing food that will keep you coming back for more. We started with marinated peppers and zucchini stuffed with fresh goat cheese and a vegetable tartare with smoked salmon. Fresh French bread was already on the table. All the main courses sounded delicious, but we finally settled on pan-seared tuna and a Thai-style chicken brochette. Both were excellent, and people dining nearby gave two thumbs up for their beef filet dinners. Dessert would have been a difficult decision, except that we're chocolate fiends and went straight for the banana-spiked chocolate mousse. Excellent choice.

■ Pointe Milou

Le Ti St-Barth
Pointe Milou Hills
☎ 590-27-97-71
Steaks, Créole, Eclectic $$$
Dinner daily 7:30-11 pm; bar open at 7 pm

Billing itself as a Caribbean tavern, this wild and crazy restaurant is a favorite with the young and untamed. Full-moon parties and outlandish theme nights draw a huge crowd, so you'll need a reservation most evenings, especially if you want to book a prime table in the torch-lit covered courtyard. A surly-faced pirate is the mascot (probably famous Barth-bad-boy, Montbars the Exterminator) and the décor could be straight off a buccaneer-movie set.

On the night we stopped in (after navigating up the steep cliffhanger road to the top of the hill overlooking Pointe Milou), prime rib for two was the big seller, but the ambitious menu also offered seafood and chicken, as well as snail cassoulet and crayfish fricassée. A great mix of lively music was playing, and vanilla rum flowed freely, so we weren't surprised when people began dancing on the tables.

Thierry DeBadereau and Carole Gruson, who own the colorful Tom Beach Hotel and its eclectic La Plage restaurant, are the masterminds behind Ti's overwhelming success.

■ Anse des Cayes

Chez Yvon
Main Road
☎ 590-29-86-81
Creole $$
Lunch and dinner daily
Check out the daily special (*plat du jour*) that's written on a board beside the menu posted outside the front door. You'll likely find a French favorite, such as boeuf bourguignonne, prepared with a Caribbean twist. The main menu features salads, quiche, and crêpes.

New Born
Main Road
☎ 590-27-67-07, fax 590-27-55-79
Seafood $$$
Dinner daily
Don't mistake this for a boutique selling baby items. No, it's a traditional island-style restaurant serving simple all-you-care-to-eat mouth-watering meals. The fresh fish and lobster are cooked over a wood grill. Owners Frankie and David catch most of the fish themselves, and we've seen four-pound lobsters from their traps on display.

WORD TO THE WISE
Most restaurants close annually for several weeks and curtail serving hours during the low season. Always call ahead to verify hours of operation.

■ Anse des Flamands

La Langouste
Baie des Anges Hotel
☎ 590-27-63-61, fax 590-27-83-44
Seafood, Créole, and French $$$
Lunch and dinner served daily during high season
Closed Mondays from April 15-December 15
Closed the month of September
Langouste is the French word for spiny lobster, so we recommend you give special attention to the seafood selections. The lobster salad made with fresh grapefruit is a mouth-tingling treat on a warm day, and the stuffed crab has a lot of zing. Interior decorations reflect a nautical theme, and you'll have a view from your table of lavish yachts moored in the cove.

■ Grande Saline Beach

Le Gommier
Grande Saline Beach
☎ 590-27-70-57, fax 590-27-54-32
Creole $$$
Dinner served daily during high season; closed Mondays during low season
A *gommier* is a boat carved out of a single tree trunk, and it was this type of vessel that transported the islands' earliest inhabitants throughout the Caribbean. The open-air garden restaurant named after this boat is near the parking lot at Saline Beach. Owner/chef Maryse Chinon and his efficient staff offer good service, delicious food, and a nice wine list. We think the set-price Créole menu is a particularly good value. It features such things as shrimp flambéed in aged rum and conch smothered in a spicy West Indies sauce.

Le Grain de Sel
Grande Saline Beach
☎ 590-52-46-05, fax 590-27-71-03
Mediterranean French $$$
Lunch and dinner daily; closed September-October
You can sit on the deck to enjoy your lunch, but we ordered sandwiches to take to the beach. In the evening, the kitchen turns out specials based on recipes from Provence and the coast of Spain. Be sure to save room for a homemade dessert.

■ Grand Cul-de-Sac

La Gloriette
Grand Cul-de-Sac
☎ 590-27-75-66, fax 590-27-56-32
Seafood and Créole $$
Lunch and dinner, Thursday-Tuesday
Many people say this is their favorite restaurant on St. Barts, which is surprising because it's so plain-Jane simple. Intentionally so, we suspect, to highlight the fabulous lagoon views outside the windows. Service is exceptionally smooth, and the food is well-presented and delicious. Albert, the owner, is a legend, and he oversees the entire operation. One of the best deals is the lobster dinner, priced at less than $40. Other choices include grilled meats, stuffed crab, and several types of fish. Be sure to try the goat cheese salad – it's one of our favorites.

La Lafayette Club
Grand Cul-de-Sac Beach
☎ 590-27-62-51
French and Créole $$$$
Lunch and dinner daily; closed May-October
Splurge on this one. It's worth it. Owners Nadine and George Labau are from Toulouse and know a thing or two about French cuisine. The huge lobster salad is large enough for dinner, but you may want to try one of the other choices as a starter (we suggest the foie gras) and save your appetite for the main dishes. Seafood is a good pick, and we especially liked the grilled chicken served with a luscious sauce. Of course, being French, most of the main courses are paired with some type of unusual topping or magnificent sauce.

Nightlife

Nightlife on St. Barts is considerably quieter than on St. Martin. There are no casinos or movie theaters, and only a few hotels offer evening entertainment; even that is more along the lines of piano music, rather than a full-production floor show. If you need a lot of all-night action, this may not be the island for you.

However, there are a few lively hot spots, and many restaurant bars stay open after dinner hours. You can find out about theme nights and visiting entertainers performing at trendy clubs by browsing through the free weekly bilingual newspaper, *Le Journal de St. Barth*.

Locals enjoy drinks and conversation Monday through Saturday at **Le Select** on the corner of Rue de la France and Rue du Général de Gaulle, a block inland from the Gustavia harbor, ☎ 590-27-86-87. Join in by ordering a drink and settling at one of the tables scattered under the trees in the graveled courtyard. This isn't a late-night spot, since the bar closes at 11 pm, but prices are low, and it's a great place to meet people.

Diagonally across the road, **Bar de l'Oubli** is a bit more chic, but still closes at 11 pm. It's right across from the harbor on Rue de la République, ☎ 590-27-70-06. Patrons tend to be young, friendly, French, and fashionable.

Nightclub action picks up after 10 pm, but doesn't really get going until about midnight. **Le Petit Club**, Rue de l'Eglise, ☎ 590-27-66-33, is the best place for music and dancing. The latest international music plays and the action continues nonstop until dawn.

Le Deck is a waterside lounge with super bartenders who make a wide variety of drinks. If you like French wine, you can order from the list that includes bottles from every region. Around 10 pm, the club plays music, including the latest international hits, and patrons dance until 2 or 3 am. Look for it on Rue du Centenaire, ☎ 590-27-86-07.

In the village of Lurin, live music and dancing begins around 10 am at **Le New Feeling**, ☎ 590-27-88-67. Call ahead to find out who's playing. It's open until 2 or 3 am.

Island Facts & Numbers

 AIRPORT CODE: SBH

AREA CODE: 590 (see *Telephone* below).

ATMS & BANKS:

Banque National de Paris, Boulevard du Bord de Mer, Gustavia.

Banque Française Commerciale, Rue du Général de Gaulle, Gustavia, ☎ 590-27-62-62.

Banque Française Commerciale, Galeries du Commerce, St. Jean, ☎ 590-27-65-88.

BUS: There are no buses or other public transportation on St. Barts.

CAPITAL: Gustavia.

CREDIT CARDS: Widely accepted by most businesses, but ask before you shop if the credit card symbol is not displayed in the window.

ELECTRICITY: 220 V-60 Hz (products made for use in North America require a current transformer and plug converter; those made for use in Europe may run hot).

EMERGENCY NUMBERS: **Fire, Police, Medical Emergency**, ☎ 18 (do not dial 0 first).

For non-emergencies: **Fire**, ☎ 590-27-62-31; **Police**, ☎ 590-27-60-12; **Sea Rescue**, ☎ 590-27-70-41; **Doctor** on call, ☎ 590-27-76-03; **Hospital**, ☎ 590-27-60-35.

GAS STATIONS: St. Jean, Main Road near Galleries du Commerce, Monday-Saturday, 7:30 am-5 pm, ☎ 590-27-50-50; Lorient, Main road, Monday-Friday, 7:30 am-5 pm, and Saturday, 7:30 am-5:30 pm, ☎ 590-27-62-30.

HIGHEST POINT: Morne du Vitet at 938 feet.

LAND AREA: Eight square miles.

LANGUAGE: French; many residents also speak English.

MONEY: Euro, but the US dollar is accepted in most places.

NEWSPAPER: *Le Journal de Saint Barth*, free weekly publication, ☎ 590-27-65-19.

PHARMACIES: **Pharmacie St. Barth**, ☎ 590-27-61-82 (in Gustavia, across from the ferry dock); **Pharmacie de L'Aéroport**, ☎ 590-27-66-61 (across from the airport); **Island Pharmacie**, ☎ 590-29-02-12 (in St. Jean).

POLITICAL STATUS: The island is politically tied to the island of Guadeloupe, which is an Overseas Region of France. (For more details, see *The 20th Century*, page 24.)

POPULATION: Approximately 7,000.

POST OFFICES: **Gustavia**, corner of Rue Fahlberg and Rue Jeanne d'Arc, ☎ 590-27-62-62; **St. Jeanne**, Galeries du Commerce; **Lorient**, Main Road.

RADIO STATIONS: **Radio Saint-Barth**, 103.7 FM, ☎ 590-27-74-74; **Radio Transat**, 100.3 FM, ☎ 590-27-60-62.

RELIGIOUS SERVICES: **Catholic**, Rue Courbet, Gustavia and Main Road, Lorient (services at each church on alternating weeks, call for the schedule), 5:30 pm Saturday and 8 am Sunday, ☎ 590-27-61-08. **Anglican**, Gustavia, 9 am Sunday, ☎ 590-27-89-44. Gustavia (call for the schedule), ☎ 590-27-61-60.

TAXIS: Taxis are plentiful at the airport and ferry docks. Drivers are licensed by the government and carry a published rate sheet, which lists authorized fares between many common destinations, such as from the airport to major hotels. Ask to see it. Daytime rates apply from 7 am to 9 pm. An additional 25% is added to the base fare from 9 until midnight; 50% is added to the base fare from midnight to 7 am. If your destination isn't listed, negotiate a price before you get into the cab, and confirm whether the rate is quoted per trip or per passenger.

Unless the driver overcharges, is rude, or takes you out of your way, plan to add at least a 10% tip to the fare. Tip a little extra if the driver gives information about the island as you travel or helps you with your luggage (50¢ to $1 per bag is standard, depending on the size and weight of each piece). US dollars and euros are accepted, but don't expect the driver to have change for large-denomination bills. **Taxi Dispatch**, ☎ 590-27-75-81 (airport) or 590-27-66-31 (Gustavia).

TELEPHONE:

DID YOU KNOW?

You must add a 0 to the beginning of each number when you dial locally. Example: 0590-xx-xx-xx.

- When dialing St. Barts from the US or Canada, dial **011** to get international service, then the area code, **590**, plus the on-island nine-digit number, which means dialing 590 twice (011-590-590-xx-xx-xx). When calling St. Barts from Great Britain, dial 00 to get international service, then follow the above procedure.

- Within the overseas French system, you must add a 0 to the nine-digit local number; so, to call French St. Martin, dial 0590-xx-xx-xx.

- To call out from St. Barts to an island in the Netherlands Antilles, dial 00 + area code + local number. So, to call Dutch St. Martin, dial 00 + 599 + xxx-xxxx.

- To call an island or country not in the overseas French system or in the Netherlands Antilles, dial 00, then the country code + area code + the local number. As an example, to call the US or Canada, dial 00 + 1 + area code + local number. To call anywhere in Great Britain, dial 00 + 44 + the number.

- You will find all country codes listed along with long-distance rates in the TELEDOM phone directory that's available at all hotels.

TELEPHONE CARDS: Most public phones are not coin-operated, but require a telephone card, which can be purchased at a post office, gas station, or convenience store. Some phones accept major credit cards.

TELEPHONE OPERATOR: ☎ 12.

TEMPERATURE RANGE: Year-round average low is 72°F; year-round average high is 86°F.

TIME: St. Barts is on Atlantic Standard Time and doesn't observe Daylight Savings Time. During the summer months, island time is the same as Eastern Daylight Time; in the winter, island time is one hour ahead. St. Barts' time is five hours behind England and six hours behind France and the rest of Western Europe during the summer; it's four hours behind England and five hour behind western Europe in the winter.

TIPPING IN RESTAURANTS: On St. Barts, as in France, a service charge is added to the price of each item on the menu. Most people leave an additional five-10% on the table for the server, since the service charge is divided among all employees. If service is poor, tell the manager or owner of the restaurant. Failing to leave a tip does nothing to correct the problem.

TOURIST OFFICE: Office Municipal du Tourisme de Saint-Barthèlemy, located at Rue de la République, harbor side, open Monday-Friday, 8:30 am-12:30 pm and 2:30-5:30 pm, Saturday, 9:30-11:30 am, ☎ 590-27-87-27, fax 590-27-74-47, www.saint-barths.com.

In the US

French Government Tourist Office, 444 Madison Avenue, 16th Floor, New York, NY 10022, ☎ 212-838-7800, fax 212-838-7855, www.francetourism.com, info@francetourism.com.

In Canada

French Government Tourist Office, 1981 Avenue McGill College, Ste 490, Montreal, Québec QU H3A 2W0, ☎ 514-288-4264, fax 514-844-8901, valerie.ammann@mdlfr.com.

WATER: It's safe to drink, but most people prefer bottled water, which is readily available. Drinking water is rainfall collected in cisterns or desalinated sea water.

St. Barts

WEBSITES: www.St-Barths.com is the official Tourist Office site. You might also want to check www.frenchcaribbean.com/StBarthFrenchCaribbean.html.

WELCOME CENTER: All types of information on activities, car rental, accommodations, and restaurants. Rue du Général de Gaulle, 2nd floor, Gustavia, ☎ 590-27-82-54, fax 590-27-69-72.

Index

Adventure Guides
from Hunter Publishing

"These useful guides are highly recommended." *Library Journal*

ALASKA HIGHWAY

3rd Edition, Ed & Lynn Readicker-Henderson
"A comprehensive guide.... Plenty of background history and extensive bibliography."
(*Travel Reference Library on-line*)
Travels the fascinating highway that passes settlements of the Tlingit and the Haida Indians, with stops at Anchorage, Tok, Skagway, Valdez, Denali National Park and more. Sidetrips and attractions en route, plus details on all other approaches – the Alaska Marine Hwy, Klondike Hwy, Top-of-the-World Hwy. Color photos. 420 pp, $17.95, 1-58843-117-7

BELIZE

5th Edition, Vivien Lougheed
Extensive coverage of the country's political, social and economic history, along with the plant and animal life. Encouraging you to mingle with the locals, the author entices you with descriptions of local dishes and festivals. Maps, color photos. 400 pp, $18.95, 1-58843-289-0

CANADA'S ATLANTIC PROVINCES

2nd Edition, Barbara & Stillman Rogers
Pristine waters, rugged slopes, breathtaking seascapes, remote wilderness, sophisticated cities, and quaint, historic towns. Year-round adventures on the Fundy Coast, Acadian Peninsula, fjords of Gros Morne, Viking Trail & Vineland, Saint John River, Lord Baltimore's lost colony. Color photos. 632 pp, $21.95, 1-58843-264-5

THE CAYMAN ISLANDS

2nd Edition, Paris Permenter & John Bigley
The only comprehensive guidebook to Grand
Cayman, Cayman Brac and Little Cayman. En-
cyclopedic listings of dive/snorkel operators,
along with the best dive sites. Enjoy nighttime
pony rides on a glorious beach, visit the turtle
farms, prepare to get wet at staggering blow-
holes or just laze on a white sand beach. Color
photos. 256 pp, $16.95, 1-55650-915-4

THE INSIDE PASSAGE
& COASTAL ALASKA

4th Edition, Lynn & Ed Readicker-Henderson
"A highly useful book." (*Travel Books Review*)
Using the Alaska Marine Highway to visit
Ketchikan, Bellingham, the Aleutians, Kodiak,
Seldovia, Valdez, Seward, Homer, Cordova,
Prince of Wales Island, Juneau, Gustavas,
Sitka, Haines, Skagway. Glacier Bay, Tenakee.
US and Canadian gateway cities profiled.
460 pp, $17.95, 1-58843-288-2

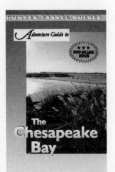

THE CHESAPEAKE BAY

Barbara & Stillman Rogers
One of the most visited regions in the US, including Maryland, Washington DC and Virginia's Eastern Shore. Fishing, paddling,
walking, cycling, skiing, riding are some of the
ways to enjoy this area. The authors tell you
about the best shopping, restaurants and hotels,
along with all other information you will need.
496 pp, $18.95, 1-55650-889-1

COSTA RICA

4th Edition, Bruce & June Conord
Incredible detail on culture, history, plant life,
animals, where to stay & eat, as well as the
practicalities of travel here. Firsthand advice on
travel in the country's various environments –
the mountains, jungle, beach and cities.
360 pp, $17.95, 1-58843-290-4

ARUBA, BONAIRE & CURACAO
Lynne Sullivan
A detailed guide to the three fascinating islands of the Dutch Caribbean. Diving, sailing, hiking, golf and horseback riding, gourmet cuisine, charming small inns and superb five-star resorts. Duty-free stores and unique island crafts. All are fully explored, with details on the history and culture that makes each island so appealing. Color.
288 pp, $17.95, 1-58843-320-X

PUERTO RICO
4th Edition, Kurt Pitzer & Tara Stevens
Visit the land of sizzling salsa music, Spanish ruins and tropical rainforest. Explore archaeological sites and preserves. Old San Juan, El Yunque, the Caribbean National Forest, Mona Island – these are but a few of the attractions. Practical travel advice, including how to use the local buses and travel safety. Island culture, history, religion. Color photos.
432 pp, $18.95, 1-58843-116-9

THE VIRGIN ISLANDS
5th Edition, Lynne Sullivan
A guide to all the settlements, nature preserves, wilderness areas and sandy beaches that grace these islands: St. Thomas, St. John, St. Croix, Tortola, Virgin Gorda and Jost Van Dyke. Town walking tours, museums, great places to eat, charming guesthouses and resorts – it's all in this guide. Color photos.
320 pp, $17.95, 1-55650-907-3

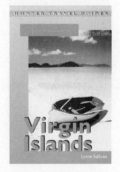

Other Adventure Guides include: *Anguilla, Antigua, St. Barts, St. Kitts & St. Martin; Jamaica; The Bahamas; Bermuda; Grenada, St. Vincent & the Grenadines; Jamaica; Trinidad & Tobago; Barbados* and many more. Send for our complete catalog. All Hunter titles are available at bookstores nationwide. or direct from the publisher.

VISIT US ON THE WORLD WIDE WEB

http://www.hunterpublishing.com

You'll find our full range of travel guides to all corners of the globe, with descriptions, reviews, author profiles and pictures. Our **Alive Guide** series includes guides to *Aruba, Bonaire & Curaçao, St. Martin & St. Barts, Cancún & Cozumel, Long Island, the Catskills, Hollywood* and *Costa Rica*. **Romantic Weekends** guides explore destinations from New England to Virginia, Florida to Texas. Hundreds of other books are described, ranging from *Best Dives of the Caribbean* to *England Revealed! What the Guidebooks Don't Tell You* and *A Traveler's Guide to the Galapagos*. Books may be purchased on-line through our secure credit card transaction system or by check.

We Love to Get Mail

This book has been carefully researched to bring you current, accurate information. But no place is unchanging. We welcome your comments for future editions. Please write us at: Hunter Publishing, 130 Campus Drive, Edison NJ 08818, or e-mail your comments to comments@ hunterpublishing.com.